American Vertigo

AMERICAN VERTIGO

ON THE ROAD FROM NEWPORT TO GUANTÁNAMO

(In the Footsteps of Alexis de Tocqueville)

Bernard–Henri Lévy

GIBSON SQUARE

To Cullen Murphy

This edition first published in 2006 by

Gibson Square
47 Lonsdale Square
London N1 1EW
UK

UK Tel: +44 (0)20 7689 4790
Fax: +44 (0)20 7689 7395

US Tel: +1 646 216 9813
Fax: +1 646 216 9488

Eire Tel: +353 (0)1 657 1057

info@gibsonsquare.com
www.gibsonsquare.com

ISBN 9 7 8 1 9 0 3 9 3 3 8 7 9 (1-903933-87-0)

Contents

LE VOYAGE EN AMÉRIQUE

I

First Visions

A People and Its Flag

IT WAS HERE, not too far south of Boston, on the East Coast, which still bears the mark of Europe so clearly, that Alexis de Tocqueville came ashore: Newport, Rhode Island. The well-kept Easton's Beach. Yachts. Palladian mansions and painted wooden houses that remind me of the beach towns of Normandy. A naval museum. An athenaeum library. Bed-and-breakfasts with a picture of the owner displayed instead of a sign. Gorgeous trees. Tennis courts. A Georgian-style synagogue, portrayed as the oldest in the United States. With its well-polished pale wood, its fluted columns, its spotless black rattan chairs, its large candelabra, its plaque engraved with clear-cut letters in memory of Isaac Touro and the six or seven great spiritual leaders who succeeded him, its American flag standing next to the Torah scroll under glass, it seems to me, on the contrary, strangely modern.

And then, those flags: a riot of American flags, at crossroads, on building fronts, on car hoods, on pay phones, on the furniture displayed in the windows along Thames Street, on the boats tied to the dock and on the moorings with no boats, on beach umbrellas, on parasols, on bicycle saddlebags—everywhere, in every form, flapping in the wind or on stickers, an epidemic of flags that has spread throughout the city. There are also, as it happens, a lot of Japanese flags. A Japanese cultural festival is opening, with exhibitions of prints, sushi samples on the boardwalk, sumo wrestling in the street, barkers enticing passers-by to come see these wonders, these monsters: 'Come on! Look at them—all white and powdered! Three hundred pounds! Legs like hams! So fat they can't even walk! They needed three seats in the airplane! Step right up!' White flags with a red ball, symbols of the Land of the Rising Sun, hang from the balconies on a street of jewellers near the harbour where I'm searching for a restaurant, to have lunch. In the end, though, it's the American flag that dominates. One is struck by the omnipresence of the Star-Spangled Banner, even on the T-shirts of the kids who come to watch the sumo wrestlers as the little crowd cheers them on.

It's the flag of the American cavalry in westerns, the flag of Frank Capra movies. It's the fetish that is there, in the frame, every time the American president appears. It's the beloved flag, almost a living being, the use of which, I understand, is subject not just to rules but to an extremely precise code of flag behaviour: don't get it dirty, don't copy it, don't tattoo it onto your body, never let it fall on the ground, never hang it upside down, don't insult it, don't burn it. On the other hand, if it gets too old, if it can no longer be used, if it can't be flown, then you must burn it; yes, instead of throwing it out or bundling it up, better to burn it than abandon it in the trash. It's the flag that was offended by Kid Rock at the Super Bowl, and it's the flag of Michael W. Smith in his song 'There She Stands,' written just after September 11, in which 'she' is none other than 'it,' the flag, the American symbol that was targeted, defiled, attacked, scorned by the barbarians, but is always proudly unfurled.

It's a little strange, this obsession with the flag. It's incomprehensible for someone who, like me, comes from a country virtually without a flag—where the flag has, so to speak, disappeared; where you see it flying only in front of official buildings; and where any nostalgia and concern for it, any evocation of it, is a sign of an attachment to the past that has become almost ridiculous. Is this flag obsession a result of September 11? A response to that trauma whose violence we Europeans persist in underestimating but which, three years later, haunts American minds as much as ever? Should we reread those pages in Tocqueville on America's good fortune of being sheltered by geography from violations of the nation's territory and come to see in this return to the flag a neurotic abreaction to the astonishment that the violation actually occurred? Or is it something else entirely? An older, more conflicted relationship of America with itself and with its national existence? A difficulty in being a nation, more severe than in the flagless countries of old Europe, that produces this compensatory effect?

Leafed through the first few pages of *One Nation, After All*, which the author, the sociologist Alan Wolfe, gave me last night. Maybe the secret lies in this 'after all.' Maybe American patriotism is more complex, more painful, than it seems at first glance, and perhaps its apparent excessiveness comes from that. Or perhaps it has to do, as Tocqueville saw it, rather with a kind of 'reflective patriotism' which, unlike the 'instinctive love' that reigned during the regimes of times past, is forced to exaggerate when it comes to emblems and symbols.

To be continued…

Tell Me What Your Prisons Are…

TOCQUEVILLE'S FIRST INTENTION was, we tend to

forget, to investigate the American penal system. He went beyond that, of course. He analysed the political system and American society in its entirety better than anyone. But as his notes, his journal, his letters to Kergorlay and others, and the very text of Democracy in America attest, it was with this business of prisons that everything began, and that's why I too, after Newport, asked to see the New York prison of Rikers Island, that city within a city on an island that is not shown on every map—a place few New Yorkers seem to take much notice of.

A meeting with Mark J. Cranston, of the New York City Department of Corrections, this Tuesday morning at 8:00 a.m. in Queens, at the entrance to a bridge that doesn't lead anywhere open to the public. Landscape of desolate shoreline in the foggy morning light. Electric barbed-wire fences. High walls. A checkpoint, as at the edge of a war zone, where the prison guards, almost all of them black, greet one another as they come on duty, and—heading in the opposite direction, packed into barred buses that look like school buses—the prisoners, also mainly black, or Hispanic, who are driven with chains on their feet to courthouses in the Bronx and Queens. A security badge along with my photo. Frisked. On the other side of the East River, in the fog, a white boat like a ghost ship, where, for lack of space, the least dangerous criminals are locked up. And very soon, clinging to New York (La Guardia is so close that, at times, when the wind blows from a certain quarter, the noise from the planes makes you raise your voice or even stop talking), the ten prison buildings that make up this fortress, an enclave cut off from everything, an anti-utopian reservation.

The common room, dirty gray, where the people arrested during the night are assembled, seated on makeshift benches. A small cell, No. 14, where two prisoners (white—is that by chance?) have been isolated. A neater dormitory, with clean sheets, where a sign indicates, as in Manhattan bars, that the zone is 'smoke-free.' A man, weirdly agitated, who, taking me for a health inspector, hurries towards me to complain about the mosquitoes. And before we arrive at the detention centre proper, before the row of cells, all identical, like minuscule horse stalls, a labyrinth of corridors sliced with bars and opening onto the series of 'social' areas they persist in showing me: a chapel; a mosque; a volleyball court from which a distant birdsong rises; a library, where everyone is free, they tell me, to consult law manuals; another room, finally, where there are three open boxes of letters, marked GRIEVANCE, LEGAL AID, and SOCIAL SERVICES. At first sight you'd think it is a dilapidated hospital, but one obsessed with hygiene: the enormous black female guard, her belt studded with keys, who is guiding me through this maze explains that the first thing to do when a delinquent arrives is to have him take a shower in order to disinfect him; later on she tells me—in the nice booming voice of a guard who has wound up, since there's no other choice, liking these prisoners—that the second urgent thing is to run a battery of psychological tests to identify the suicidal temperaments; prisoners call to her as we pass, insult her because they've been denied the use of the recreation room or the canteen, make farting noises at which she doesn't bat an eye, stop her sometimes to confide a wish to live or die; it's only when you look at them up close, obviously, that things become more complicated.

A man with shackled feet. Another one, handcuffs on his wrists and gloves over the handcuffs, because just last week he hid eight razor blades in his ass before throwing himself on a guard to cut his throat. Wild-animal glares—hard to endure. Prisoners for whom a secure system of serving hatches had to be invented, because they took advantage of the moment when their scrap of food was slid over to them to bite the guard's hand. The little Hispanic man, hand on his ear, streaming blood, screaming that he should be taken to the infirmary, under the shouts of his black co-detainees—the guard tells me he has a 'Rikers-cut,' a ritual gash made to the ear or face of an inmate by the big shots of the Latin Kings and the Bloods, the gangs that control the prison. The shouts, the *fuck yous*, the enraged banging on the metal doors in the maximum-security section. Further on, at the end of the section, in one of the three 'shower cells,' which open onto the corridor, the spectacle of a bearded, naked giant jerking off in front of an impassive female guard, to whom he shouts in the voice of a madman, 'Come and get me, bitch! Come on!' And then the cry of alarm my guard lets out when, dying of thirst, I bend toward a sink in the hallway: 'No! Not there! Don't drink there!' Marking my surprise, she regains her composure. Excuses herself. Stammers out that it's all right, it's just the prisoners' sink, I could have drunk there. But her reflex says a lot about sanitary conditions in the jail. Rikers Island is actually a 'jail,' not a 'prison.' It accepts those who have been charged and await sentencing as well as those sentenced to less than a year. What would this be like if it were a real prison? How would these people be treated if they were hardened criminals?

On the way back with Mark Cranston, taking the bridge that leads to the normal world and noticing what I hadn't noticed when I arrived—namely, that from where I am and, most likely, from the volleyball court and the exercise yard and even certain cells, you can see, as if you were touching it, the Manhattan skyline—I can't dodge this question. Does the impression of having brushed with hell arise because Rikers is cut off or because it is so close to everything? And then another question occurs to me when Cranston, anxious about the impression his 'house' has made, explains that the island used to be a huge garbage dump where the city's trash was unloaded. Prison or dumping ground? A kind of replacement, on the same site, of society's trash by its rejects? First impressions of the system. First briefing.

On Religion in General, and Baseball in Particular

LEAVING THE CITY behind. Yes, leaving New York, which I know too well. Fast, and through a driving rain. We are on the way to Cooperstown, a miniature village in the central part of the state that has managed at least three times to be in the heart of high-tension zones in American history. It was the town of James Fenimore Cooper, and thus of the symbolic responsibility for the slaughter of the Indians. It lies in a region that, before the Civil War, fleeing slaves and their smugglers passed through. And last but not least, since this is the claim to fame to which it seems most attached, it is the world capital of baseball.

I spend the night in a wooden chalet that has been transformed into a bed-and-breakfast, with ceramic rabbits in the garden and a magazine in the bedroom that explains how to 'live comfortably at thirty,' how to be 'older than seventy and still be in love,' and 'six ways to get your daily glass of milk.' The house is run by two commanding women, mother and daughter, who wear identical bloodred canvas aprons and look the spitting image of Margaret Thatcher at two stages of her life. I spend time in the morning listening to these ladies tell me the history of their house. The building was actually created a century ago by an officer in the Civil War, but it has been renovated so as to hide all antique traces. 'Are you interested in the bed-and-breakfast business, which is the passion of our existence?' one of them asks. 'Is this your first experience? Did you like it? I'm glad you did, since there are as many bed-and-breakfasts as there are owners. Everyone puts their mark on it—it's an art, a religion. No, that's not the word, "religion." We don't make any difference here between religions—no more than we would with the Yankees and the Red Sox. Who won, by the way?' (She has turned toward a customer in shorts and under-shirt who is sitting at the table next to mine. He shrugs as he wolfs down a huge slab of bacon.) 'See, he doesn't know. That means it doesn't count. And you—what are you? Oh! Jewish. Oh! Atheist. That's okay.... Everyone does what they want.... In this business you have to like ninety-nine percent of your clients....'

The breakfast was a little long. But now I'm in the immense museum, completely disproportionate to the dollhouses in the rest of the town, where this great national sport is honoured—baseball, a sport that contributes to establishing people's identi-ties and that has truly become part of their civic and patriotic religion. There, in the Hall of Fame adjoining the museum, is a plaque devoted to those champions who interrupted their careers to serve in American wars.

This is not a museum; it's a church. These are not rooms; they're chapels. The visitors themselves aren't really visitors but devotees, meditative and fervent. I hear one of them asking, in a low voice, if it's true that the greatest champions are buried here—beneath our feet, as if we were at Westminster Abbey or in the Imperial Crypt beneath the Kapuziner Church in Vienna. And every effort is made to sanctify Cooperstown itself—the cradle of this national religion, a new Nazareth, the simple little town that nothing prepared for its election and yet which was present at the birth of the thing. Consider the edifying history, told in the exhibition rooms and the brochures, of the scientif-ic commission created at the beginning of the twentieth century by a former baseball player who became a millionaire and launched a nationwide contest on the theme 'Send us your oldest baseball memory'. He collected the testimony of an old engineer from Denver who in 1839, in Cooperstown, in front of the tailor's shop, saw Abner Doubleday—later a Northern general and a Civil War hero, the man who would fire the first shot against the Southerners—explain the game to passers-by, set down the rules, and, in fact, baptise it.

It was in honour of this story that the year 1939, exactly a century later, was chosen for the inauguration of the museum. It's because of this story that, in a well-known article in *Natural History*, the paleontologist and baseball fan Stephen Jay Gould recalled that a long-ago exhibit at the museum noted that 'in the hearts of those who love baseball' the Yankee general remains 'the lad in the pasture where the game was invented.' It's because of it, again, that the big stadium nearby—where, they say, some of the finest games in the country are played—is called Doubleday Field and bears on its front the fine, proud inscription BIRTH-PLACE OF BASEBALL. And what can one say, finally, of the commissioner of baseball, Bud Selig, who at Arlington a few years ago placed a wreath on the tomb of the Unknown Soldier and publicly remembered Abner Doubleday—that son of Cooperstown, also buried in the National Cemetery? Before the eyes of America and the world, he officially proclaimed him on that day the pope of the national religion. That day not just the town but the entire United States joined in a celebration that had the twofold merit of associating the national pastime with the traditional rural values that Fenimore Cooper's town embodies and also with the patriotic grandeur that the name Doubleday bears.

The only problem, Tim Wiles, the museum's director of research, tells me, is that Abner Doubleday, in the legendary year of 1839, wasn't in Cooperstown but at West Point; that the old engineer who was supposed to have played that first game with him was just five years old then; that the word *baseball* had already appeared in 1815, in a novel by Jane Austen, and in 1748, in a private letter found in England; that a baseball scholar, an eminent member of the Society for American Baseball Research, had just discovered in Pittsfield, Massachusetts, an even older trace; that the Egyptians had, it seems, their own form of the game. The only problem, he says, is that we have always known—since 1939, in fact, since the museum's opening—that baseball is a sport of the people, and even if, like all sports of the people, it suffers from a lack of written archives, its origin is age-old. The only problem is that this history is a myth, and every year millions of men and women come, like me, to visit a town devoted entirely to the celebration of a myth.

The False as Will and Representation

TWO HYPOTHESES TO work from. Either the visitors in question are ignoramuses who believe, in good faith, that it's all true. Or, on the contrary, they are in the know; they are aware that the story doesn't hold water; but the subject excites them so much that they keep informed about the discoveries of the thousands of baseball scholars who form one of the most curious, yet also one of the most serious, learned societies in this country and who are all in full agreement about the falsity of the legend; they celebrate a myth without for a moment ignoring that it's a myth and a hoax.

Here is another scene, which makes me lean toward the second hypothesis. I'm still in Cooperstown, but now I'm in the Farmers' Museum, which owns many artefacts and exhibits the crafts and traditions of rural American life—brand-new nineteenth-century costumes.

There is a canoe that smells of green wood, from which a copy of an Indian knife is dangling. A tomahawk with its wooden handle freshly cut. A cardboard cow, warranted to be a faithful reproduction of the cows of that era. Dr. Jackson's office, his instrument case, his water pitcher, his stethoscope, his washbasin. The garden where the plants he must have cultivated at the time have been reinvented. A cemetery whose gravestones are real but where no corpses are buried. Finally, women who, in their caps, their aprons, their unbleached cotton dresses, act like real farmers running actual businesses, whereas here again, everything is false. 'What do you do for a living? I'm a nineteenth-century weaver at the Farmers' Museum in Cooperstown (or an herbalist, or a baker). Every day I put on my costume and go play my role.' I'm sure the museum possesses relics, actual objects from the era, vestiges, but they prefer facsimiles. They want the new to simulate the old. The whole idea is not to preserve but to reconstitute a false truth and celebrate it as such. Defeat of the archive. Triumph of kitsch.

And then here's another case, even more extravagant. Far off, right in the middle of the reconstituted village, there is a tent where a crowd larger than the one in front of Dr. Jackson's office or the herbalist's garden is gathered. As we come near it, we see an empty zone beneath the tent surrounded by thick braided ropes, the kind used in museums. And in the middle a gypsum statue just over ten feet long, lying down, its ribs jutting out, one hand on its stomach, as if mummified. They call it the Cardiff Giant, and its history goes like this. The scene is Cardiff, New York, in 1869: workmen digging a well on a farm belonging to William C. 'Stub' Newell unearth this mummified giant. Word spreads to Syracuse. Much discussion in the county about whether it's a fossil or a work of art. A consortium is created, which, leaning toward the fossil thesis and thinking it's the remains of a prehistoric man, exhibits the discovery, first in a tent on Newell's farm, then throughout the state, transporting it from town to town. Except there's a catch. The object has a strange look to it. Certain details—the toes, the penis—are too well preserved. Some witnesses, moreover, begin to gossip that they saw a wagon transporting a block of gypsum to a marble sculptor's place in Chicago, and then others saw the same wagon arrive here, loaded with a large wooden crate. So the idea is first insinuated, then asserted, that the whole business is a fake—that the pores of the skin, for instance, were made by pounding the gypsum with a piece of wood studded with nails, and that Newell's friend George Hull, a cigar manufacturer from Binghamton, New York, buried this false mummy on Newell's farm. But how does the world react? The hoax giant is still exhibited, as if nothing had happened. P.T. Barnum, the great showman, tries to buy it and, furious at being refused, has a copy made, which he exhibits in New York City. During this time, the original false giant goes to the Pan-American Exhibition. It is bought in the early 1930s by a rich publisher from Iowa. Then, in 1939, by the New York State Historical Association. Finally, in 1948, it's transported to Cooperstown, where it has been on display ever since, after its truly national funeral. So today people come from all over the United States to admire the biggest, most famous, most official example of the fake.

To revere a counterfeit as if it were real. To prefer in a museum, even when one has a choice, recent artefacts over relics. To rewrite the history of an age-old pastime as if it were a national sport. What is at stake in each case is a relationship to time, and in particular to the past. As if, for this nation so eminently oriented toward its future, having a past can only be sustained by reappropriating it through well-calculated words and deeds. As if with all one's strength—including the strength and power of myth and forgery—one had to reassert the power of the present over the past. Or the opposite, which comes down to the same thing: as if the pain were having not enough past rather than too much; and as if people fell back on the theme of 'Since we weren't there for the child's baptism, let's at least be there when the man's last words are spoken.' I think back to the Hall of Fame in the Museum of Baseball. And I see that, in the end, the real void, the real unspoken thing, has to do with the absence of a word ('*cricket*') and a fact (the English origin, dating back to the first English colonists, of an American sport when all is said and done). Cancel the debt. Revoke 'the name of the father.' It is the self-generation of a culture that wants to be descended from its own handiwork and, accordingly, rewrites its great and small genealogies. An American neurosis?

They Shoot Cities, Don't They?

THAT A CITY could die for a European—that is unthinkable. And yet...

Buffalo, a city that was once the glory of America, its showcase, where two presidents once lived (and where one was shot and another inaugurated), a city that on this late July afternoon—the anniversary, by the way, of Tocqueville's visit, in 1831—offers a landscape of desolation: long avenues without cars, stretching out to infinity; not a single good restaurant to dine in; few hotels; improvised gardens in place of buildings; deserted lots in place of gardens; trees that are dead or diseased; boarded-up office buildings, disintegrating or about to be torn down. Yes, a city where you can still find some of the finest specimens of urban architecture in America and some of the earliest skyscrapers is now reduced to destroying them, because an unoccupied building is a building that is breaking apart and, one day or another, will fall on your head. The library is on the verge of financial collapse. There are streets that seem not to have any running water or mail delivery. Even the main train station, which during the era of the steelworks was a major hub, is now only a shell, an enormous abandoned sugarloaf, with rusted metal signs, wind howling, crows flying around it, and, in big letters, THE NEW YORK CENTRAL RAILROAD, already half effaced.

Lackawanna, about ten miles south of Buffalo: the worst thing here is the factory. It was once a modern enterprise, and the region's heart. All that's left are cone-shaped mounds of coal or iron in lots overgrown with weeds. Extinguished chimneys. Blackened, unmoving freight cars. Warehouses with broken windows. And inside one of the warehouses, which I sneak into: sagging armchairs; shelves of twisted metal where files have been left; yellowed photographs of beaming employees, confident of the eternal greatness of their factory; crumpled copies of *The Buffalo News*; charred plastic gas masks; on one wall, an assembly of manometers, barometers, steam gauges, rubber thermometers eaten away by humidity; clocks—I count four—all stopped at the same hour. If I didn't know the history of Bethlehem Steel; if I didn't know that they closed this factory twenty years ago because of tragic but routine foreign competition; if I didn't know that the city itself still lives, with a tiny life indeed, but a life all the same; if I hadn't, for instance, read the story of those six Arab Americans who hid here after September 11 (the ones the FBI arrested) I could almost believe in a natural catastrophe, a cataclysm—of the kind that leaves standing the calcified facades of those towns that had to be evacuated, with no time to carry anything away, because of an earthquake, a tsunami, a volcano.

Cleveland. Not so sad. Not so broken. A real will, above all, to revitalise the destroyed neighbourhoods. At a meeting in a church at breakfast time, with Mort Mandell and Neighborhood Progress Inc., are gathered in great austerity a dozen or so men of means, with their slightly old-fashioned pearl-gray suits, white hair, and fine austere faces, successors to the Gunds, the Van Sweringens, the Jacobses, those Protestant and Jewish philanthropists who flourished with the greatness of the city. With slides and diagrams at hand, they're thinking about how to rehabilitate the heart of this city which remains their 'little homeland,' even if they have deserted it, even if they went elsewhere to make their fortunes or their lives. Here, too, deserted neighbourhoods. Empty parking lots. Cars prowling along Euclid and Prospect, between East Fifth and East Sixth. Winos in municipal buildings. Empty or bricked-up churches, yet I keep being told about the renewal in America of evangelical faith and morality. A fire station with a sign, BUDGET CUTS ARE SUICIDE. A rotary planted with flowers that women feel sorry for and water since no one goes there anymore. And this detail, which didn't strike me in Buffalo; the absence of billboards on certain avenues. But on a wall next to a razed building, an inscription, in capital letters from the last century, reappearing the way wreckage washes up: ATTORNEY AT LAW. Further on, in a vacant lot, on the last remaining wall of a vanished building, a sign from another time, a preposterous witness to a previous life: THE HOTTEST JEANS ON TWO LEGS.

And finally Detroit, radiant Detroit, the city that during the war, because of its car and steel factories, called itself 'the arsenal of democracy,' but that once one has entered it—whether in the Brush Park area, north of downtown, or, worse, East Detroit— seems like an immense, deserted Babylon, a futuristic city whose inhabitants have fled: more burnt or razed houses; collapsed facades and roofs that the next heavy rain will carry away; trash heaps in former gardens; prowlers; dumpster divers; nature reasserting its rights; foxes, some nights; crack houses; closed schools; a liquor store ringed with barbed wire. The Fox Theatre intact, with its winged golden lions at the entrance; intact, too, the Wright houses and Orchestra Hall, where people walk decked in tuxedos into a doomsday environment; but the Book Cadillac Hotel and the Statler Hilton (architectural wonders whose corbelled construction is museum quality), they are empty, and padlocked. At times you'd think it was a plague. At other times, Dresden or Sarajevo. An observer who knew nothing of the history of the city and the riots that accelerated the exodus of the white population to the suburbs forty years ago might think now that he was in a bombed metropolis. But no. It's just Detroit. It's just an American city whose inhabitants have left, forgetting to close the door behind them. It's just the experience, unique in the world, of a city that people have left as one leaves a spurned partner and that, little by little, has returned to chaos.

The mystery of these modern ruins. It is the enigma of an America about which I feel, at this stage of my journey, that a certain sensibility (essential to Europe's civility, twinned with its urbanity) is perhaps on the verge of vanishing—a love of cities.

The Revenge of the Little Man

HE CAN'T MANAGE to say 'stem cells' without tripping himself up. Stumbles over numbers and acronyms, beginning with that of the National Urban League, the black civil-rights defence organisation to which he has been invited. He fumbles with unemployment rates and the number of primary school teachers in Ohio. He has, in his expression, in his eyes, which are set too close together, that faint look of panic that dyslexic children have when they think they're going to make a mistake and will be scolded for it but simply can't stop once they've started. He frowns with concern when he talks about the city's poor neighbourhoods. Takes on a fake tough-guy look when he broaches the subject of Iraq. When he utters the word *America* or *army*, he stops short or, rather, stiffens as if at the sound of an invisible bugle.

I think about all that has been said about the ambivalence of his relationship with the earlier President Bush. I think about the discussion Alan Wolfe and I had the other evening about whether he started the war in Iraq in order to take revenge (Saddam humiliated my father, so I will humiliate Saddam) or in order to issue a huge Oedipal challenge (I'll do what he couldn't do—I'll obey another father, who is higher than my own, and who inspires me to actions he couldn't inspire in my father). The truth is that this man is something of a child. Whether he's dependent on his father, his mother, his wife, or God Almighty, he looks to me this morning like one of those humiliated children Georges Bernanos was so good at creating, showing that their hardness stemmed from their shyness and fear.

That said, watch out. This shy man is shrewd, too. The child is a cunning child. He's clever enough to call the president of the National Urban League, Marc Morial, by his first name, and to begin his speech, just after a prayer, with praise for the Detroit Pistons, the local basketball team. He has the talent to tell joke after joke and, like a good comedian warming up a difficult audience, to be the first to laugh, noisily, at his own wisecrack. He has the intelligence to call the two important black leaders who are sitting in the front row, Jesse Jackson and Al Sharpton, by their first names, too, so as to defuse their hostility. He does this also, after admitting that his party must earn the vote of African Americans, by saying to Reverend Jackson, 'You don't need to nod your head so hard at that, Jesse,' and to Reverend Sharpton, 'It's hard to run for office, isn't it, Al?' Everyone in the audience remembers the battle Sharpton has just lost for nomination by the Democratic Party.

Detroit is a city where Bush has, as he knows, 'a lot of work to do' to win the hearts of a community that four years ago voted 94 percent for Al Gore. He is in enemy territory. The two thousand people present came to see the man but don't share his ideology. Yet the trick is working. His riffs on the American dream and on small business; his audacity in attacking the power of bureaucracy and Washington, as if he hasn't been in the White House for four years; his vision of America as a blue-chip corporation in which all citizens are shareholders and that wants everyone to get only richer; his talk about Sudan, finally, and about the genocide (though he does not use the word, he says that he will do what he can, if he is elected, to see that the rulers of Khartoum bring an end to the slaughter)—all of this ends up working. Nerve and naïveté. Tactical cleverness along with a certain candour. A delegate, as we are leaving, in the crush of radio and television teams that are asking the opinions of the attendees, says: 'The son of a bitch—he got us…' Another one: 'That was good, the part about Sudan!' That's what strikes me, too, of course. But, even stranger, it's also that look of a resourceful little boy, a bit mischievous, who has to work hard to be a candidate and a president.

I picture him, in his native Texas, as a difficult youth, an average student, rowdy, worrying his parents no end. I imagine him—like Sidney Blumenthal described him to me in Washington the other day—at Phillips Academy, and then at Yale, trailed by the reputation of a well-connected boy and snubbed by the rich sons of East Coast families who find him useful but a little country-bumpkinish. I see him then, quite clearly, as a provincial narcissist and a frustrated dilettante, a bad businessman, an overgrown daddy's boy whom the family manages to save from each of his semi-failures. When was this pattern reversed? And how? Under whose influence, or under what influence, did the metamorphosis come about for the lover of backfiring cars and drinking bouts with his buddies, for the failure, the nice guy, the man no one for a long time would have thought had a chance of becoming anything at all? How did this man become a formidable machine capable of winning the most difficult competition in America and, when it comes down to it, on the planet? There are men—Bill Clinton, for example—you feel were born to be president. Others—John Kennedy—who were formed, trained, for the office. He is the opposite: born to lose; raised above all not to win. And, for this change of direction, this late-blooming grace that hasn't even had time to imprint itself on his face, no one has any real explanation—except him, when he talks about 'grace,' actually. And being 'born again.' Who knows?

A Jewish Model for Arab Americans

HOW CAN ONE be an Arab—I mean, Arab and American?

How can one in post-9/11 America remain loyal to one's Muslim faith and not be taken for a bad citizen? For the inhabitants of Dearborn, Michigan, a few miles west of Detroit, the question doesn't even arise. This town is a little special, of course. Its McDonald's, for instance, is halal. A supermarket is called Al Jazeera. There are mosques. I spot an old Ford with one of those personalised license plates that Americans love; it reads TALIBAN. And I quickly find that around River Rouge—the old Ford factory, parts of which are now reduced, like the Bethlehem Steel plant in Lackawanna, to rusted steel carcasses, useless pipes, empty silos, and half-destroyed warehouses in the middle of which trees are growing—conversations switch easily from Arabic to English and back. But all the people I meet, all the businessmen, politicians, community leaders, when I ask them how in these times of al-Qaeda these two interlinked identities can be combined, reply that actually everything is for the best in the best of all possible worlds. The question of twofold allegiance that is poisoning the debate in France is not an issue here.

Ahmed, wearing a turban like a Sikh, who sells utterly American sodas on Warren Avenue, says, 'Of course there were problems; of course there was a backlash; of course the FBI agents came here to look for terrorists; but they didn't find any; we are exemplary American citizens, and they couldn't find any.' Nasser M. Beydoun is a high-spirited young businessman, married to a Frenchwoman. It takes me a while to pick up that when he says 'we,' he doesn't mean 'we Arabs' but 'we Americans.' He tells me, in the large conference room of the American Arab Chamber of Commerce, of which he is a board member, 'I was against the war in Iraq, but less for them, the Arabs, than for us, the Americans, this great nation with its fine culture, this exemplary democracy that's preparing a fate for itself as an occupying power.' And then there's Abed Hammoud of the Arab American Political Action Committee, a small organisation whose role, he tells me, is to interview, review, and eventually endorse candidates at all levels of local or national power. When Bush wrote him, in 2000, a beautiful page-and-a-half personal letter beginning with 'Dear Abed', when Kerry asked him what procedure he should follow to gain the support of the Arabs in Detroit and he sent Kerry a copy of the letter to inspire him; when, last January, he organised a series of telephone interviews for Kerry and for Wesley Clark and a representative of Howard Dean; when he had one of his teams follow around a candidate for the Illinois legislature and be present at all his appearances and press conferences, even the smallest ones; when he finished off, this very morning, the information letter he sends to all his members—in all this, do I realise what his example is?

The Jews, obviously. The incredible success story that is the power of the Jewish community. What they succeeded in creating, the power they knew how to buy, to earn with the sweat of their brows; the path they made that led them to bring together all influences. 'How can one not be inspired by that?' he asks. 'We are fifty years late, I'll grant that; today they are ten times stronger than us; but you'll see, we'll get there; one day we'll be equal.'

I'm not saying this argument is deprived of dubious undertones. Perhaps the restraint is purely tactical and the idea is still in the end to do not just as well as but better than a Jewish community that is identified as the very face of the enemy, without its being said. And I felt in Beydoun also a strong reticence about Israel, whose existence he is careful not to question, but where it is 'out of the question' for him to travel as long as the 'Palestinian resistance' hasn't been granted its rights by the 'occupiers.' But, the fact still remains. We are far from Islamberg, tucked away near the Catskills, the fundamentalist phalanstery I discovered during my investigation into the death of Daniel Pearl, where the terrorist ideologue Ali Shah

Gilani is revered. And we are even farther from those French suburbs where they shit on the flag and hiss at the national anthem, and where hatred for the country that has taken them in is equalled only by an anti-Semitism eager to shift into action. Fine American lesson. Admirable image of democracy at work—that is, of integration and compromise.

There are 115,000 Arab Americans in the Detroit metropolitan area. There are about 1.2 million scattered through Michigan, Ohio, Illinois, and the rest of America. And despite Iraq, despite Bush, despite the hawks of the so-called clash of civilisations, these two traits dominate: the American dream, neither more nor less alive than in all the generations of Irish, Polish, German, or Italian immigrants who came before them; and, linked to that, a passion, an obsession, a copycat rivalry, with a Jewish community that is regarded as an example and, ultimately, an obscure object of desire; a yearning to be, if I may say so, as happy as the Jews in America—parodying the famous motto of French Jews before the Dreyfus affair.

The Left Lane

ON THE ROAD again. The highway. The great Interstate 94 that leads to Chicago, which we must reach before tonight. Distance. Space. Centimetres on the map, so deceptive to a European. This sense of space and thus of time passing, which is the real sixth sense one has to acquire when travelling in America. And then the legalism, too, this extraordinary sense of the law and the rules, which shapes people's conduct in general and that of motorists in particular. No excessive speeding, for instance. No screaming matches from car to car, as we have in France.

No way, either—even on the outskirts of Battle Creek, where the traffic is at a complete standstill—to persuade Tim, the young man who is driving, to try to make up a little time by using the breakdown lane. Or this other detail, perhaps even more bothersome, which says a lot about the anthropology of American automobile customs: in Europe the point of having a road with several lanes is to reserve one for slow cars, so that the fast ones, the ones in a hurry, which often happen to be the prettiest and most expensive cars, can drive as fast as they like in the lane reserved for them. Here that is not the case. Both lanes are being used at the same speeds. Quick and slow, big and little, and thus, whether you like it or not, rich and poor, powerful and weak—all use their lane of choice interchangeably. If you're late, try to blow your horn at the asshole who's blocking your way— and who, in France, would comply and move over. You can shout 'Get out of the way, moron, and let me pass!' all you like. (That would make him give way in France.) Here, not only will he not give way, not only will he keep going at his imper- turbable pace, sure of his right of way, but you'll see through his window, if you finally manage to pass him, his indignant, alarmed, incredulous look: 'Hey! Big fella, we're in this together—this is an automobile democracy!' A real lesson, in the field, in equality of conditions, where in France we flaunt our social distinctions, our privileges. And a real example, once again, of the perspicacity of Tocqueville, who, more than a century before the birth of the highway, noted that 'the first and liveliest of the passions inspired by equality of status' is 'the love of equality itself.'

There we are.

Another incident, mid-afternoon, no less Tocquevillean: seized by a strong need to piss and tired of Starbucks, McDonald's, and Pizza Hut, where there are almost always signs telling you the name of the guy who 'cleaned this bathroom with pride' and the name of the 'supervisor' whom you should call 'for comments and compliments,' I ask Tim to let me off at the edge of a quiet field bathed in sunlight. Scarcely have I begun when I hear behind me the roar of an engine followed by a screeching of brakes. I turn around. It's a police car.

'What are you doing?'

'I'm getting some fresh air.'

'Getting fresh air is forbidden.'

'Okay, I'm taking a piss.'

'Taking a piss is forbidden, too.'

'So, what on earth is allowed?'

'Nothing: it is forbidden to stop on highways, to hang around, to dawdle, and to piss.'

'I didn't know—'

'I don't give a damn what you know. Keep moving.'

'I'm French—'

'I couldn't care less if you're French—the law's the same for everyone. Keep moving.'

'I wrote a book on Daniel Pearl.'

'Daniel who?'

'And a book on the forgotten wars.'

'What kind of wars?'

'I'm writing about following the path of Tocqueville—'

And suddenly, as the name Tocqueville is uttered, a sort of miracle occurs! The cop's face goes from suspicious to curious to almost friendly.

'Tocqueville—really? Alexis de Tocqueville?'

After I tell him yes, Alexis, I'm following in the footsteps of this great compatriot who 170 years ago must have passed somewhere near here, this temperamental guy, red with rage, who for all I know is getting ready to book me for inappropriate behaviour, for sexual display on a public highway, or, in any case, for 'loitering with intent,' looks at me with sudden affability and begins to ask me what, in my opinion, continues to be valid in Tocqueville's analysis.

Three conclusions may be drawn. First, this 'loitering with intent,' which shows how paranoid American society after 9/11 has become. (Didn't I read the other day a story about a twenty-four-year-old Pakistani, Ansar Mahmood, who in the fall of 2001 was surprised as he was lingering near a water-treatment facility on the Hudson and was held in custody for almost three years before being deported?) Second, this command to 'keep moving,' which I had already noticed in the airports, and at the office in Washington where I went to get press badges, and in front of my hotel, which had the misfortune of being opposite the White House, and then again in New York, in front of the Ground Zero barricades: Paranoia again? Security obsession? Or a much deeper anxiety, ingrained in the American ethos, when faced with the very idea that movement can stop? And third, despite all that, the extraordinary image of this ordinary Michigan cop, a little stubborn, whose face lit up at the mere mention of this French friend of his country. What better reply to those who keep telling us that America is a country of backward cowboys and uneducated people? And what a magnificent challenge to those who want to use Francophobia as the last word these days in our transatlantic relations.

Chicago Transfer

'OH, NO', RICHARD Daley, the mayor of Chicago, exclaimed yesterday evening during the inauguration of Millennium Park, which will be the pride of his city. 'You aren't going to write us up, like all the visitors who are in a hurry and greedy for the sensational, as just the homeland of Chicago gangs, are you?' Daley, standing, somewhat tipsy, flushed in a slightly too tight tuxedo, boasted about this other Chicago, the real one, the one that, through his father's willpower and then his own; through the talent of Daniel Hudson Burnham and then of Edward H. Bennett, the city's architects, its landscapers, its Haussmanns; and thanks also to the simple decision to open up the city onto the lake and let the light in, has become this magical, beautiful city, perhaps the most beautiful city in the

United States, whose apotheosis he is now celebrating along with two thousand handpicked guests. Mayor Daley is right. And I like the passion he shows as he talks about his taste for urbanism itself. His obsession with ecology and art, his crusade for 'green roofs,' hanging gardens, lakeside towers, and also for Frank Lloyd Wright and Mies van der Rohe. I like the idea of the other artists (Anish Kapoor and Frank Gehry, Jaume Plensa and Kathryn Gustafson) he has managed to attract for this park, with the help of the successors to the old magnates of steel, chewing gum, and sausages who made the city's first fortunes— with the help and money of all these new philanthropists parading past him in their evening gowns, their tuxedos, their face-lifts.

Except... except that there is also the city conjured by James T. Farrell. There is, despite Daley's protests, the Chicago of junkies, bums, whores, freaks, and hoodlums portrayed by Nelson Algren (and filmmaker Otto Preminger). There is—still on the subject of Nelson Algren—an astounding story that says a lot about the propensity of the city's inhabitants to forget its shadowy side. On Evergreen Street one can still see the apartment where Algren lived. After Algren's death the street was christened Nelson Algren Street before being quickly, almost immediately, rechristened Evergreen Street after formal protests by residents who did not think the novelist of the dregs of society was worthy of such commemoration.

There is this other part of the city, about which no one wants to speak, but which I took time this morning to explore a little: Chinatown; the neighbourhood of the insane, released en masse decades ago; the slums on Sacramento Avenue; the division between Lawndale and La Villita, 'The Little Village,' mostly black on one side and mostly Hispanic on the other; there is this other city, where the signs are in Spanish, where you can eat only tortillas and tacos, where the supermarket is called La Ilusión and the butcher is Aguas Calientes. There is this other city, where the Latin Kings gang is still, after thirty years, waging its long war against the Two Sixers gang.

'Two Sixers,' I am told, not without scorn, by the young Hispanic who is guiding me down Broadway to the famous Green Mill—half jazz club, half cocktail lounge, where, it is said, Al Capone was a regular. 'Just 'Two Sixers.' Two and six. Like Twenty-sixth Street. Isn't that totally stupid—to call yourself the name of the street where you were born? We don't give a damn. We're the biggest gang in the city, with branches all over the country. The only problem is when the bastards come taunt us or try to pick up one of our girls right in front of us. We don't put up with that, and there can be fighting.'

And there was a lot of fighting. Gunfire near the Pilsen neighbourhood. A punitive expedition against two blacks who, eight days before, had disrupted a Latin Kings wedding. Another member of the Latin Kings had discovered on the Internet that the Two Sixers had made fun of the famous crown, the gang's symbol. Another incident: a member of the Two Sixers who witnessed a Latin King mimicking the victory sign that, in principle, is the rally sign of the Sixers. And yet another settling of accounts, linked to a matter of unpaid rent.

The result of all this shows at the courthouse on California Avenue where I have a meeting this morning with Judge Paul B. Biebel: forty-five men, mostly black and Hispanic, arrested overnight. That's a lot, forty-five. It's too many for the handsome courtrooms whose coffered ceilings go back to the days of Mafia capos and a different kind of crime. And it's so much too much that they have to be assembled elsewhere, in a basement room, where they get processed by videoconference: 'Do you speak English? Name? Age? Occupation?' And the procession on the video of the faces of these small-time juvenile delinquents, shabby and blank-looking, most of them with no home or job, who seem to have stepped out of the pages of one of the city's native sons, the writer Richard Wright. One monitor for the families, also packed in, but within waiting rooms with bulletproof glass, and another monitor for the judges, who yawn as they listen to these meagre, frightened narratives in which the same stories keep emerging, of drug addiction, unemployment, mentally retarded people who never should have left the institution, two-time losers.

The big shots of crime are merry. Thinking the city had become dangerous for their beloved children, they emigrated to the fashionable suburbs, where they live a perfectly bourgeois life as elegant, almost respectable followers of law and order. Perhaps—God knows—a few of them even present, last night, at the inauguration of Millennium Park.

The God of Willow Creek

THE BANKS IN America look like churches. But here is a church that looks like a bank. It has the coldness of a bank—futuristic, sombre architecture. No cross, no stained-glass windows, no religious symbols at all. It is ten o'clock in the morning. The faithful are beginning to pour in. Or perhaps one should say 'the public.' Video screens light up pretty much everywhere. A curtain rises to the side of the stage, revealing a picture window that opens onto a landscape of lakes and greenery. And now the bank begins to resemble a conference.

On the stage, under a tent, a man and a child in shorts discuss the origin of the world, eating popcorn.

A female rock singer is thunderously applauded, her shouts repeated in chorus by the five thousand people present: 'I'm here to meet with you… Come and meet with me… Drive me into your arms….'

Another man, in jeans and sneakers, jumps onto the stage: 'Let's speak to our Creator.' Then, to heaven, his hands cupping his mouth: 'Yes, Creator, talk to us!' This, too, is repeated by the audience.

And then the same man turns back to the congregation, his voice scarcely able to rise above the noise of the guitars and drums: 'Lee Strobel! Ladies and gentlemen, please welcome Lee Strobel, who's coming back to us from California with his new book! On *The New York Times* bestseller list! TV celebrity! Give him a big round of applause, ladies and gentlemen!'

At which point Lee Strobel arrives, a man about fifty years old with a sales-rep smile on a plump face, also wearing jeans and sneakers, and a nylon jacket—and between the two men, in this place of faith and prayer, this dialogue:

'My goodness! Our minister has changed his hairdo!'

'Bingo! You got that right! Barbra Streisand sent me her hair-stylist!'

'And what have you come to talk to us about today?'

'I hesitated between "Saving Your Marriage," "Rediscovering Your Self-Esteem," and the "Fit for Him" program that teaches you how to lose weight through faith. But I finally decided in favour of the subject of my last book, *God Proven by Science and Scholars*.'

A few gags. A quotation from the Epistle to the Romans. Then the lights go down. Now, on the main screen, sound effects blaring, a video begins, titled *In the Heart of DNA*, which shows a camera zooming inside a cell, exploring it, getting lost, encountering a thousand obstacles. Then interviews with 'former atheists' who have a whole string of academic titles explaining how at the end of this maze, à la *Raiders of the Lost Ark*, there is God.

'The problem is Darwin,' Lee Strobel says, in a tone that makes him sound as if he's advertising a product rather than preaching a sermon. 'That's the subject of my book: if Darwin is right, then life develops all on its own and God is out of a job. Do you want God to be out of a job?'

The faithful murmur—no, they don't want God to be out of a job.

'It's like the miracle of bacteria—take one atom away from bacteria and it's no longer bacteria. Isn't that proof that God exists? Isn't that proof that the Bible tells the truth? That, too, is demonstrated in my book.'

This former journalist—who in another book tells how his marriage nearly foundered when his wife became a Christian and was then salvaged when he converted, too—finds ways to quote himself eight times in one hour. So when the time for book signing arrives, several hundred of us are waiting quietly in line in the cafeteria, between airport-security cordons, to have him scribble for us 'Hi, Matt!' or 'Hi, Doug!', accompanied by a promotional smile.

'French?' he asks me, looking slightly put off, when my turn comes. 'French, yes. And atheist.'

Then this reply, as though he has changed his mind: 'Oh! That's okay… In that case, say the atheist's prayer—that works for the French, too.'

He closes his eyes, puts his left hand on his heart while continuing to scrawl an almost illegible 'Hi, Bernie!' with his right, and says, "God, if you are there, show yourself." That's the atheist's prayer.'

Lee Strobel is not the pastor of Willow Creek. Because the holder of that title happens to be away, Strobel is just filling in. But the scenario, I am told by a couple, my neighbours in line, is always the same. The other churches are dying because they're churches of yes-men who come there without knowing why. Not us. We're a living church. Our ministers are of our time, just as Christ was of his time. And we make it a point of honour to have a useful religion: prayer channels, sharing and discussing visions, organizing telephone services transmitted to brothers and sisters in distress, mowing old people's lawns, feeding the neighbours' dog when they're on vacation, cleaning the toilets at Starbucks… 'There's a lot for a Christian to do!'

Inspired by a former member of the Baptist church on the

Avenue du Maine in Paris, deliberately 'non-denominational' and, because of this, using every marketing technique to target a maximum number of customers—sorry—potential faithful, the Willow Creek Community Church in South Barrington, Illinois, draws 17,500 worshippers every weekend and has 10,000 affiliated churches dotting the country. Power? Political influence and aim? That remains to be seen. What is obvious is the power of a religion whose secret is, perhaps, simply to get rid of the distance, the transcendence, and the remoteness of the divine that are at the heart of European theologies. A present God this time; a God who is there, behind the door or the curtain, and asks only to show himself; a God without mystery; a good-guy God, almost a human being, a good American, someone who loves you one by one, listens to you if you talk to him, answers if you ask him to—God, the friend who has your best interests at heart.

The Sense of the Tragic. Knoxville Style

THEY GIVE ME, at the Hotel Fort Des Moines, the room that's reserved, eight days from now, for John Kerry. I write down this detail because it's the first thing the receptionist tells me as I'm registering.

Better than that, they've taken care to display on my night table, next to a framed photo of the candidate playing the guitar, a plate of cheese wrapped in cellophane identical to the one that will be served to him on the evening of his arrival and, in another frame, a copy of the fax sent by his press secretary detailing his minibar preferences: 'Mixed nuts; chocolate chip cookies; diet soda (preferably Diet Coke in the can); bottled water; plain M&M's (no peanuts); regular Doritos.'

The craze for the relic—this time. A taste for preservation and for the museum, taken to the nth degree. No longer, as in Cooperstown, the artificial as opposed to the authentic. Nor is it as in Dearborn, where, the other day, I visited Henry Ford's Americana museum. Everything that has existed will, one day or another, end up in a museum; even if it's under the heading 'fake,' we might as well make a museum of everything right away. But, even more striking, more extravagant: yes, everything is becoming a relic; a mere plate of cheese is becoming a museum piece, but the museum piece is a plate of cheese that has not been eaten yet, or even served—it's a kind of antemuseum, a pre-relic, an extension into the realm of memory of what has not yet taken place.

Tour of Des Moines, this city with such an odd name, 'Of the Monks.' Lost in the middle of nowhere, without charm, it must have been a significant stopping place during the time of the French.

A quick visit to the Iowa State Fair, which opened this morning and which, with its life-size cow made of butter, its prize for the fattest fowl, its giant hot dogs, seems to be a festival of American kitsch.

But my real aim—what I came here for—is Knoxville, twenty miles east, where what *The Des Moines Register* (which, it must be said, doesn't skimp on adjectives for the Iowa State Fair) calls 'the greatest car race in the world,' the Knoxville Nationals, is beginning its forty-fourth series.

WELCOME TO KNOXVILLE, says a little road sign. Right next to it on another, larger sign are written the names of all the churches in town, most of them evangelical. Then, at the end of a complex of warehouses that contain the drivers' pits along with pizzerias and stands selling hamburgers, T-shirts, and French fries, is another Hall of Fame, where spectators are lining up. This is, in effect, another church, where the names of the greatest drivers—A.J. Foyt, Jr., Mario Andretti, Karl Kinser—are venerated. And then, finally, the oval track, surrounded by stands full to the brim but surprisingly quiet. Five or six thousand people are there, mostly white, wearing shorts, cowboy hats or hunters' caps and plaid shirts. It's a while before I realise that they're so quiet—so far from the European image of wild crowds of fans—because they're praying.

Taking a closer look, I see that the drivers, too, are praying. There are about a hundred of them in the central part of the oval, gathered in groups in which one can make out, despite the distance, a sort of subtle hierarchy of allegiances and merits. They have embraced their families. Exchanged a few last words with their managers. Thanked the 'dirt crews,' the paid volunteers who came from all over the country for the honour of riding around the track in their pickup trucks several hours before the race in order to pack down the sacred ground and give it good traction. The race drivers are getting ready to climb into their cars, built to their size and almost moulded to their bodies; topped with the two airfoils that are meant to keep them on the ground; heads in helmets, helmets attached to the seats, so that the drivers, however often they roll over, will still be one with their machines. Perhaps, at that instant, the most superstitious among them have one final thought for the martyr Mark Wilson, who died in a crash here in 2001. And so they pray.

When, after the final parade, the contest actually begins; when, after they've turned and turned again around the track like Achilles and Hector before the ramparts of Troy, the heroes really speed up in earnest—in bunches of eight or ten, in a deafening, hellish roar; when the real champions detach themselves and, with the crowd holding its breath, confront one another in a swift and violent duel that never lasts more than a few dozen seconds, the match takes on the feeling of a joust, an ordeal, an epic and merciless tournament. And then one senses that it is death that is leading the dance. One senses that the drivers are taking all the risks and that the spectators—excited but still silent—deep down, both dread and hope for an accident. A theatre of cruelty, waiting as in duels or at public executions for the moment of first blood. The ferocity, violence which was common in American society, but which has on the whole been eliminated over the centuries and to which it succumbs nowadays only through fringe ceremonies like this one.

Knoxville, or the memory of the accursed share of the American past.

II

Moving West
FROM KALONA TO LIVINGSTON

A Black Clinton?

'BERNARD-HENRI LÉVY,' he repeats, mocking me a little, because when I introduced myself I must have exaggerated the syllables. 'With a name like that, you would have been a big hit at the convention.' I have interrupted my westward drive for a few days to see the formal nomination of John Kerry at the Democratic National Convention, in Boston. In this hotel dining room where some of us have been waiting for him for over an hour, I ask, 'And what about 'Barack Obama'? With a name like that, and with the success you had last night, you should be able to become president of the United States in a heartbeat.' He laughs. Thumps me on the chest, pulls away a little as if to gather momentum to land a better punch, gives me a hug, laughs again, and repeats, like a nursery rhyme, 'Barack Obama, Bernard-Henri Lévy…'

This is the man who brought the house down yesterday, in the big Fleet Center. This is the perpetrator of the most authentic single event in an evening whose other attractions included the First Lady of Iowa; the mayor of Trenton; Tom Daschle, the South Dakota senator; and hundreds of people wearing hats draped with flags shaped like donkeys, skyscrapers, World Trade Centers. True, he didn't say much. In his insistence on claiming to be a follower of the Founding Fathers, in his repeating over and over that America is a religious country and that he himself is a religious man, in the faith with which he exclaimed, 'There's not a black America and white America and Latino America and Asian America; there's the United States of America,' in his way of saying that the problem is not another president for 'another policy but a new president for the same policy the old one no longer has enough credit to follow'—in all these things there was something desperately accommodating for a Frenchman who's used to big political disputes. But in the end there was his ease; his cheeky humour, a black Clinton; his bad-boy, Harvard-grad good looks; his white mother born in Kansas City, his black father born in Kenya; there was a twofold mixture, mixed origins squared, a lively disavowal of all identities, including—and this is perhaps the most original of all—the southern African American identity. Hadn't his opponent in Illinois, the black Republican Alan Keyes, just reproached him for not being 'black enough'? Who is this white black man who isn't even descended from a slave in the Deep South?

His eloquence... His speech, which, like all the speeches over the past two days, was calibrated down to the slightest intonation, but whose smallest sigh he seemed to be improvising... the hall trembled. As soon as he stood up, you could feel that something important was happening. And the first one to realise this was, as it should have been, the one whose role was being usurped—the Reverend Al Sharpton. The born agitator, the man of all the insolent remarks, and the author, incidentally, of the only unconventional speech of the entire convention, the only one who dared to jump the rails of party speech-writers and quote Ray Charles and shout, fist raised, that poor blacks were still waiting for the forty acres and a mule that had been promised a century and a half ago to the freed slaves. But at that point, suddenly, things didn't go as planned. His rage fell flat. His indignation sounded false. Obama was there, and it was as if all the charm had gone out of the faded old star.

Barack Obama. We should consider of the image of him when, at 11:00 p.m., he leaped onto the stage with his slightly dancing gait, was lit up by the spotlights, and turned his brown American face to an amazed audience. And we should also consider the image of him today, at the hotel, light-hearted, facetious, and then suddenly tired, a little slow, drugged by his success last night—almost boring when he undertakes to explain, in a drawling voice, inventing a stammer for himself as if he wanted to talk even more slowly, the fragility of all this. We should consider the moment of suspense, almost of uncertainty, when he says we shouldn't go faster than the music, that America is the country of meteoric careers, and 'next month somebody else will be the story.' I look at Obama. I remember reading an article explaining that *barack*, in Swahili, means 'blessed.' And I feel that, whatever he may say, something is at stake in this very posture, in this marked distance from all kinds of communities. The first black man to understand that you should stop playing on guilt and play on seduction instead? The first one to want to be America's promise rather than its reproach? The beginning of the end for identity-based ideologies?

Hillary and the Stain

DID SHE KNOW? Did she put up with it? Has she forgiven him by now? Is it true, the story of the sofa to which he says in his memoirs she banished him before she let bygones be bygones? Is it possible for things to work that way with the Clintons, as with any middle-class American couple? Is there a degree of complicity in this case? Equal parts solidarity and rancour? How can you live when the whole country, the whole planet, has come into your bedroom to spy on you? And what about the White House—what, in this context, about her own supposed aspiration to enter the White House one day? Does the affair have anything to do with it?

Or, more precisely, how could it not? How could a betrayed spouse contemplate, without thinking about it, entering—working in, coming and going to, every morning of her life—the place of her humiliation? Why, in that case, would she do it? Why does she imagine herself sitting down in her turn in the infamous chair? For love of the public good—all right. For the sake of America—okay. Because she is a modern woman and a modern woman has her personal career—true. But beyond that? Who can swear that in her head, at night, other reasons aren't swirling around? Will she go there to avenge herself or to avenge him? To occupy the terrain, signal her victory, display, both to the world and to him, what an unstained Clinton presidency can be like? Or to help him, to finally erase the stain and let us turn the page? And would she then be like a film noir heroine whose husband has committed a murder—who, after she's hidden the corpse, returns to the scene of the crime to erase the clues?

That's what I'm thinking about while Senator Hillary Rodham Clinton talks, very poised, very much at ease, in this fashionable Boston restaurant to which Tina Brown has invited us.

One way or another, that has to be what the Michael Moores, the Caroline Kennedys, old Senator McGovern, and all the other guests who are busy questioning her on terrorism, Iraq, the flaws in the health-care system, the deficit, are thinking about.

For people can say whatever they like. They can go on acting as if Hillary were a person in her own right who doesn't owe anything to her retired husband. They can go on repeating that she, alone, was elected senator for the State of New York, and that the same will be true if she ever runs for president. The situation was so unusual, the moral tidal wave so devastating, the traces it left in people's minds so vivid, that when one listens to her one can't help having one ear open to what she's saying and the other, or even a third, to the strange situation in which she finds herself.

Soon she will have to declare her intention.

She will say whether or not she'll be a candidate.

And since the White House is not New York, I think these questions will take on an even greater importance that day. I think there will suddenly be nothing more important politically than, first, what the senator has in her head in planning to enter this office associated with the escapades of her husband and, second, what the voters have in their own minds when they see the craziest vaudeville in contemporary history rebound this way.

I imagine the betrayed wives of America feeling themselves truly avenged by this admirable and dignified woman, so modest, so upright—Tocqueville would have said so 'chaste,' and would have seen in this 'chastity' the privilege of the 'equality of social conditions'—who holds her head so high beneath the showering insults.

I imagine all of American political correctness falling in line behind this saint who married a lout, who suffered a thousand deaths in silence, and who now presents him with the gift of cleansing the family honour: never will the celebrated (and silly) saying about woman being the future of man seem so true.

I imagine the furthest-right lady Republicans shouting 'No! It's just the opposite! No morality! No respect for anything! Don't those Clintons have any principles? Hasn't that woman got any class? Any pride? If my husband cheated on me, and with a tramp no less, I would insist on moving out, since the place where it happened would be irrevocably cursed; so the White House? Give me a break.' Yes, I can imagine a chorus of furies shouting that in the very situation itself there would be an outrage to good manners and to reason: 'Do you want a female president who, instead of having a head for business, would only be obsessed, morning to night, with what happened there—no, here, beneath this desk, on this corner of the carpet?' Vertigo of signs… memory of places: evil venom of jealousy… Is that how one leads a country?

And then, finally, I try to imagine the public's reaction to this strange vision of a female President Clinton succeeding a President Clinton in this Oval Office, which is not a very normal office in America's history. If only America were France! There's no Oval Office in France. No symbolism of the office! The presidents change, and if they feel like it, they change their office. But in America that's not the case. No going against authority, no passing fancies! Since America is a real democracy, the place wins out, once and for all, over the occupant of the place. In the 'libraries' that former presidents build, which are supposed to bear witness to the excellence of their term of office, isn't it the Oval Office that occupies the place of honour every time? How, then, in the newspapers, on TV, in the minds of people in general—how could there be room, on that day, for anything other than the crazy, unimaginable, and at the same time fascinating image of the virtuous Hillary returning to the scene of her husband's vice?

America being what it is—that is to say, a country where Hollywood has supplanted Hegel and where, consequently, the maxim 'What is reasonable is real; that which is real is reasonable' of the philosopher has given way to the 'What is real must be spectacle; that which is spectacle must, in one way or another, be real' of the producers of reality shows. The United States being, as it were, a country where no one can ever resist a good image (unlike France, where no one can ever resist a quip), I'll bet that, if only for that reason and that instant—if only for the pleasure of seeing the scene filmed or, in any case, recorded by the great media spectacles that are the new version of universal history—Hillary Rodham Clinton might well one day enter the White House.

The Place of the Fanatics

I HAD SEEN Peter Weir's film *Witness*, with Harrison Ford.

I knew there was a strange, vaguely Anabaptist sect living ascetically, in accordance with the old rhythm of harvests and nature.

So, here I am. Back in Des Moines. And, from Des Moines, before continuing my journey to the West Coast, I set out in search of the legendary Amish, the Plain People, whose precise whereabouts no one at first seems able to tell me.

I begin with the Pella Historical Village, guaranteed to be 100 percent fake and thus open from 9:00 a.m. to 5:00 p.m. 'No, we're not Amish,' a man tells me, a little annoyed. He is in charge of the twenty or so buildings erected exactly as if they were nineteenth-century. There's Vermeer Windmill, certified to be the same as a Dutch windmill from the 1850s, and the founder's office, an actual historic building, where the evocation of the past has been pushed to such a point that they've leaned a cane against the table at the exact place where the founder used to put it. 'We aren't Amish; they gave you the wrong information.'

I go on to the Amana Colonies and their seven villages— almost all the way to Cedar Rapids—founded in the mid-nineteenth century by a sect of German 'True Inspirationists' who had been persecuted by ordinary Lutherans. 'We're not Amish,' says Meg Merckens, the young actress who, every afternoon, in a blue dress and a white cap, delivers 'Home on the Iowa,' a long monologue telling the stories of the good old times in the Amana Colonies. 'People often confuse us, but despite the similarity of our names, we don't have anything to do with the Amish. You'll find them about forty miles farther on, in Kalona.'

So I continue on to the Kalona Historical Village, another Potemkin setting, once again empty, with its post office of the era, its saloon, its general store, still the same trompe l'oeil, the same set—except this time the set isn't just a set. On the neighbouring farms there are actually men and women living according to the ancestral laws of the Amish.

The farmers I see in the distance, working with the same kinds of tools they used a century and a half ago, are Amish.

Roads that are purposely not paved, where the wagons—for the Amish drive only in wagons—raise blinding clouds of dust in front of us, are Amish.

Men in brown trousers and wide suspenders, who look as if they'd stepped out of a painting by Le Nain, are Amish. As are the women wearing homespun dresses and white caps who never cut their hair.

The refusal of electricity—except for the very ill—is Amish.

The rejection of higher education—and, in fact, of any education above eighth grade—is Amish: everything for the Plain People is in the Bible—existence must be completely governed by what they read in the Bible.

The other farmers, back from the fields, who shun my camera, are Amish. God said, 'Thou shalt not make any graven image'. All the more reason, then, not to make images of the face or the gaze.

Amish, finally, is the Community County Store, where they sell Amish bread, Amish barley sugar, Amish bobbins (stainless steel), Amish wrapping paper (handmade).

'You're using a calculator?' I ask the old, bent-over Amish woman who's running the till.

'Yes,' she says in a surprisingly sharp, fluty voice. 'Since it runs on batteries, it doesn't need electricity.'

And when I try to find out more about the difficulty of

being Amish in contemporary America—I ask what kind of citizens the Amish are; if they vote, and if so, for whom; if they read the newspapers, and if so, which ones; what they think of September 11; if they feel concerned by the terrorist threat, and if so, in what way—a brief conversation begins, which is, unfortunately, too quickly interrupted by the woman's nephew, who is suspicious of me. No, the Amish generally don't vote; yes, the Amish are bad patriots and bad citizens; an Amish can't be in the civil service or in the army; to be Amish is to not give a damn about September 11, al-Qaeda, the security of Americans, and all the rest of it.

The old lady, moreover, doesn't say 'Americans' but 'the English.'

For the Amish, the United States is not a country but an abstraction, a phoney idea.

Who are the Amish, then? Who are these men and women who live in an economic autarky, their gaze fixed on eternity?

A counter society? An anti-America within America? A case, unique in the West, of an acommunal community, putting into practice the biblical precept to set one's camp apart, separate? I remember how in the 1960s people talked about hippies who had modelled themselves on the Indians—maybe not, in the end. Maybe the model was the Amish.

Unless we ought to look at the thing in quite a different way. Unless we should regard the stubbornness of the Plain People as one aspect of the political philosophy—let's call it 'exceptionalist'—that I'm sure is just as present in American hearts now as it was in the time of Tocqueville. A rider to the social contract. An additional paragraph in the pact. The implied clause, an extra article that was not foreseen by the Founding Fathers but is in accord with their intentions. Any logician knows that this is a necessity if a totality is not to become supersaturated, and that a society with built-in flexibility can better bring its designs to realisation.

Or the opposite. They are witnesses not of God but of America. The real and final pioneers. The only ones who haven't given in, haven't summed up their religion as the 'In God We Trust' of banknotes. They are witnesses to a lost purity. The true heirs of the *Mayflower*. The silent witnesses (truly silent, since, unlike the Indians or the blacks, they don't say anything, don't demand anything, and, above all, don't reproach others for anything)—the silent witnesses, then, to the values that were those of America but on which America has turned its back since it sold itself to the religion of commodity.

Not anti-America but hyper-America. A conservatory. A shard of the Bible's meaning. America's living bad conscience but, once again, silent. You betrayed the ideals of the Founding Fathers? Turned your back on your principles? America is a failed country? An unrealised utopia? Well, then, here we are. Just here. We don't criticise anything. But we are the Amish. The profound, hidden, forgotten, denied truth of America is alive in us.

The conundrum—and grandeur—of a country that tolerates that. I try to picture the Amish in France. I can't imagine those 200,000 men and women, their testimony, their perseverance, their positive demography, in my old Jacobin country, so finicky about the rites of its own national religion.

Tocqueville in Minnesota

IT'S A MALL. The biggest one in the United States. The second biggest in the world, after the one in Edmonton, Alberta. It's a complex of five hundred stores, placed on the southern outskirts of Minneapolis—we have driven north from Iowa—where, let it be said in passing, I saw baseball bats MADE IN HONDURAS; T-shirts MADE IN PERU; garden gnomes and beachwear MADE IN BANGLADESH; dolls MADE IN MEXICO, in the likenesses of Reagan, Kennedy, and Clinton;

all kinds of 'Americana' made in Sri Lanka, Egypt, Jamaica, the Philippines, Chile, India, Korea; but not all that much made in America. It's a New Age temple of consumption. It's a church—yet another—to the glory of triumphant capitalism and neo-American living for business. Except—and this is where things get interesting—it's meant to be a lively gathering place. It's the one place in maybe all of Minnesota where lonely social misfits, addicted to the Internet and to the glamour of the virtual, come to experience reality and get a shot of physical community. There are day-care centres here. Restaurants. Cinema multi-plexes showing the best Hollywood has to offer. A bank where you can deposit your money before you spend it. An amusement park, Camp Snoopy, with a roller coaster and elaborate fountains. Lego dinosaurs in the Lego Imagination Center. A business school, the National American University, for hardworking teenagers. Greenery. A health clinic. What haven't the mall designers thought of? What possible circumstance of existence hasn't found a setting in this cocoon, a happy metrop-olis, where you could, in principle, spend your entire life?

People come here in the morning, before the stores open, for pleasure. At noon, instead of having lunch, they take a walk here. There are 'mall walkers,' about two hundred a day, who come here not to buy anything but just to walk, because it's free, the weather is always clement, never too hot or too cold, and, above all, it's safe, under surveillance 24/7. Management even ended up forbidding children under fifteen to enter after 6:00 p.m. on Fridays and Saturdays unless accompanied by an adult when word got out that bands of wild children were preparing to sow terror here, like wolves. Hence the patrols of volunteer 'Mighty Moms' and 'Dedicated Dads,' who come on the weekends to watch over and chaperone unruly children. Hence the teenagers who need to wait till they turn fifteen to have the privilege of attaining the holy of holies and becoming a true Mall-goer. The ideal thing is to celebrate your eighteenth birthday here at the

Mall. There is an entire population in the Twin Cities of Minneapolis and St. Paul whose dream is to come here on the major occasions of life, to these long, windowless galleries, devoid of fresh air, dotted with surveillance cameras and the occasional sniffer dog, noisy, stifling. They come here to pick one another up. Flirt. Lift their spirits when things aren't going well. Hang out. Treat themselves to a festive honeymoon.

Get married. Yes, marriage is very important. There is a place on the third floor, next to a store that sells wedding gowns and accessories, where a stout little woman with a machine-gun delivery offers you a choice of weddings: 'Premiere' (a one-hour ceremony with music, champagne, and prewedding consultation, all for $669 on Mondays and Tuesdays, $699 other weekdays, $799 Saturdays), 'Petite Plus' (half an hour; fifty guests instead of seventy; $569, $599, $699), 'Petite' (thirty guests; $469, $499, $599), 'Dream' (twenty minutes; two guests; $269, $299, $399), or 'Dream Plus' (same thing, but with twelve guests; $369, $399, $499).

The Mall of America is an adventure—a great, modern, total adventure. Judging from the number of customers in the souvenir shops, which sell coffee mugs, glasses, beer mugs, T-shirts, and other trimmings marked with the arms and colours of the Mall, it's an experience in and of itself. What does this experience tell us? What do we learn about American civilisation from this mausoleum of merchandise, this funereal accumulation of false goods and nondesires in this end-of-the-world setting? What is the effect on the Americans of today of this confined space, this aquarium, where only a semblance of life seems to subsist?

It brings to mind the easily led, almost animal-like face Alexandre Kojève said would be the face of humanity at the arrival (which he described as imminent) of the end of history. It brings to mind the famous 'absolute, minute, regular, provident, and mild' authority predicted by Tocqueville, the

From Kalona to Livingston

dominant characteristic of which would be a state of 'perpetual childhood' in which the master is 'well content that the people should enjoy themselves, provided they have only enjoyment in mind.' And in both cases we are gripped by an obscure terror, as though we had suddenly discovered another face of Big Brother—enveloping and gentle, pure love, and thus all the more perilous.

Who Killed Ernest Hemingway?

NINETY MILES SOUTH. In Rochester, Minnesota, this bleak little city, infested with mosquitoes in summer and freezing cold in winter, roughly equidistant from Boston and Los Angeles (hence a central stopping point for the coast-to-coast traveller), I immediately think of Ernest Hemingway. It was on the way here that he almost threw himself out of his air taxi while in the throes of manic depression. And it was here, at the Mayo Clinic, the high-tech clinic that is the aim of my visit, that he was admitted on November 30, 1960, and then again in April 1961. Officially he was admitted for diabetes mellitus and hypertension. But actually he came here (taking the assumed name of George Saviers) under a suicide watch, to undergo the two series of electroshock treatments that to this day a number of Hemingway scholars believe precipitated his demise.

I soon discover that the clinic has a choice between two accounts.

The literary memory, which it doesn't seem particularly fond of. No trace of Dr. Howard Rome, who was responsible for both decisions—to give the author of *A Moveable Feast* intensive psychiatric treatment, and to let him leave. No picture of Dr. Rome, that I saw, in the Plummer Building, where the photos of all the great doctors who left their mark on the institution can be found. No photo of the suicide from Ketchum, Idaho, either. No such documentation in a country where everything is documented. Only embarrassment when I bring up the subject. The eyes of the clinic's public relations representative show disbelief when I quote Martha Gellhorn, one of Hemingway's ex-wives, as saying after 'Papa's' death that 'the Mayo made terrible mistakes' and that its major mistake was letting the false George Saviers's real identity leak out. Astonishment, apparently unfeigned, when I mention recurring suspicions among the most devout Hemingway fans of possible complicity between the good Dr. Howard Rome and J. Edgar Hoover's FBI—which allegedly tried to bring about the ruin of the old Red, veteran of the Spanish Civil War and friend of Fidel Castro. The file is not available, in any case, they end up telling me. It all happened a long time ago. It's classified. Curtain.

And then there's the other, happier legend of William Worrall Mayo, a military doctor during the Civil War, who, by himself at first and then with his sons, William James and Charles Horace, established 120 years ago the clinic that remains, for all other clinics in the country, a model of technical progress and multidisciplinary approaches as well as humanity in patient relations. Ultramodern treatment for certain kinds of lung cancer. A new medicine, donepezil, for some cases of Alzheimer's disease. A sophisticated system of checkups that attracts clients from all over the world, who reside in the luxury suites at the Kahler Grand Hotel, which is linked to the clinics—as are other hotels in the city—by passageways, both elevated and underground, that turn the neighbourhood into a giant hospital complex. The formation, in cooperation with IBM, of a genome data bank boasting six million names. Records of diseases. Stem cells. Research on stem cells.

Bush is against it, of course. These stem cells are an issue in the campaign, and a battle is being waged around the allocation or nonallocation of federal funds for research that Ron Reagan claimed, the other day in Boston, might have saved his father.

But Mayo is a private clinic. Mayo is an academic institution that makes it a point of honour to depend mostly on itself and to ask the minimum from the federal and the state government. Mayo, moreover, is an exemplary place, an ethical clinic, an establishment where doctors are paid as in a kibbutz, and where their wish to cure is equalled only by their desire for knowledge. So at Mayo, they do not have to wait for the outcome of the battle before they move to the front lines of stem-cell research.

Well. Given the sorry state of the American health-care system; given everything I've been hearing since I got here about doctors paralysed by fear of malpractice suits, and about clinics that are cutting their budgets for lack of sufficient profits; given, this morning, an article in *The Spokesman-Review* about how the Sacred Heart Medical Center, in Spokane, has just laid off 174 people, many of them highly qualified nurses, because it wasn't sure it could reach the 3 percent profit that management had sought; given that here lies one of the core issues of the country, one of its bleeding wounds; given that reform of the public health system is the most difficult challenge America will have to meet over the next few years—given all that, I choose, legend against legend, just this once, to forget the literary legend and buy into the medical legend.

Long live the Mayo Clinic. Long live its consulting physicians. Long live its philosophy of recruiting from within and its so proudly nonlucrative aims. Long live its culture of excellence and its practice of achievement. Long live its brilliant researchers, who seem like the living illustration of the scholars in Tocqueville who put the same 'unparalleled energy' into the 'practice of sciences' as the scholars of an 'aristocratic nation' apply to their 'theory.' Long live the gentle madness of these free-thinking men, who have declared war on disease and who—gaze fixed on their computers, with their fund of observations and illnesses, their experimental techniques more refined every day—know that they are the strongest, that they are leaving no chance to the enemy, and that therefore they will win. May Mayo set a precedent. May the example of Mayo win out over the dominant counterexample. Faced with its ruined health-care system, overwhelmed by all the vices—which in principle ought to be incompatible—of rampaging neoliberalism and the irresponsibility of state-funded medical care, may the United States give itself the means to create two, three, ten, new Mayos.

Dances with a Wolf

I HAVE, AFTER Sioux City, entered South Dakota. Prairies. Motorcyclists. Bands of bikers headed out of Rapid City with their leather jackets, high boots, metal insignias on their backs, bandannas over their hair, aviator sunglasses. The Corn Palace of Mitchell. Chamberlain and its St. Joseph Indian School, where for a long time Indian children were 're-educated.' The prairies again. The desert. Long, well-defined clouds. At the end of the day, after ten hours on the road, descent into the Lower Brule Indian Reservation. Sagebrush, shrubs, bumpy road, old cars, signs posting the number of fatal accidents due to the hairpin turns, bony animals inside ramshackle pens, herds of cows in the distance, drunkards lying by the side of the road, little lakes.

And then finally Lower Brule—Lower Brule proper. I was expecting a village, but I find scattered houses, mobile homes; one last pond, gray and swamplike; a shabby casino, the Golden Buffalo—nothing like the glittering temples I hear Indian tribes have such a monopoly on. Just grimy slot machines in an old-saloon decor, a handful of woozy, sad little white men weaving in and out among the tables, clutching their chips. And then a little farther on, in the middle of a field, a circle marked out as if for a rodeo, with plastic chairs and wooden stands beneath tents. This is where the powwow will take place, the sacred dance at which, as a signal honour, two groups of white people will be in attendance—my assistant and me; and one of the senators from South Dakota, Tom Daschle, in a tough re-election bid, and his family.

I ask John Yellowbird Steele—the president of the Tribal Agency, a small, portly, healthy-looking man, baseball hat and jacket, Ray-Bans—why the American Indians haven't thought of creating a memorial, as the Jews have done. 'Our memories are here,' he replies, hitting his chest. 'Here, inside of us. A memorial would only make things harder. It would point a finger at the whites and irritate them. It's much wiser to exploit the suffering of the Indians. Yes, I did say 'exploit.' Wait for the senator—you'll see what I mean.'

Replies Linda Vargas, a social worker in Lower Brule, dancer's waist, sexy, pretty gray bun beneath a cowboy hat, a lot like Bardot in *Viva Maria!*, who hears the end of the conversation and explodes: 'Crooked traitor! The people who peddle Indian suffering like that are horrible. There is a reason to reject your idea for a memorial, but it has nothing to do with what that sell-out tells you. You build a memorial to signify that the war is over, but this war isn't over—just look at the expropriations that are continuing, the broken treaties, the genocide that's still going on. The war isn't over, so a memorial has no reason to exist.'

Meantime, the stands and the plastic chairs are beginning to fill with people: gaunt, sly-looking children; women prematurely aged; men in jeans and leather jackets, with only their tied-back hair—and, alas, their broken faces, devastated by alcohol and poverty—distinguishing them from average American farmers. The entire local Bureau of Indian Affairs is here, along with employees from Wells Fargo and from the Lower Brule Farm Corporation (the nation's largest producer of popcorn), people from the Indian Health Services and from the casino, and the unemployed, the tramps. In Lower Brule there are 1,362

Indians registered, of whom at least a third are disadvantaged. It looks like all of them are here.

And then, finally, the crowd perks up. Senator Daschle has arrived, hair neatly arranged, clean-cut, beige trousers a little too short, red-checked shirt with no jacket, accompanied by his wife, his daughter, his son. Photos, autographs, a light touch on the shoulders of the disabled, handshakes with Yellowbird, kisses for the young Indian girls in yellow polo shirts, not particularly Indian-looking, who are holding placards that say TOM DASCHLE: A STRONG VOICE FOR INDIAN COUNTRY, and the masquerade can begin.

When I say 'masquerade,' I am not thinking of the dance itself, which is very beautiful, very moving, with its hundred or so women covered in jewellery, its warriors with painted faces and blissful looks, its medicine men wearing large angel wings on their backs, its elders at the head of the procession rhythmically striking the ground with their spears, its feathered flutes and its drums, its smooth, modulated chants suddenly rising in pitch. "'I am a Lakota, I suffer for my people"— that's Crazy Horse's song,' my neighbour whispers to me, moved to tears.

No. I'm thinking of the Daschle family leading the dance. I'm thinking of the image of Linda, the senator's wife, sweater tied over her shoulders as if she were going to Newport for the weekend, dancing to the wrong beat. I'm thinking of his awkward son, his mind elsewhere, stiff, softly tapping his foot without bothering to follow the rhythm. I'm thinking of his daughter, all smiles, gracefully waving her hand between two Indian women in a trance. And I'm thinking of Daschle himself, angling for the photo op, between the lead dancers. A strange ballet, a little macabre, but one that without him would have been beautiful. One Lakota warrior brandishing the American flag and another carrying a Lakota banner—long sliding steps, genuflections, modulated cries, then heads thrown up to the sky as a sign of ecstasy or despair—and him, Daschle, happy with himself, oh! so obviously happy with his meagre political coup.

How can we forget what these dances signified, and what, perhaps, they still signify? How can we not recognise that these are the same ghost dances that a century ago aroused such keen terror in Daschle's ancestors that they forbade them under penalty of death? How can we not recall Wounded Knee and the end of Sitting Bull? How can we not keep in mind those thousands of Indians massacred because they devoted themselves to these same dances that Tom Daschle and his family are aping? When I say 'masquerade,' I'm also thinking of the Indians who consent to this aping. I'm thinking of the chief who, afterward, standing next to the senator, declaims that the Lakota people took the flag from Custer's hands, and now the flag belongs to them. I'm thinking of the soup being passed out by the senator's majorettes, in T-shirts and orange caps, at the end of the ceremony.

I think of Tocqueville's disappointment when he arrived in Buffalo and, instead of those 'savages on whose face nature had left a trace of some of those high virtues the spirit of freedom engenders,' met men 'of small stature,' their 'ignoble and mischievous faces' marked by the 'vices' and 'depravations' of both their civilisation and our own. And the melancholy of Chateaubriand, then of Fenimore Cooper, faced with the 'last of the Mohicans.' What would any of them have said about this sacred ceremony in Lower Brule that turns into a distribution of bread and circuses?

Rushmore as a Myth

THREE SMALL FACTS that I'm not sure the countless tourists who come every year in pilgrimage to Mount Rushmore know and that I, at any rate, was unaware of.

First, the architect: the famous John Gutzon de la Mothe Borglum. To him we owe the idea for, and then most of the construction of, the four stone faces that are the symbol of American democracy the world over, especially since Hitchcock's film *North by Northwest*. In Wounded Knee I learn, from the mouth of an old Indian woman I meet at the entrance to the little monument built on the site of the 1890 massacre, that he was a member of the Ku Klux Klan; that his first great project was a memorial in Georgia to the glory of the Confederate heroes Robert E. Lee, Jefferson Davis, and Stonewall Jackson. And that it was only after the failure of this first project—and thus his break with the dubious United Daughters of the Confederacy—that he fell back on Rushmore.

Then the site itself. This magnificent place, chosen for the way it takes the light, the profundity of its granite rock, and its resistance to erosion through the ages. But its other characteristic is its location in the heart of the Black Hills, a holy place for the Indians and for the Lakota Nation in particular—to whom it had been guaranteed by the terms of the Treaty of Fort Laramie. Other options had existed. The Rockies, even the Appalachians, weren't lacking in superb places where the admirer of Rodin could have given shape to his dream. But he chose this one. He and his sponsors, beginning with the secretary of the South Dakota Historical Society, Doane Robinson, could think of nothing better than to stick their monument in this highly disputed area, in the heart of what the Indian nation holds as most sacred.

Finally, the name. Rushmore I had always thought, because the sound of it was unfamiliar to my French ear, was some sort of traditional Indian name. Not so. There is nothing less age-old than the name of Mount Rushmore. For here is an extraordinary detail I discovered a little later on, as I was surfing Internet sites devoted to tourism in the region. It's the name of Charles E. Rushmore, a lawyer who in 1885—in the midst of the gold rush, when people were looking for all the military and legal methods of expropriating the last Indians—crisscrossed the

Black Hills on behalf of an American mining company. What is the name of this rich mountain? he is supposed to have asked his guide. No name, the guide replied. It's an old Indian mountain without a name. Give it your name, and this act of naming will justify expropriation.

Add to this the pathetic quality of the humble memorial at Wounded Knee, set down in the middle of nowhere, at the intersection of two roads where the village of the same name used to be, and where I met the old Indian woman. It is a simple block of cement, round, very basic; an atmosphere of half-light and chapel of rest, where, the day I passed by, there were only two young people, who had come from the next village over to buy VOTE FOR RUSSELL MEANS banners.

Add to this the bizarre impression left, a little further away, by another Indian memorial, the one dedicated to Crazy Horse. According to the intentions of its promoters—or, in any case, of Chief Henry Standing Bear, the Lakota leader who in 1939 commissioned it from the Polish American sculptor Korczak Ziolkowski—it was supposed to overshadow Rushmore. (Ziolkowski was an assistant to Borglum and, so, had worked on the Rushmore site.) Monumental indeed. Lyrical. Standing up to the comparison, in principle. But incomplete. Underfinanced. The glorious body of the Indian hero and his winged horse still caught in the uncut stone. And the absurdity of the museum next to the statue, whose star attraction—the one that, this afternoon in any case, drew the only crowd—is an old, yellowing cardboard model not of the monument itself, or even of what it will be on the day of its completion, but of what they thought twenty years ago it would end up looking like when it was finally finished. Here, then, is yet another variation on the American museographic delirium. And above all, a pathetic confirmation of the perfect virtual reality—unlike Rushmore—in which America has set up its Indian memorial! On the one hand, Rushmore, a fully completed monument, a cathedral of stone. On the other, this rough draft, this botched work, this incomplete relief carving whose very incompleteness, as the entire environment indicates, has already lasted for two decades and will last until the end of time.

The least one can say is that all of this is troublesome—very sad, very troublesome, and, as to the display of American memory, finally embarrassing. Regarding Rushmore, one thing at least is certain. This temple of the Idea, this semi-sanctuary where millions of Americans come believing they can find the elemental spirit of their country's manifest destiny, this cluster of icons that a former member of the Ku Klux Klan sculpted on land that was stolen from the Indians and christened by a gold prospector (I discovered later that, after his break with the KKK, Gutzon Borglum never completely renounced his anti-Semitism or his ideas on the supremacy of the white race)—all this is an outrage as well as a memorial. Do the Americans know? Do they feel, even obscurely, that their Founding Fathers are, here, also Profaning Fathers? Is that the reason the memorial, which was originally meant to be enlarged, to make room for and honour other figures, finally remained as it was? All I can say is that the American Idea is too important, too beautiful, and also too indispensable to the symbolic economy of the world to be left in the care of the fetishists of Mount Rushmore.

An Indian Hero Stricken with Anti-Semitism

MOOT QUESTION: DOES the status of being a victim, or a spokesperson for victims, entitle you to every right?

Recce: a meeting with Russell Means, the famous activist, a veteran of the 1973 takeover of Wounded Knee, friend of Marlon Brando, indefatigable advocate of the Indian cause, icon, hero, colourful and legendary figure. I am happy and proud to meet him.

Where the scene takes place: the heart of the Pine Ridge Indian Reservation, in the middle of some deserted land between Potato Creek and Porcupine, at a dilapidated house reached by a path leading through wild grass and then over dilapidated boards that straddle a stream of wastewater. His house? His house.

Setting: untidy little kitchen; long table around which we take our places when the interview begins; books on the floor; a big fax machine from twenty years ago; watercolours I think at first are stained-glass windows, which he tells me he painted himself; photos from films in which he appeared, as Chief Big Tree and Chief Thundercloud did before him; poster saying DON'T BLAME ME, I VOTED FOR RUSSELL MEANS; leaflets from the campaign he's running now, for the presidency of the Tribal Agency, against the man from yesterday's powwow, John Yellowbird Steele; and leaflets in support of George W. Bush, whose side I already knew he had joined.

His first sentence, while he's still standing in the doorway, very tall in the harsh noon light, imposing, long black hair tied in a ponytail reaching the middle of his back, shorts and ink-blue undershirt, sneakers, strong biceps under bare skin, energy, charisma, rings on his fingers, a bracelet—this is his welcoming sentence, accompanied by an immense burst of laughter: 'You here, Mr. Lévy? Not in Israel yet? But I heard on the radio that Sharon wanted all the Jews in France to emigrate to Tel Aviv! Ha, ha!'

And when I give a start, when I let him know that I haven't come all this way to listen to this kind of bad joke, and show that I don't find this sort of thing particularly funny, that I'm a Jew who is sympathetic to the Indian cause and that I came expressly to ask him why on earth no one ever had the idea to create a kind of Yard Vase of Indian suffering rather than the casinos that are a slow-working poison, I get this terrible reply, which is hammered out, word by word, in a restrained, affected tone of rage. 'I don't need advice from Zionists; you understand? I don't need their advice; when I needed them, they weren't there; I went to see them, I went to see the Jews in Cleveland, and I waited, oh! I waited a long time and no one—you hear me?—no one answered my call; so don't try to give me advice! A little respect, no advice!'

And then: 'What? The Moonies? Yes, sir, that's right, it's not a rumour—it's true that I gave a series of lectures sponsored by the Moonies. They've done less harm to me than the Catholics. Unlike you Jews, they held out their hand to me. When you're in our situation, Mr. Lévy, when the whole world is against you, you're not choosy, you take what you can.'

The rest of the interview is weird, vehement, sometimes zany, but, all the same, more controlled. When I tell him about the powwow, Russell Means replies that 'Tom Daschle is a snake,' the 'worst human being in America,' and that's why he's a leader of the Democratic Party. He explains to me that 'Indian politics,' as it was formalised in the Indian Reorganization Act of 1934, accomplished the feat of being the 'secret model for Hitler' in its treatment of the 'unwanted'; the 'carbon copy,' 'thirty years early,' of the Bantu Development Act, which 'institutionalised apartheid in South Africa'; and, today, at the beginning of the twenty-first century, the last case in the world of 'pure and simple communism.' He warns me, with fiery gaze and stentorian voice, that 'every official Indian person you meet in this country' is corrupt and a collaborator. You understand? he asks. A collaborator. (He actually says, straining at a French accent, 'a Vichy.') An 'apple Indian,' red outside and white inside. He talks, not without eloquence, about Indians, his people, who are sitting on 'forty percent of the wealth of natural resources in America' but who remain 'the poorest of the poor,' the 'most diseased people in the Western Hemisphere.' I am treated to a comical but sincere exposition on the necessity of 'kicking out the white man'—

in other words, seceding—and, at the same time, without his appearing to realise any contradiction, on the fact that the Indians could take advantage of the fact that reservations 'don't have to worry about minimum wage,' don't have 'health-benefit problems,' and, especially, 'have no unions' in order to 'attract industry.' He says fine things about neglected Indian languages. He preaches about the greatness of this culture that, like the culture of the ancient Greeks, emphasised, and continues to emphasise, heroism. Don't talk about Indians in the past tense, he thunders! Don't think that the death of their world and their values is an established fact! That was the big miscalculation of the whites. The whites started off assuming that nature would take over and that this dirty race of Indians would slowly die out. Well, that's not the case. That's the surprise. We are the community in America with the highest growth rate; there were 250,000 of us a century ago, but there are more than two million of us today. That's our answer, Mr. Lévy, to the policy of genocide…. But nothing can make me forget his first few sentences. Nothing, no fine phrase or emotion, will erase from my memory the fetid brutality of his welcome.

To whom should the crown of martyrdom be awarded? Who should be assigned the terrible role of king of suffering? Aren't the Jews, with their Shoah, their obsessive memory, their lobbying, causing us, the Indians, irremediable harm? That, roughly, is what he said. And as long as there are Indian leaders who use this kind of language; as long as they don't break with the insane logic of competition for victimhood and outright war for the construction of ethnic memory; as long, consequently, as they give in to an anti-Semitism that has always found its most facile arguments in this very war, there will be a shadow over the legitimacy of the cause that they defend.

Meeting with Jim Harrison

HERE I DISCOVER someone who is not surprised by Russell Means's reaction. The meeting takes place the next day at Chatham's Livingston Bar and Grill, in Livingston, in the heart of Montana, where the poet Jim Harrison moved because he'd had enough of seeing his Michigan invaded by Republicans and stockbrokers. God knows he liked them, the Indians.... God knows he still likes them when they have the faces of Louis Owens, Ron Querry, Sherman Alexie—his writer friends. But Russell Means... He doesn't know Russell Means. But he can guess. He knows the ravages the white culture makes when it corrupts hearts and souls. He knows how it can transform the best into pathetic clowns, mimes, phantoms of themselves. A memorial? Fine, a memorial. We could even, if I insist, start an international committee for the memorial. But it's not a memorial that will give Crazy Horse his soul back or save the sublime heritage of Sitting Bull. Have I read the book by James Welch, by the way, on the Battle of Little Bighorn? Since my arrival have I felt the electric, still magical atmosphere that reigns over Wounded Knee? No, of course I didn't feel anything. The cause is lost. We don't feel anything anymore. Only the writers remain, those guardians of the dead—but good-bye to living souls, farewell to Indian culture.

Big Jim is sad. He looks at me with his one eye, and then looks at the already empty bottle of Côtes du Rhône, which his friend Chatham replaces pronto, following a wordless but seemingly regular ritual, and he is sad. He becomes more animated when he talks about his house in the mountains, where he hears the song of nature. Or when he talks about the return of wolves to Montana and the fact that never—understand? never—has a case of a wolf's attacking a human being been authenticated. Or when he talks about his taste for Faulkner, whom he prefers to Hemingway—it's annoying, in the end, the way journalists who are in a hurry always compare him to Hemingway, whereas Faulkner is his real brother, Faulkner is the true writer. His enthusiasm revives, too, when he talks about France, which gave him so much, at a time when America was treating him like trash. He gets excited when he begins to talk about jet lag, that delicious state when you're not only between two spaces but between two times, earlier or later, twilight or morning in the world. You'd need a poem to express the blessing of this in-between state when you're in Paris, at the Hotel de Suède, or at your friend Bourgois's place! But as soon as the conversation turns back to America—not just the Indians but America in general, this America that, he says, has never been so poor, so commonplace, or so freedom-stifling since Nixon—as soon as we start talking about that, a look of over-whelmed weariness settles on his old swashbuckling face, which becomes streaked with red and tinged with mauve the more he drinks.

Okay, I say to him. But Nixon's America was also the America of the 1960s revolution, wasn't it? Can't we imagine the same thing? Doesn't he feel, in the inmost depths of his country, a burst of the same kind of freedom? And shouldn't he put his fame, his legend, at the service of… ?

He looks at me then as though I am teasing him. Gestures to me to stop speaking. Empties his glass. Looks at the ceiling like a blind man who is trying to remember what light looks like. Then he lets out an enormous, completely unexpected laugh that makes the restaurant customers in the other room turn around.

Stop with the legend, he says. That was exactly what I couldn't stand about Hemingway. And that's what ended up killing him. As for me… I'll die of something, obviously—maybe from that (he points to the new bottle, already diminished). Or from something else (he looks at Anika, my assistant). But definitely not from that damned legend, which has nothing to do with me!

There's no comparison, he goes on to say. The situation now, he insists, is much worse than it was under Nixon. There are the far-right Republicans and the politically correct left. The ones greedy for business, on the one hand; on the other, the morons who want to prevent us, my pal Nicholson and me, from smoking, drinking, and (another look at my assistant) appreciating the beauty of the world. The real problem—I'll tell you what it is. It's Yale. Yes, Yale. The school of Bush and Kerry. I knew that, one day, Yale would take over. Well, here it is—that day has come. And this triumph of the great predator, this victory of greedy pigs over progressives, that's the absolute truth of America. Do you know that I told Hollywood to fuck off the day I thought the system was going crazy and, by paying me too much, was about to transform me, too, into a big, insatiable, greedy bastard? All you can do is refuse. And laugh. And write literature. And, like the Indians, save the dead. And since we're back to the Indians, all that's left is for each one of us to save the Indian part that's inside himself.

The Indian as a category of the soul? A region of being and of the spirit? Harrison, at this moment, is talking the way Bohumil Hrabal did in his Prague apartment in 1989. He is talking more or less as my dissident friends in Russia did during the Iron Curtain years when they wanted to believe in nothing but moral resistance, hidden away in the heart of every person. He wants to be a writer and dissident. Writer, hence dissident. The image he gives me is of a man discouraged and uncompromising, without illusions but on the offensive, who, as long as there are free men, that's to say, writers and Indians—even if they are, like him, white Indians—will despair neither of life nor of America. I am not sure, now, if I follow him. And I'm even less sure I like this idea of an America summarily compared to a totalitarian country that leaves no choice for its citizens but withdrawal, inner exile. But it's all right. I'm too fascinated to interrupt.

Too entranced to argue. So I let him talk. I listen, and I let him talk.

The Return of Ideology

WHAT IS A Republican? What distinguishes a Republican in the America of today from a Democrat? Does this division of the two Americas exist, the blue and the red, the progressive and the conservative, which Barack Obama challenged but in which Jim Harrison seems to believe?

On the one hand, I keep meeting Democrats who think like Republicans and who, without any qualms, without thinking for a single second of leaving their original party, go and vote for George Bush (the former mayor of New York Ed Koch, the former CIA chief James Woolsey). In the same vein, I keep seeing Republicans who—also without a qualm, and without even understanding my surprise—go and vote for John Kerry (Ron Reagan, the son of President Reagan) or abstain (the association of conservative gay men the Log Cabin Republicans, one of whose leaders, Chris Barron, I interviewed in Washington, who don't want to 'endorse' Bush's stance in favour of a constitutional amendment that would forbid gay marriage).

On one hand, then, a unique system of membership, which bears no comparison to what we know in Europe and in which one's attachment to a party is both very strong and very pliable, extremely tenacious and in the end somewhat empty: an essentialist attachment, if you like (Koch, for instance, wouldn't renounce it at any price, and he proudly shows me, in his Fifth Avenue office overlooking his beloved New York, hanging next to hallowed images of Anwar Sadat, Dizzy Gillespie, Teddy Kollek, and Mother Teresa, his photos with Hillary Clinton), yet devoid of all content and even of direction (when I ask him what it can mean, when you vote Republican, to declare yourself a Democrat, he hesitates, becomes a little flustered, looks at the photo of Hillary as if she could whisper the answer to him, and ends up blurting out, 'Stubbornness and nostalgia— a mixture of stubbornness and memory, habit and loyalty, that's all').

But on the other hand, as I've already said, I attended the Republican convention in New York. I listened to speeches given by Rudy Giuliani and Governor George Pataki. I listened to Bush. I saw Arnold Schwarzenegger tell us—with an emotion that didn't seem entirely put on—about his experience as an immigrant coming from a socialist country (sic) to discover this America that opened its arms to him. Mostly, I interviewed crowds of delegates from Wyoming, Idaho, Nevada, Kansas, Arkansas, each of whom I asked what being Republican and being there meant to them. And the surprise, the big surprise, is that the answers they gave me had nothing to do with the old French—but also American—cliché of a political parade filleted to its purely festive, playful, carnivalesque dimension and thus without anything at stake.

Some talked to me about abortion and gay marriage. Some explained that nothing seemed more important to them than reinforcing the role of the churches or reducing the role of the urban elite. Others advocated a return to Main Street instead of Wall Street, the rehabilitation of the values of rural America as opposed to those of interventionist and cosmopolitan America, the defence of a concept of human rights that embraces the right to bear arms to defend one's freedom and property. For others, hatred of the Clintons was a good enough reason. And for still others, the senator from Massachusetts and his plutocrat wife, Teresa, were embodiments of a France that was likened to an uneasy mixture of 'femininity,' 'decadent immorality,' 'snobbish intellectualism,' and 'chic radicalism.'

You can think what you like about these issues. You can deem them naïve, retrograde, indefensible, contradictory. You

can find it amusing to hear the same virtuous people condemning Teresa's millions and defending, in the same breath, the
hedge funds against the welfare state.

But what you can't say is that it's a question of a watered-
down or half-hearted position. Or one that is purely pragmatic
and reduces the ideal government of the United States to a
glorified board of directors. What you can't claim is that you
were present here at one more bazaar, another stopover of the
travelling circus, a second summit of the same nihilism that
offers its two symmetrically standard Democratic and
Republican versions. What you can't argue without bad faith is
that between the position of these people and that of the
delegates in Boston who gave standing ovations to Howard
Dean and Senator Ted Kennedy there is no difference in
content or ideology.

For you can take that word, *ideology*, in whatever sense you
like. You can understand it in the ordinary sense of a representation of the world. You can understand it in the sense of an
illusion that conceals from people the reality of their situation.
You can think about the grand philosophical 'systems' and other
'utopias' that Tocqueville thought Americans 'mistrusted.'

Or, by contrast, you can think of the mania for 'general
causes,' the submission to ideas and broad social forces that act
'on so many men's faculties at once'—a tendency that can
paralyse individuals and societies, Tocqueville warns.

We have reached that point. These people who say 'values
matter more', these activists for whom the struggle against
Darwin is a sacred cause that should be argued in the schools;
the blue-collar man from Buffalo who, when I explain that the
promise of the current president to reduce federal taxes will
have the automatic effect of impoverishing his native city even
more, replies that he couldn't care less because what matters to
him is the problem posed by inflation in a quasi-Soviet state;
these are men and women who are ready to let the questions

that affect them most directly take second place to matters of principle that—in the case, for instance, of the legalisation of gay marriage in Massachusetts—do not have, and never will have, any effect on their concrete existence. Aren't they reacting as ideologues would, according to criteria that have to be called ideological?

A peculiar matter. And a peculiar reversal. It surprises me as a Frenchman—coming from a country that has lived under the rule of ideological passion brought to white heat, and yet has recovered from it. But I can clearly see that it is all the more disconcerting to the most discerning analysts of the evolution of a society in which each person's appreciation of the just dividends he can get from the social contract seemed to be the first and last word in politics. 'What's the matter with Kansas?' Since when has politics stopped obeying the honest calculation of self-interest and personal ambition? How can knowledgeable, reasonable, pragmatic men work for their own servitude, thinking they're struggling for their freedom?

That, Thomas Frank, is what is called ideology. That is precisely the mechanism that La Boétie and Karl Marx described in Europe, and which we, alas, have experienced only too often. Now it's your turn, my friends. And, as we say in France, *A votre santé!*—Cheers!

Poor Israel

IT'S THE ONE day I would have preferred not to endure.

I returned to Washington and then to New York for the Republican convention. And since I had a little time to spare, I decided to spend it in Brooklyn, in effect the fourth-largest city in the United States. Yes, that's something we tend to forget in Europe, and that I, in any case, am always forgetting. The city of Arthur Miller and Henry Miller, Barbra Streisand, Mel Brooks, Hubert Selby, Jr., Spike Lee, the city that symbolises (in France, at least) the vitality of American Judaism, is, with its 2.5 million inhabitants, the fourth-largest city in the United States—or would be, had it not been incorporated into New York.

Signs in Yiddish. Landscape of garages and warehouses, giving way to houses and kosher restaurants. Men in black. Tefillin. The heavy clothes, despite the summer heat. The hats, the yarmulkes, the long coats, and, for the women, the long skirts and the head scarves. Time standing still. Contemplation. The only sign of activity in this unusually silent world—whose only equivalent I know is the Mea Shearim in Jerusalem: the passage, sirens wailing, of the new ambulance of the Hatzolah, the Jewish volunteers who devote a third or a half of their week to helping people with medical emergencies.

And then, finally, the two events for which I have come. A meeting at the office of the Ohel Children's Home and Family Services, where everything—from the old wood wainscoting to the black-and-white photos from the era of the pioneers of Israel, the very Warsaw ghetto-like caps on most of the men, the cloche hats and old-fashioned makeup on the women—seems to bear witness to a time gone by that here, in the midst of New York, has been mysteriously recovered. And then, at the neighbouring yeshiva, on the corner of Forty-seventh Street and Sixteenth Avenue, in an even more austere setting that reminds me of the shuls of Lithuania, a meeting of the Council of Wise Men of the Torah. Sitting around a long table where an old master with a white beard is enthroned—Rabbi Yaakov Perlow, rebbe of Novominsk and spiritual leader of the Agudath Israel of America—an assembly of rabbis, quite handsome, quite poetic. I don't think I've ever seen anything like this, it seems to come out of a story by Isaac Bashevis Singer. And then two strange characters appear who have come, to put it bluntly, to negotiate the support of the Orthodox Jews for President Bush and his camp.

One of them, Norm Coleman, Jewish, a Republican

candidate for a Senate seat from Minnesota, is a sort of blond yuppie with exceedingly white teeth and the smile of a wolf.

The other is Rick Santorum, Catholic, a Republican senator from Pennsylvania; I will interview him the next day, during a break in the convention, and he will explain that, as a Catholic, he is a fervent supporter of Israel and that traditional Catholics and Orthodox Jews see God and the world in similar ways.

Thank you, Coleman begins, under the suspicious and faintly bemused gaze of the rabbis. Thank you, not just for being here but for being, for existing.... I was born not far from here, but you embody another world....This world is an example....Your world is a model....Vote for me.

Your faith, Santorum adds, even more ingratiatingly, desperately trying to meet the gaze of Rabbi Perlow—who, in the big black satin coat that he won't remove during the entire meeting, his face sealed off, gazing into the distance, seems completely withdrawn, completely absent—your faith is my own; the example of your faith and your belonging is what helps me live and believe; tomorrow I have to talk to a devout assembly of Christians; well, I hope you know that when I talk to them about faith, about the power and grandeur of hope, it's you I'll be thinking about; it's your example I'll bear in mind.

And the rabbis—diffident, ironic, with an air of immense disdain and the drifting attention of people who have seen everything, heard everything, and who observe this sales pitch from their age-old summit of history and wisdom—are silently bored, ask a few questions, consult one another with a glance, and end up saying, just like that, without insisting, without abandoning their conspicuous detachment from whatever is not directly or indirectly linked to their religious concerns. Well then, since you must know, here is what our community needs for its schools, synagogues, health services, and support for Israel in its struggle against terrorism...

In this scene, in this confrontation between faith and greed, between the highest demands of the spirit and the crass indifference of vote fishers, I don't know who should be blamed. Maybe there's no need to blame anyone, and I'm merely present at one of those operations of bargaining or lobbying that are the common bill of fare of the 'civic pragmatism' Tocqueville spoke of, which at least has the merit, compared with European hypocrisy, of putting its cards on the table. But there's one thing, nonetheless, I'm sure of. I have my own radar. I have my personal instrument panel on which, on a certain number of sensitive subjects, the signs that indicate the best and the worst begin to flash. Well, then: didn't feel that Rick Santorum and Norm Coleman were the sincere friends they claimed to be, or that they would make this country an unfailing supporter of Israel. I listened to them. Observed them. I saw clearly, in each of them, the requisite consideration for a powerful, close-knit community that holds a part of their political destiny in its hands. But what of a situation in which the community in question is less powerful? What of the day when another community, one that makes hatred of the Jewish people the heart of its program, acquires more power? And beyond all that, what about the brilliant evangelical Protestant idea of the need to ensure a peaceful, faithful, and, above all, Jewish Israel for the time when the Christian Day of Judgment comes? How can one not feel that this is the very kind of argument that lasts as long as great misunderstandings last? Perhaps I'm wrong. But I wouldn't like to bet on American support for the survivors of the Shoah if it comes down to depending, really depending, on an outlook of this sort.

III

The Pacific Wall

FROM SEATTLE TO SAN DIEGO

Seattle, Mon Amour

NOTHING MORE STRIKING in Seattle than the arrival. I loved the city itself, of course.

I loved that sensation of wide-openness on Puget Sound, the current of brisk air that touches you despite the summer heat.

I loved Seattle's delicate, sun-speckled docks. Its pulsing, colour-studded marketplace, where highly specialised book-stores, shops displaying collectible posters, myriad bars, are all wedged between two shimmering fish markets. During the day I loved the breeze that rises from the water as if to widen the streets, and, in the evening, the summer mist, wispy, a little gray, which stops, mysteriously, at the waterfront. I loved the city's hills and its interminable steps, the floating bridge over Lake Washington, the boats leaving for Alaska and Panama. I loved those 'boulevards without movement or commerce' around First Avenue, and I loved the 'drunkenness of a big capital' that soars over Capitol Hill and its sidewalks inlaid with bronze dance steps. I loved the Jimi Hendrix museum—or is it the Paul

Allen museum? Or the Frank Gehry museum? I don't quite know what to call it; what can you say, really, when the most generous patron helps the greatest architect build the most extraordinary rock-and-roll museum? I loved the air of freedom, of nonconformism, that reigns over the economic capital of this state about which they said, during the time of the great strikes after World War I, 'There are forty-seven states in the United States, plus the Soviet of Washington.'

And I loved the fact that this city that, in a distant past, endured the most savage anti-Asian riots in the history of the United States is the one that continues to welcome the greatest influx of people from Taiwan, Hong Kong, Seoul, Beijing. I loved the fact that this post-American metropolis—where, if it has to invent itself somewhere, the American civilisation of tomorrow will invent itself—remains, despite everything, so obstinately European. I liked Frank Blethen, a young man with a white beard, imitation Hemingway and genuine publisher and part owner of *The Seattle Times*, who is fighting against the Hearst empire for the survival of his paper, and through his paper, for the survival of the family press, whose fate, by his lights, is linked to that of democracy.

In Redmond I visited that city-within-a-city, surrounded by pine trees, green lawns, and little lakes, that is the headquarters of Microsoft. I met some of the engineers from Mexico, France, and India, who are inventing the language and social fabric of the future. And here, too, I loved the feeling of imagination, youth, chic and atypical bohemianness, irreverence, cosmopolitanism, civilisation, intelligence, that this peculiar group of people radiates. All the recent research, for instance, into graphic recognition. The enthusiasm when the idea arose to apply the method to the manuscripts of Joyce, Dickens, Dostoyevsky, Hugo, and with the same method, with the most up-to-date computer science, to encourage the writers of today to go back to the tradition of handwriting. The uplifting wind of elation that rose in the tiny room, empty and white, aseptic yet warm, at the mere idea of having in their hands—they, the offspring of Bill Gates, whiz kids of science and culture—the means of crossbreeding the wildest modernity with the very symbol of archaism.

I visited the Boeing factories. I spent half a day in a landscape of girders and giant winches worthy of a sculpted Fernand Léger; of mini-buildings inside cavernous hangars; of walls of monitors, monstrous pipes and chrome caterpillars, immense Jetways, colossal scaffolding, open bellies and steel guts, fuselages and armour plates—the miracle of high technology that is the assembling of a new plane. And I loved the fact that the officiants at this miracle, on whose shoulders rests a responsibility made twice as pressing by security issues and terrorist threats, looked like hippies with ponytails as they worked coolly to a Rolling Stones song.

I loved, on the corner of First Avenue and Virginia Street, the bistro Le Pichet, whose sign says in French that it's 'a bar during the day and a cafe at night' and serves 'regional specialties all day.' I met Ron Reagan there, son of Ronald and Nancy, whose speech on stem-cell research was one of the big events of the Democratic convention, and I liked seeing him this way—in a jean jacket and a khaki T-shirt, looking unkempt and sleepy, improvising a dance step in the morning sun (for, he told me, he was once a dancer, a professional ballet dancer). I liked seeing him that morning, relaxed and joking, imitating President Bush's diffidence on the day of Reagan's funeral. 'Come on, George,' Nancy whispered to Bush when she caught sight of him, completely terrified, arms dangling, as unpresidential as could be, faced with the circle of the Reagan family that so impressed him. 'Come on, George, say something to us?' And he, petrified with timidity, his Adam's apple quivering, could find nothing to say other than a little strangled 'How are you?' And I also liked hearing Ron Reagan tell me about what was behind his Boston speech, and how that very morning the Democratic speechwriters had tried to unload on him a ready-made speech full of clichés. No, thanks, can't say that, it'll be my text or nothing, and if it's nothing, no problem, I'll go back to Seattle, where I feel happy....

I liked absolutely everything about Seattle.

If I had to choose an American city to live in—if I had to pick a place, and only one, where I had the feeling in America of rediscovering my lost bearings—it would be Seattle. If I had to choose one moment in this voyage of discovery—if I had to say at what instant everything was settled and, in the blink of an eye, the genius of the place was revealed to me—it would be the moment when, arriving from Spokane on Highway 90, having stopped at a motel in Moses Lake for a late-afternoon sandwich, having crossed the orchards of Wenatchee, having passed Mercer Island and then the Homer M. Hadley Bridge, I saw, floating like a torch between two motionless clouds, in a dark-pink sky entirely new to me, the tip of a skyscraper, the Space Needle. Already completely lit up, it suddenly condensed in my imagination everything that America has always made me dream of—poetry and modernity, precariousness and technical challenge, lightness of form meshed with a Babel syndrome, city lights, the haunting quality of darkness, tall trees of steel. Ever since I was little I've so loved saying '*gratte-ciels*'—'skyscrapers.'

An Evening in Gayland

AT THE ENTRANCE to Power Exchange, a partner-swapping club in San Francisco at the corner of Otis and Gough, is this uncompromising sign:

NO ALCOHOL. NO DRUGS. NO SLEEPING. NO UPROARIOUS OR LOUD LAUGHTER. CONDOMS OBLIGATORY. TURN ALL CELL PHONES OFF. IF

SOMEONE SAYS NO TO YOU, PLEASE DO NOT INSIST.

The interior follows suit. Libertine and conventional. Depraved and proper. On the one hand, menacing labyrinths and cells surrounded by wire mesh and painted cobwebs where torture devices are set up that look straight out of either the Marquis de Sade's *The 120 Days of Sodom* or Francois Reichenbach's *Sex o'Clock USA*—the film that was so effective in the 1970s at popularizing in Europe the image of a free, bold America, one that was throwing the last conventions out the window and continuing to push the limits of dissoluteness ever further. And on the other hand, a quirky clientele, friendly, almost well behaved, and, incidentally, surprisingly old. Hesitant cordiality of first encounters. Courteous nods. A fat Japanese lady with red hair and a whip who asks a gentleman if he'd like to be tortured; the gentleman answers 'Yes, but not too much, please—make sure you don't hurt me, and no biting.' Women's clothing demurely folded at the entrance to the pleasure tents. An atmosphere in the changing rooms like that at a gym or a pool. And beneath the fake Egyptian pyramid they hinted about at the entrance (with knowing looks that left everything to the imagination and made you suspect that the most inventive and unspeakable acts occurred there), a woman wearing a garter belt who has curled up in a corner and gone to sleep and two old gay men in conversation, their voices low so as not to wake her up, towels tied around their waists and draped over their shoulders because they're cold.

It's like the gay clubs in the Castro. How weird, by the way, this name—Castro—is. Ironic that the city's gay district—a place where two men walking down the street can hold hands and kiss each other full on the mouth, where at nightfall all the bars, restaurants, nightclubs, and cinemas are gay and where not being gay makes you feel ill at ease, how ironic that this open-

air Cage aux Folles, carnival of liberated and assertive homo-
sexuality, permanent Gay Pride, this Gayland—bears the name
of the most homophobic of caudillos.

The Power Exchange is like the Castro, then. There the floor
shows have a certain boldness. Tonight, for instance, a drag
queen dressed as Rita Hayworth performs and sings like Gilda,
not about the ''Cisco quake' of 1906 but about the other one,
the real one, the enormous 'Big One,' the sexual liberation of
the sixties and the welcome disintegration of all unnatural pro-
hibitions: 'They said that old Mother Nature was up to her old
tricks / Put the blame on Mame, boys.' Further on, in a New
Age cabaret open to the street, its walls plastered with photos of
naked men, are two over-the-top drag queens gesturing frenetically on a makeshift stage. One, in a figure-hugging dress, black
stockings, mammoth silicone breasts, and blond wig, sings and
acts out songs that feature Michael Jackson, who 'shook his baby
out the window. Why? To shake off the sperm.' The other, also
blond, but lanky, flat, fake boa around her neck, hurls herself at
the clients, goes out to the sidewalk to fetch them, throws
herself at their feet, pretends to jerk them off between her fake
breasts, utters little cries, swoons. You can find joke-and-trick
stores selling SUCK BUSH pins, T-shirts saying FUCK BUSH,
postcards showing Bush dressed as a queen, with wig, panty
hose, and garter belt, and the caption 'Bush lied, thousands died.'

The trouble is that the only people here to laugh at all this
are old gays with neat hair, white legs emerging from ironed
shorts, silk ankle socks in high-tops, shirts that say VOTE FOR
KERRY or POVERTY IS A WEAPON OF MASS
DESTRUCTION, looking actually as if they're disguised,
almost more disguised than the drag queens they've come to
applaud. They have the restrained laughter, the ultraconvention-
al bearing, of nice middle-class men out for a good time, with
their high-tops that, in moments of great emotion, just the tips
of rub against the top of their ankle socks, average age about

sixty, fear of AIDS, fear of sex. If we've escaped the wildness of our youth, it's not so we can succumb today to the vertigo of a remake. Reichenbach, all right. And even the Foucault of the last years; but firing only with blanks; pro forma; making sure to neutralise whatever liberating but dangerous effects gay practices may have had in the past.

San Francisco and its ghosts. San Francisco and its frozen revolution. Once upon a time in San Francisco, the city of all excesses and the wildest orgies. The city, too, it should be said in passing, where, in one night, in a former garage at the intersection of Union and Fillmore, the literary generation was born that, from Kerouac to Lamantia, from Michael McClure to Philip Whalen, Allen Ginsberg, and Gary Snyder, most transformed America—and thus the world—for half a century. Today this city has become a reservation of audacity, a museum of successful liberations, a tomb for 300,000 activists, escapees from the merry apocalypse of the sixties—the proof, again, that the time has come for America to choose between reality and commemoration, between the position of the living and that of the survivor.

Morality among the Leftists

A HOUSE IN the Berkeley hills. A graduate-student sort of living room. A piano. The score of 'Für Elise' open on the piano. Black-and-white family photographs. A library where I notice a history of the Russian Revolution, a memoir by Eleanor Roosevelt, an anti-aging handbook. Children's toys lying on the floor. A dog that keeps barging in from the garden and getting fussed over each time. And a woman, pretty but somehow plain, arms and shoulders too thin, a long shapeless blouse that hides her figure, glasses, no makeup—the prototype of the eco-friendly Californian who makes it a point to play the part 100 percent naturally. I am in the home of Joan Blades, the lawyer—

or, rather, the mediator—originally a specialist in divorce, and author or co-author of two popular books: *Mediate Your Divorce* and *The Divorce Book*.

Six years ago she dropped everything in order to create (along with her husband, Wes Boyd) one of the most significant and innovative American alternative political movements in recent times. I am in the holy of holies where the extraordinary Internet network began that is at the origin of at least three large citizen mobilisations: the 2003 petition called 'Let the Inspections Work,' which was delivered by volunteers in person to all the congressmen and senators in the country; the thousands of phone calls imploring the same members of Congress to vote no on the $87 billion Bush requested to finance the occupation of Iraq; and the huge campaign to get unregistered voters, especially the youngest ones, onto electoral lists and out to vote. I am at the headquarters, in other words, of MoveOn.org, which people have been talking to me about ever since my arrival. But what exactly does 'Move On' mean? What is it referring to, specifically?

It's very simple, Joan Blades replies. It's 1998. We're in the middle of the Lewinsky affair. And we're so shocked. We—my husband and I—are so sick of this conservative offensive to put the president out of the running; we can so clearly see the trick that allowed them, by entertaining the crowd with a sex case, to avoid the real problems that should have been at the heart of any public debate worthy of the name. We're so deeply scandalised by this that I end all my activities as a mediator and we sell the software company we have and we devote all our energy, all our time, and all our resources, to launching the slogan whose full wording is not 'Move On' but 'Censure and Move On'. Or, if you prefer, 'Censure (President Clinton) and Move On (to pressing issues facing the nation).'

I hear her. I have her repeat it, but I've heard it all. The idea at the time was to destroy the Republican trap but also, in the same movement, to censure the Democratic president. The target was the special prosecutor Kenneth Starr and the campaign he was spearheading, but it was also Clinton himself, who in the view of Blades and Boyd had committed a genuine sin and thus 'deserved'—that's their word—to be censured. I am in the temple of American radicalism. I am in contact with what could be morphing into another New Left.

I am in Berkeley, near Oakland, with the heirs of the great liberation movement born here in the sixties around Eldridge Cleaver, Huey Newton, Bobby Seale. I am in the company of resolutely modern people connected nevertheless with the long memory of American cultural and social struggles. I am with unorthodox activists who, when they publish a book that is supposed to offer a fair image of alternative America, title it *Fifty Ways to Love Your Country*—in homage to the iconic '50 Ways to Leave Your Lover.' What these activists are telling us, though, what they are conceding through the very name of their movement, is that Clinton was just slightly less guilty than his persecutors—that the sin shocked them just as much as the impeachment. These liberal thinkers could have argued what some of them privately believed—that they thought that this business of the 'stain' was a nonaffair. They could have proclaimed that the president's sex life was his private affair, and that in any event it was out of order to let senators, congressmen, and the press have the least opinion on the subject. But no. They chose to call, at one and the same time, for the American people to 'move on' (out of the crisis) and 'censure' (the licentious president). They put side by side the promoters of the new witch hunt and the venial sin that was its first pretext. These progressives, in the very act of founding their organisation, ratified the keystone of the conservative argument and thus let people think that here was a kind of axiom, an inviolable norm, a kind of prolegomenon to all political reasoning—present or future. In the eyes of a Frenchman this is absolutely astounding.

I am not, I should point out, intent on diminishing the merit of MoveOn. Nor do I know if its work even has a future—perhaps MoveOn is a seasonal product, the fruit of a passing moment in history. But one can see something here that is larger than the specific phenomenon itself. A detail that is in fact not a detail, a genealogical slip of the tongue, a way of having to stipulate agreement with the core of the opponent's premise—and obviously giving it weight by doing so—says much about the form of American ideology. Moralism… puritanism… the confusion of the realms of politics and ethics, which a democracy worthy of that name should keep separate… a desire for purity… rigid moral standards and transparency erected as categorical imperatives…. Nothing new here, on this subject, for readers of Tocqueville, who will recognise some of the characteristics of the well-known 'tyranny of the majority.'

The real surprise is in the facts, and especially in the oddity of a situation that was not foreseeable, and in which we can see the so-called tyranny vindicated, comforted, and basically legitimised by the very citizens who should have been its natural challengers.

The Absolute Prison

ALCATRAZ IS THE prison from which no one ever escaped.

That is what literature tells us.

That is what each and every movie inspired by Alcatraz tells us; they all have to do, to a greater or lesser degree, with this idea of impossible escape.

That is what the museum, which has occupied most of the island since the prison closed, tells us (for Alcatraz, too, has caved in to the trend toward the museumification of everything).

And that is what the two Native American boatmen I met on Fisherman's Wharf, who agreed to take me to 'the Rock,' tell me. I try my best to get them to talk about something else.

I try to question them why Bobby Kennedy decided to close the most famous federal penitentiary in the country in 1963.

I would like them to tell me more about the strange and beautiful story of the eighty-nine Sioux, Blackfoot, Mohawk, Navajo, Cherokee, and Winnebago activists who a few years later, in November 1969, invoking American legislation concerning unoccupied federal territories as well as the broken but still valid old treaties that were signed after the victory of Red Cloud, offered, not without humour, to buy back the island for a little more than the price the whites paid them, long ago, for Manhattan, and who established a kind of Indian commune there for nineteen months.

I would like—since they say, not without pride, that they are longstanding citizens of San Francisco—for them to tell me all they know about the life of the prison, its system of punishment, its fiercest criminals: Al Capone, Machine Gun Kelly, and Robert Stroud, 'the Bird-Man of Alcatraz.'

They could at least talk about what we see from the boat: the Transamerica Pyramid, standing tall on its anti-earthquake foundations; the Golden Gate Bridge, on our left, with its enormous pylons, its suspension cables that seem to be mocking heaven, its orange colour made to glow in the fog; the baby seal who's escorting us; the colony of sea lions on the shore behind us; the long-beaked pelicans, known as 'Alcatraz birds,' circling over our heads.

But no. Nothing's any good.

Nothing interests them but incessant commentary about the records of this absolute prison.

Nothing makes them happier than to tell about all those escape attempts, each one crazier, more fantastic, more inspired than the previous, not one of which ever succeeded.

Steering around the island, we find the enormous water tower mounted on pilings that films have so often shown. We make out a building, gutted, that looks as if it was a forced-labour workshop. We can see elements of the fortifications that appear to date back to when Alcatraz was just starting up—to the time when it wasn't yet a prison but a fort, the first one on the Pacific, built to defend San Francisco. We can see a stairway that climbs up into emptiness. The barred, rusty framework of cells. Nearby would be the 'hole' where the most intractable prisoners were isolated and sometimes forgotten. We recognise two white stone buildings, still in pretty good shape, where the supervisors must have lived. But my two guides have eyes, and voices, only for the lighthouse, the watchtower, the remains of the 'gun gallery' from which the guards could shoot at fugitives. They become talkative only when we manage (at the risk of running into the rocks) to approach the half-effaced notice PERSONS PROVOKING OR CONCEALING ESCAPE OF PRISONERS ARE SUBJECT TO PROSECUTION AND IMPRISONMENT and when, all excited, they can show us the ruins of the bakery that, they explain, allowed the prison to function as a self-sufficient system.

I wonder about this fixation.

I am surprised at the bizarre pleasure they derive from enumerating the names of fugitives recaptured (Fred Hunter, Huron 'Ted' Walters, John Giles, John Bayless) or drowned (Ralph Roe, the Anglin brothers, Theodore Cole) or killed by a bullet while in the process of escaping (Joseph Bowers, Dale Stamphill, James Limerick, Arthur 'Doc' Barker, James Boarman).

And I wonder if there isn't something at stake here, something that touches on the very way America had, and perhaps still has, of conceiving its prisons.

In Europe, or France at any rate, people debate whether prisons should be used for surveillance or punishment, rehabilitation or rectification. People reflect on the severity of the crime and the punishment, and on the duration of the penalty and the hope for rehabilitation. Once those questions have been answered, and once it has been decided who should seek and obtain justice—the person wronged or the sovereign power—one still has to think about the place of the prison in society and the chances that prisoners will have when they leave the former to reinsert themselves into the latter. In America the main concern seems to be the imperviousness of both worlds and the radicalism of exclusion. The concern, the obsession, and thus probably everything at stake here, involves reassurance that at any moment in time the separation has been successfully carried out and the two worlds have indeed been isolated.

The freezing water. The wind. The violence of the currents and the beating of the waves against the indented shore. The thick, cold fog that, in the winter, must isolate 'the Rock' even more. The bay itself, so cheerful, so beautiful, which, when you consider it after Alcatraz, seems like a kind of Styx separating the world of the living from the house of the dead. Alcatraz is the completed form of what I saw sketched out on Rikers Island. It's the confirmation of the concept of the prison as pure machine to exclude, enclose, and, in a way, purify. Not that Alcatraz is the only island prison in the world. Not that I'm forgetting Solovki, in Russia; Lipari, in Italy; Devil's Island, in French Guiana—or even the Château d'If, in France. But Edmond Dames escaped from the Château d'If. The Italian *confino*, harsh as it might have been, was still part and parcel of the mainland. What happens here is that space itself is split in two, and this changes everything. It makes the prison the heart of another world.

If it is true, as Foucault believed, that the Western penitentiary mentality oscillated for a long time between two rival models—one, of leprosy and plague, of power that excludes and banishes, and the other, the more modern power that knows, calculates, and in the end includes—it seems that Alcatraz represents the former. The prison as leper colony. To lock people up the same way you would draw a sacred circle. No escapees from Alcatraz. Just the damned of Alcatraz. And perhaps, beyond Alcatraz, a whole segment of the American penal system.

On the Road to Los Angeles

HIGHWAY 101. THEN Highway 1, the legendary highway that follows the seacoast and that I've pictured so many times in books that I feel I know it before I even take it. Warmth and speed. Desert. Sea sky. The Pacific Wall that Jean-Francois Lyotard spoke of—about which I no longer know whether the mountain is the wall, or the cliffs over the sand, or even the immense, towering white waves that crash onto the beach.

In Monterey the landscape suddenly shifts to rounder hills, a coast of deep red, then green, then yet again red, because of the kelp—a kind of very long seaweed, spread out in beds over hundreds of feet, of which we see only the tips. But mostly one notices steep hillsides; sharp bends winding through the hillsides; well-defined cliff ridges dotted with dwarf cacti in some places and giant redwoods in others; grandiose, jagged contours; huge masses and overwhelming skies; a scenery not of the end but of the morning of the world, from which man could have been erased; and down below, in the other direction, more waves, the sun glittering in the waves, seals, the new endless luminosity of this inhuman desert that has thrown itself into the ocean.

Lunch stop in Carmel Valley, at a bikers' restaurant, where we eat bad tacos and boiled corn on the cob that remain leaden in the stomach. Another stop, at a campground for RVs, where in the torrid heat a group of white youths are playing. Everything about them—their trousers with the crotch falling down to their knees, their backward baseball caps, the shape of their T-shirts, their slang, their tone of voice, their disaffected look—is trying hard to imitate black kids in American movies. A gas station in the middle of nowhere. A McDonald's, at a turn in the road, where an American flag is flying listlessly and a billboard urges SUPPORT OUR TROOPS. A farm where a roaming pack of coyotes was reported yesterday. An obliging phone booth—after Monterey, cell phones can't get any signal. Needless to say, the least sign or detail of this sort, any billboard (like the one in front of the phone booth, JESUS SAVES, COME TO US), any Greyhound bus (all of which bring Ginsberg and Kerouac to mind), seems in this dusty landscape miraculous, almost like a mirage....

In Big Sur I discover in the woods, set back a little from the highway, the humble memorial set up to the glory of Henry Miller by a literature buff: library; little museum; bookstore where anything that has to do, however remotely, with the author or his work can be found; in a clearing, a movie screen on which a documentary will be projected in a few days; a platform, also out in the open, where the best Miller scholars in the country sometimes give lectures before a tiny audience of literature-loving locals; an old guitar-playing hippie; beneath a canopy of greenery and low-lying trees, on a pedestal of television screens artistically crushed and piled, a big crucified Jesus made of wire intertwined with branches and meant, I imagine, to incarnate the suffering of the author of *Sexus*, *Plexus*, and *Nexus*.

And then further down the road the Hearst castle, set on an arid mountain facing the ocean: San Simeon—bombastic kitsch, as big as one-fourth of Rhode Island—where I arrive full of emotion (isn't this, after all, the model for *Citizen Kane's* Xanadu, the fortress of solitude where Orson Welles brought to life and circumscribed his character?) but which I leave, an hour later, torn between an uncontrollable and conflicting urge to laugh, vomit, and yet at times to applaud.

Why laugh? The incredible images of those sleuths sent all over Europe to flush out an altarpiece the owner was mad about, and the two-hundred-and-twelfth piece of a mosaic that was shattered ten centuries ago but that he wanted to restore, or a Greco-Roman temple he caught a glimpse of in a book and decided to buy, dismantle, number stone by stone, pack up, transport, and rebuild exactly as it was before.

Vomit? The predatory aspect of it all. The caprice of it. The almighty dollar, the cave-of-Ali-Baba side of it—the fruits of one of the most formidable enterprises of contemporary pillaging all stored in a jumble. Your culture and mine; this is what I make of your memory. I buy and I stockpile. I steal and I heap up, move and possibly remodel as I please, since I'm lord of the world and patron of the arts. The world (of yesterday) was created in order to end up in my house. The most sumptuous collections of artworks and objects are destined to find their way here, to this nowhere land, temple of bad taste erected to my glory and to the glory of my mistress, the actress Marion Davies. On his good days William Randolph Hearst must have thought he was making these works live again, that he was offering them a new baptism. Isn't that, in a sense, what American religion calls 'Anabaptism'? On his bad-humoured days he must have told himself that the Europeans were dwarfs, subhumans, and that he had the supreme right to walk over, sit down, shit on, all that heritage they were so ridiculously proud of.

But why in the world do I feel like applauding, too? Despite everything, there's still a genuine love for these works, a dream of civilisation, and—in the very act of placing on the same level an ancient marble bust and a fifteenth-century statue, an Italian Venus from the twentieth century, a Moorish Spanish ceiling, and the Venetian glass tiles in the pool—a desire (pathetic certainly, but touching, and one that has a certain nobility) to make the beating heart of Europe live again here, in the wild heart of America, in an archive of the Old World. The ark of a new Noah saving from who knows what obscure disaster (perhaps the great European catastrophe…) animals turned into objects and species metamorphosed into masterpieces, each one unique. Hearst or the stocky version of the grand American gesture that the salvation, the revitalisation, the reinvention, of European culture has represented through myriad collections, museums, libraries, and university resources. Faced with this gesture, shouldn't the traveller not only applaud, but bless the New World?

At nightfall, the coconut palms of Santa Barbara. The cascades of flowers in Santa Monica. Melancholy palm trees in a Riviera-like landscape. And very quickly, without forewarning, a scene of wide rectilinear avenues, lit up like nowhere else in the United States, phosphorescent—from which I deduce that I have entered Los Angeles.

The Anti-city

A CITY IS like a text, Roland Barthes once wrote.

Just as there is a language of dreams, so there is a language of cities, more or less well articulated, more or less elegant or legible.

I wonder, then, if the prototype of a city with a poorly developed language, the prototype of unintelligible, illegible communication, isn't Los Angeles.

For, after all, what must be true for a city to be legible?

First, it has to have a centre. But Los Angeles has no centre. It has districts, neighbourhoods, even cities within the city, each of which has a centre of some sort. But one centre, one unique site as a point of reference (the law of isonomy the Athenians believed was the principle behind every city), a hub or focus with which the inhabitants of Beverly Hills, Hollywood, Venice, Chinatown, Koreatown, Little Saigon and Little Tokyo, Malibu, Inglewood, Pico Union (and I could go on, since Los Angeles officially numbers 84 neighbourhoods, where 120 languages are spoken), could have a relationship at once distinct and regular. Nothing like that exists in Los Angeles.

Second, it has to have a border beyond which it dissolves or breaks apart. But Los Angeles has no border. Along with Tokyo, it is the limitless, indeterminate city par excellence. Or if there is one—if there is, necessarily, a space that is the city proper and another that is not yet or no longer the city—the characteristic of this border is that it is undetectable, impossible to determine or situate.

I looked out for it yesterday, when I arrived from San Francisco. I will look out for it tomorrow, when I leave again for the south. But it's like the border that separates night from day or day from night, about which I swore to myself every night and every morning when I was a child: 'There, that's it, I'm going to trap it, I'm going to keep my eyes wide-open, and this time I won't miss it.' But no, I failed, every time, I bafflingly failed. Night fell, day broke, and once again I had missed the instant of transformation—just as here I missed the borderline of Los Angeles, this burgeoning city that goes on indefinitely, like an interminable stutter, a huge slow animal—lazy but quietly out of control.

Third, it has to have a vantage point, or several, from which, as in the Paris of Hugo's *The Hunchback of Notre Dame*, it can be embraced with a single glance. But is it because of its gigantic size? The immensity of the five counties—Orange, Riverside, San Bernardino, Ventura, Los Angeles—over which it is spread? The fact that the County of Los Angeles alone, with its nine million inhabitants (seventeen million in greater Los Angeles), extends more than fifty miles from east to west and sixty from north to south? Is it this precautionary horizontality, the product of earthquake threats, that so clearly distinguishes it from New York and Chicago? Is it the smog, the smoke and fog, that envelops it for most of the year and makes it one of the most polluted cities in the country contrary to legend?

The fact is, these vantage points do not exist. Nowhere can the traveller find a place from which the city in its entirety can be the object of this panoramic gaze—Hugo likened this gaze to 'the flight of a bird'—that alone would qualify it as a city. There is the U.S. Bank Tower, of course. In the east, the Gas Company Tower. In the west, next to the Spanish Steps, the 444 South Flower Street building. In the south, the First Interstate World Center, which, with its seventy-three floors, is the tallest building on the West Coast. But again, from none of these buildings is Hugo's sweeping gaze possible. From none of these heights is the city as a whole visible. And I realise—as I reflect on this and gather the few memories I have of arriving by plane in Los Angeles—that not until you see it from the sky is there the same perspective, from whatever direction you're approaching, of a city that isn't just formless but also elusive; I see that because it is always identically illuminated as far as the eye can reach, as in the opening scene of *Mulholland Drive*, it has the singular quality of systematically concealing itself from the double hold of both the eye and the intelligence.

In the end, a legible city has to have a heart, and this heart must be pulsating. It has to have, somewhere, a starting point from which one feels the city was produced, and from which its mode of production is still active today. It has to have a historical neighbourhood, if you like, but one whose historicity continues to shape, provoke, inspire, the rest of the urban space.

But this place, too, is nonexistent. In Los Angeles there is nothing like the old neighbourhoods from which you feel, almost physically, that the European cities, or even New York, have emerged. They may well show me an old neighbourhood. Kevin Starr, the excellent California historian, takes me not far from Chinatown to Olvera Street and Old Plaza, which are supposed to be the nucleus of what was once called El Pueblo de Nuestra Señora la Reina de los Angeles. But they are dead places. It's a neighbourhood frozen in time. However much

Starr leaps from house to house, his considerable bulk proving surprisingly agile with his ink-blue, too warm suit and his bow tie that makes him look like a private eye out of Raymond Chandler, explaining to me how gargantuan Los Angeles was born from this tiny seed, something doesn't work. You don't feel any possible common denominator between this stone museum, its relics, and the vital, luxuriant enormousness of the city. And the truth is that, with their pedestrian islands and their restored façades, their profusion of typical restaurants and their stands selling authentic Mexican products, their wrought-iron bandstands, their cobblestoned streets, or the varnished wood of the Avila Adobe (which is supposed to be the oldest house in the neighbourhood), these streets make me think either of all the fake streets of all the fake cities that, from Pella to Kalona and from Des Moines to Rapid City, I keep visiting. Or, in this very place, Los Angeles, in the grotesque City Walk of San Fernando Valley, of the reconstitutions, guaranteed free of gangs and beggars, of Venice, of Sunset Boulevard, or of the beaches of Santa Monica. Or yet again of a tiny brass plaque that, hidden in a corner of the Mall of America in Minneapolis, reminds modern consumers that, once, a long time ago, when there was life, humans, and, thus, history, a baseball stadium existed with real players and real spectators.

For an illegible city is also a city without a history.

An unintelligible city is a city whose historicity is nothing more than an eternal atonement.

And a posthistorical city is a city, I fear, about which one can predict, with some certainty, that it will die.

Who's Afraid of the Obese?

OF COURSE THERE are obese people in America. Yet… Are there really as many of them as they say there are and, especially, as much as anti-American literature lay claim to?

And isn't the matter of obesity more complicated than the caricature of it—and thus too, of course, the American type?

From Newport on, in all the little towns I went through, I kept my eye out for those notorious clusters of fat people photographed in European tabloids. Perhaps I didn't look carefully enough; perhaps I travelled through the wrong places. But I didn't find many more fat people here than in any provincial French town.

I read the American statistics meant to alert public opinion to this new epidemic that is supposedly in the process of becoming the leading cause of death in the country, ahead of cigarette smoking and cancer. I read a study this very morning that, in the exaggerated 'state of emergency' tone the press loves to use when it declares war on crime, drugs, terrorism, or now, obesity, said that the proportion of officially overweight people in America has just risen above 65 percent—and that number is increasing and will continue to increase by at least 5 percent a year. Imagining the future with alarm, like all readers of the study, I pictured a time when at this rate 100 percent of the population would be afflicted by the virus—until I realised that the method of calculation used, the well-known BMI (body mass index, which measures the relationship between height and weight), placed the bar so low that if the same measure were applied to many European countries, roughly the same percentage of people would be affected.

I looked at other statistics, alleged to show the correlation between obesity and mortality. I read the studies of the Behavioral Risk Factor Surveillance System (what a name!) and the American Obesity Association (which calls, flat out, for the institution of 'fat taxes' like the taxes levied on tobacco). I read all the government investigations of obesity, investigations whose comparative alarmism is such that it reduces AIDS to the rank of a flu epidemic. But I also read studies from Cornell University and the National Center for Health Statistics. I read a study by Glenn Gaesser, a professor at the University of Virginia; I read an essay by Paul Campos on the 'myth' of obesity. And I discovered that here were a handful of experts who—not content with questioning the previous studies or with denying a cause-and-effect relationship between the increase of BMI and mortality, demonstrate, for example—that overweight nonsmoking white men die from cancer less often than non-overweight subjects.

In short, lost in these arguments and numbers, no longer knowing what expert to turn to—and incapable of reaching a decision in the connected battle over the responsibility of junk food or of McDonald's, Pizza Hut, Burger King and Wendy's, for this degenerative transformation of American bodies—I end up going this morning to the Lindora weight-loss clinic, here in Los Angeles, which is said to be one of the leading establishments in the battle to the death against obesity.

I interview Cynthia Stamper Graff, Lindora's president and CEO—dark green suit, red hair, artificially perfect smile, forehead smoother than nature, photos of Reagan and Thatcher over her desk. Did she know them? No, but she admires them, she says. Wasn't it after they left office that this epidemic began? she adds. It could hardly be pure chance, is the implication, that the most famous of America's overweight people, Bill Clinton, became president soon after.

I look with her at the other pictures mounted on the walls, before-and-after photos of some of the 'big losers.' It's suddenly unclear to me whether they went through this clinic or the NBC reality show *The Biggest Loser*.

I interview one of these 'losers,' Traci Smith, thirty-six years old, 488 pounds on arrival, who can't say enough about how much her life has changed since she entered the system and, for about $1,200 each year, could take a brief course of treatment in one of the thirty or so centres belonging to the company.

Especially after meeting Traci, after seeing this newly thin woman who has strangely kept all of the gestures, postures, ways of walking and thinking—in short, the entire destiny of a fat person—I think I understand a few things.

I understand that there is a weight-loss business that is as big as the junk-food business.

I understand that the former has an advantage over the latter in being able to rely on the prestigious testimonials of science and medicine.

Even better I understand that inventing obesity—that is to say, claiming first that being fat is a disease, second that this disease must be treated, and third that it will never, despite treatment, be completely cured—creates a type of dependency that is at least equal to the one produced by the inventors of tastes, smells, and packaging that are designed to develop a loyal following among junk-food consumers.

So we can't put the blame on junk food, fly to the rescue of citizens intoxicated by the new engineers of flavour, support them in the lawsuits they are bringing against McDonald's, for example, unless we add right away that they are the guinea pigs of not just one but two competing lobbies—one gaining the advantage over the other by having discovered a regime of subjection that is almost more restrictive.

Big Brother once again.

No longer a cop but a doctor in everyone's body.

Worse than a doctor, a statistician, engraving his relentless demands onto the quick of live flesh.

Will we end up penalizing the fat?

Will we forbid them access to food deemed harmful?

Will we put scales at the cash registers of fast-food restaurants to weigh people before selling them Super-Sized Happy Meals?

And will we see, thanks to these new norms, the return of forgotten attitudes that existed during Prohibition?

We understand very well the mechanisms at play here.

We know how, starting with the control over bodies, one

imperceptibly reinforces control over society.

We can't ignore how, beginning in Europe, the medical establishment lent a hand to the political establishment by offering procedures of examination, classification, diagnosis, evaluation.

The United States has reached that stage—later than Europe, but making up for lost time. It's the last of those 'open medical governments' that Foucault, in *The Birth of the Clinic*, amusingly contrasted with Fichte's closed commercial state, and in which he saw one more decisive step forward in the history of servitude.

Bush According to Sharon Stone

SHE RECEIVES ME in her home, in a vast living room with gilded mouldings and coffered ceilings, in the Beverly Hills house where she lives with her cook, her secretary, and her black bodyguards. She is wearing a beige skirt and blouse. A sand-collared shawl. Her hair is short, a little tousled, revealing a very white forehead. A cross around her neck. Bare feet raised on the flowered sofa. I have the feeling that the conversation picks up exactly where we left off two years ago when she was participating in Not in Our Name, the patriotic movement opposing the Iraq War along with Sean Penn, Al Pacino, Susan Sarandon, and a few others.

'Things are finally starting to move,' she begins. 'A little. People are asking themselves, What's happened to us? How could we have fallen into such a trap, with such a loser? They're like sleepwalkers who are waking up. And they're ashamed.'

I object that one day soon America will pass the mark of one thousand dead, and that the press doesn't talk much about this sad record, the growing cost of the war, or people like the soldier's mother I saw yesterday in the North Hollywood Starbucks who told me how her son, Sergeant Evan Ashcraft, died a year ago because the American army is no longer able to equip its soldiers with well-armoured Humvees....

'Yes, you're right, of course. The press is hopeless. But still...'

She unfolds her legs, refolds them, pulls at the hem of her skirt with the gesture of a flirt who's trying to act virtuous, sighs deeply, takes her time, and finally gives me a look that is already outraged by what she's going to say.

'Still, I don't understand either why the press is so fixated on American deaths. I am a mother, you know. A mother above all. And for the mother I am, every Iraqi child who gets killed is as important as our thousand dead.'

An indictment of the American press, which is no longer entirely a free press.

An indictment of the conservative wave that, even more than the press, is flooding people's minds and corrupting them.

And then the city, her city, where it's becoming increasingly difficult for her to accept the contrast between this neighbourhood where we are—and where she is ashamed to have to admit that she lives as if in a gilded ghetto—and the blighted zones downtown.

'Are you aware,' she says to me with a contained fury in her voice, 'are you aware that this glamorous Los Angeles is also the leading American capital of homeless people?'

'Yes, of course, I know that. I actually witnessed, just this afternoon, a terrible scene. On Twenty-ninth Street, near the corner of Jefferson and Normandie, a group of *morenitos*, of blacks were sleeping half naked near a rubbish heap. A detachment of mounted police arrived to check up on them and tried to disperse them. One of the policemen, seeing that one of the tramps was holding a pair of scissors, beat him with a club.'

'Scenes like that are happening all over, every day, in all the dangerous neighbourhoods in the city. That's why I'm angry. And that's why, along with my sister, we created an association, Planet Hope, that organises summer camps for homeless children and which, incidentally, has never got a penny of public funding.' The telephone rings. It hasn't stopped ringing, in fact, for the hour we've been talking. But this is the first time she picks up the receiver. A newfound softness in her voice. A few words. She hangs up.

'The problem,' she resumes, 'is Bush. That ignoramus, that loser, that guy you'd hardly even want to go out for a beer with, who ends up being president.'

'Do you know him? Have you already met him?'

She laughs.

'Why are you laughing?'

'Because I've never met him, but I have a recollection, and a hypothesis, about him. It was a few years ago. I was at the height of my stardom.'

She says 'at the height of my stardom' with a scarcely perceptible touch of melancholy.

'I was visiting a marine base, I don't remember why. And at the infirmary I came across a young soldier who was crying and crying, but no one knew why. 'Why are you crying?' I asked him after I got everyone to leave. 'I'm from a family of soldiers,' he answered. 'My father, my uncle, my other uncle, they were all soldiers, and that's why I was forced to become a soldier.'

(I think, without telling her, that this was the case with Sgt Ashcraft as well.)

'And I said,' she continues, '"But you're not forced! Come on! No one is ever forced to become a soldier!" And he, can you believe, was so grateful that someone dared to say that, just that, "You're not forced to be a soldier," that he instantly stopped crying! Well, it's the same thing with Bush. Maybe he never really wanted to be president, either. President of his club, yes. President of a band of buddies, okay. But president of the United States? It's his father who wanted that for him, and his mother, and his wife. And it was to make them all happy that he wanted to be president. And there was no one to tell him, "But you don't have to, come on, no one was ever forced to want to be president!" He is the most powerful man in the world, but he's in exactly the same situation as the desperate young recruit at my marine base.'

She laughs as though she isn't too sure of the relevance of her story. An added touch, on the contrary, to the portrait of this little man, a child that never grew up and now rules the United States.

One Flew over the Migrants' Nest

THE HELICOPTER RISES high up, very high, heading first toward the ocean, then into the sun, inland. On one side the suburbs of San Diego, California's second-largest city, the last one before the border crossings at San Ysidro and Otay Mesa, where thirty thousand pedestrians, sixty-five thousand cars, and, in all that crowd, hundreds if not thousands of people without papers attempt to pass through every week.

On the other side Tijuana, San Diego's Mexican twin city, more widespread than I had imagined. Greyer, too; dirtier; endless parking lots that look like cemeteries; the flames of rubbish heaps on the outskirts of the city; cars so dusty they seem to be dried-out chunks of mud; rare dapples of colour (an old colonial house, the remnants of a zocalo) that are all that survives of the quaint little village that numbered barely a few dozen houses a century ago.

And between the two sides, dividing the shore, the stockade fence that, seen from the sky, looks like a long black sheet of metal eaten away by rust. It is lined with a sort of barred grille—not very high—which on the Mexican side has been spray-painted with skulls and which shows, inscribed on a white panel, the names of those who have died trying to cross. To my great surprise I see that the fence extends just a hundred or so feet into the ocean and that its other end stops abruptly, less than fifteen miles inland.

How come? I ask the pilot. Less than fifteen miles for a border that's two thousand miles long? Is this the famous separation—the scar, the border between two worlds, the wall of shame and death—that American left-wingers and Mexican human-rights NGOs compare to the Iron Curtain?

'Well, yes,' he replies. 'There's no need for more. Nature takes over the job soon enough—you'll see.'

A cloud of dust lifts up at that instant. A whirlwind of red earth clashes with a whirlwind of white earth, which blinds us and causes the helicopter to sway. 'If you need to throw up, tell me,' he shouts through my headphones. 'Don't be shy, tell me—I'm the one who gets landed with cleaning up later.' When visibility returns, I discover below us a landscape that has been virtually transformed—first marshes and then, very quickly, bare mountains and hills. No more ranches. No more maquiladoras, those American-funded factories hugging the border that use Mexican labour and have migrated to Mexican territory. The river becomes a thin stream and then disappears altogether. From time to time little white crosses on top of hillocks. The dry, parched land which looks now like scales, now like huge brown slabs. The scorching heat that comes in through the door. Not one bridge to cross the steep ravines. We are over the Imperial Valley desert, which does truly seem to serve as a natural barrier.

The pilot, at my request, begins to descend for a closer look, and to approach the *Linea*, visible on a GPS display. He explains that the Mexicans will react immediately and will order us over the radio to resume our altitude if we get too close.

Same attempt, farther north: no objection this time. We hover for a while and then circle around and observe our black shadow rolling over the scorched plateaus.

Then another helicopter appears which for a second I think is coming to accompany us back to the base. But that's not the case. It's a helicopter from the Border Patrol, taking over for a patrol SUV that found a group of Mexicans looking for a night-time passage through a dried-out riverbed—but this happened on the Mexican side, and thus out of the Border Patrol's jurisdiction.

How many people are out there who are preparing for the great leap into the unknown like those Mexicans?

How many kids ready to brave the SUVs, the helicopters, and then the desert to escape poverty?

We won't see any more of them during the remaining two hours of our flight.

We'll see other SUVs, winding their way over invisible dirt tracks or parked like wild animals lying in wait and gathering their strength before they pounce—but no more potential travellers.

Nevertheless, the numbers are there. There are, I know, tens of thousands of people every year who entrust their fate to unscrupulous 'coyotes' who take their money and then sometimes abandon them halfway. There are hundreds of people who die the most inhuman of deaths here in the desert—dehydrated, their skin burnt, their brains cooked, burrowing into the searing sand to find a cool place to die. And, as long as a border exists, one has to wonder if it might not have been more sensible, more effective, and on the whole more humane to lengthen the fence. And if so, why is it not done?

Money? The prohibitive cost of a structure that would extend for more than two thousand miles from San Diego to Brownsville? It's hard to say if that would cost so much more than the thousands of new gatekeepers they've just been authorised to recruit, or more than the radar and the infrared and seismic detectors provided by the Pentagon that are designed to reveal suspicious movements.

Image? The negative publicity that a continuous iron fence would generate for a country that Thomas Paine, quoted by

Tocqueville, said should be a land of asylum for all humanity? Perhaps. But that, too, is not so definite. For the image of those border patrols, supported by organisations of citizens, which expend so much energy, imagination, and science to organise a hunt for illegal immigrants, is certainly no better.

So I wonder if there isn't, above all, an unconscious perversity in the current arrangement—a Mexican-American version of the 'Most Dangerous Game.' I wonder if there isn't in this very incompletion an implicit, and cynical, way of saying to the Mexican prey, 'Go on—give it a try. I'll give you one chance; try to find it, and if you find it, take it.'

Or, even worse, I wonder if we aren't at the very heart of the hypocrisy of a system that as everyone (in California and elsewhere) knows needs these illegal immigrants and uses them as fuel for its economy. Isn't it true that its very spokesmen, the leading lights and standard-bearers—who, like the former congressman Michael Huffington, seem in their public speeches to be the most hysterically intent on reinforcing border patrols and crackdowns—are in general the first to be caught red-handed hiring illegal immigrants themselves for their own private use? A cunning system, then, that gives itself a way of having them without wanting them, and thus of controlling both the flow and the cost of this Hispanic proletariat that is as necessary as it is undesirable.

I don't like any of these explanations. And yet…

How to Become an American

'DON'T YOU FIND it difficult, as a Hispanic, to be on the front line of this hunt for illegal immigrants?'

And then: 'What do you say to the Mexicans you arrest when they accuse you of being a *tejano*, a traitor to the race, a false friend?' Angel Santa Ana stiffens.

The chubby face of this young officer of the San Ysidro

Border Patrol suddenly becomes purple.

'I am an American,' he replies. 'An American first of all. And I'm doing my duty as an American.'

Then, regaining his composure: 'It's true that by ending the fence they're only encouraging people to keep going and run into danger....'

He points out, on the wall behind him, a yellow metal sheet that looks like a highway road sign and on which are simple pictures representing a snake, a man drowning, a sun, and steep mountains, accompanied by the warning CUIDADO! ZONA PELIGROSA! NO ARRIESGUE SUV VIDA! NO VALE LA PENA! in big black letters.

'It's also true,' he continues, 'that a part of me understands these people. I have a kind of admiration, or at least sympathy, for them. That's what I tell my men when they arrest one of them. I order them to listen, to talk with them, and especially to sympathise, since we have so much to learn from these bread-winners who have taken such risks to come to this country. But at the same time, what do you want me to do? You have to obey the law. And I'm here to uphold the law. Come on, *vámonos*, I'll take you into the field.'

I look at him at the wheel of his SUV, winding his way over the scorched road that runs alongside the fence. He is frowning, his face tense and serious, watchful, the look of a lawman in the process of turning into a hunter.

When we stop, twenty miles farther on, surrounded by mountains, I observe his demeanour: a scout on the lookout for his prey. 'It's a science,' he explains, 'tracking down illegal immi-grants. The golden rule is never to have the sun behind you. But if I keep it in front of me, if I'm facing the sun, then nothing can escape me. The smallest trace of a foot-step in the dust, the slightest rustle of grass, alerts me—I know all the signs!'

I listen to him tell me stories of the thousand and one tricks of these people he knows so well—no one in the world knows them better than he, Angel Santa Ana, does whose own family was here, he hints, a generation ago, maybe two, crossing the same border, feeding the same dreams, and taking the same terrible risks that are supposed to fill him with admiration and sympathy. I listen as he, strong with the double knowledge acquired from family memory and the U.S. Border Patrol Academy, tells me about all the ruses of these poor people he is hunting today just as, probably, his own people were hunted before. A child chained beneath the chassis of a car. A woman acrobat who managed to press herself into a space under the hood. A tunnel that began under a billiard room in Mexico and ended up in the stairway of a house in Arizona—that takes years! These people have an incredible imagination. But we know all the tricks they can dream up, and that's why, in the end, we're the ones who win out.

What does win out here? His sympathy parade or law enforcement? The sensitivity of someone who's been through all this, and who insists on the obscure tenderness that seizes him when he arrests an illegal immigrant who reminds him of his parents? Or is it the other reflex, also classic, that consists of closing the door behind him precisely because he's been there, and doing so with even more spite because he knows all their tricks? Hard to say. I suppose both possibilities are true. I also suppose that there is in the situation itself the source of a thousand crises of conscience, when officers, shattered, torn apart, no longer know if they should serve their family or their country. But I'm certain about this: if you put these questions aside. If you momentarily overlook the psychological aspect. If you make an effort, above all, not to think for an instant about the terrible dramas that are the real cost of these fine phrases in order to consider only the structural effects of all this, two elements emerge.

By recruiting only agents who speak Spanish or those willing to learn it—by choosing a form of positive discrimination that in a country like France would be unthinkable—you demonstrate that Hispanics can hunt other Hispanics, you emphasise that *La Raza* (Mexicans) is neither a unit nor a tribe, and, paradoxically, you put a wedge in American kinship.

And by allowing people like Santa Ana to suggest to the desesperadoes of Tijuana that merely wanting to be American isn't enough. By making them spell out that America has to be earned, and that American citizenship is not a gift but a conquest. By setting them up as guardians of the terrible stations of the cross their own people have already followed, in tears and blood, not one stage of which can be skipped over today, perhaps you are also maintaining, no less paradoxically, the ancient forms of a thirst for America that is as old as the country.

I see two patterns of immigration in California, and, I believe, in the United States today.

The Korean, Armenian, Iranian, and Chinese immigrations maintain newcomers in established economic and cultural cocoons that merely communicate with other cocoons. And then this kind, the Hispanic kind, in contrast, places its participants in a situation that is structurally not so different from the situation of immigrants of long ago who, once they had passed through the filter of Ellis Island, once they had let themselves be deloused and examined to verify that they weren't syphilitic, still had to endure a generation of labour and sweat before they 'deserved' to be truly American.

At that time it was 'First papers, then sweat.' Whereas today it is 'First sweat, and later on, if all goes well, papers.' But the structure is there. And along with it, this constant of a 'becoming American,' which is complicated, painful, caught in the patience and frenzy of things, solitary, for a long time uncertain. In Europe newcomers arrive with a sense of entitlement. In America newcomers take nothing for granted. For them, America is a place that must be earned.

IV

Desert Vertigo
FROM VEGAS TO TEMPE

Sex Comedy

LINDA IS ONE of the dozen or so girls officiating at Spearmint Rhino, the best lap-dancing club in Las Vegas, just off Industrial Road. She is quite beautiful. Quite naked. Wearing just stilettos that make her seem as tall as I am and a tiny sequined thong accentuating a perfect waist, the curve of pretty tanned buttocks, and, over her sex, a thin, gleaming sheath.

'It's a hundred bucks,' she tells me, starting to sway her hips, hands on her thighs, breasts thrust forward, her shoulder-length blond (glaringly blond) hair caressing my face, but her gaze hard, cold, as completely devoid of emotion as a robot's.

'It's a hundred bucks,' she repeats, louder, since the music has become deafening. 'Two hundred in the private lounge. Plus the champagne, of course.' Considering that I've circled this room, with its beer drinkers who have flocked here in groups and are sitting mesmerised in front of dancers who all have pretty much the same buttocks, the same hair, the same exceedingly round breasts as Linda—who seem, actually, to be her clones—I say yes, why not, let's try the private lounge. So she takes me by the hand and—using her hips to bump aside the clones we pass who try to tempt me away, or pushing them abruptly, sometimes with a word I don't understand—leads me into a smaller room, upholstered in mauve, with low tables, soft music, dim light. The only problem is the label 'private,' since there are already a good half dozen men here, also mesmerised, whose outlines I can at first barely make out. Each has one or several dancers by his side.

'Come sit down,' I tell my dancer, whose mechanical wriggling, fixed smile, and stereotypical poses have already begun to bore me. 'I'd rather talk a little first.' Another girl in her place, even a whore, might be surprised. Get anxious. What's wrong? she'd ask. Don't you like me? Are you gay? Not Linda. Not at all. Still mechanical, she sits down unquestioningly on the banquette opposite me and holds out her empty champagne glass for me to serve her, her eyes hazy, strangely befuddled.

'How old are you?' I ask her.

'Twenty-one.'

I'd guess at least three years less than that, easily. But I've just read in the hotel magazine that after political and legislative battles in August 2002 the county became vigilant about minors. The morality squads had wanted even more. Their idea at the time was to restrict dancers to the stages, to prohibit any physical contact with clients, and to regulate even the way the tips are distributed, since a client's hand prying into a dancer's panties signifies the height of horror and vice. But alas for the squads, the clubs won out. I am told they invoked the First Amendment to argue that lap dancing was a form of expression, not of conduct, and that as such it should be protected by the Constitution. So the squads won only regulations that were a bit stricter about the participation of minors in these little orgies.

'And how long have you been doing this? When did you start at Spearmint Rhino?'

'Oh! This is my first time,' she simpers, pulling the face of a little girl who's been caught red-handed playing forbidden games. 'I'm a student. I live in Los Angeles. This is my first night.'

I doubt it, of course. Especially since that's almost word for word what the girls in the other room told me—beginning with the super-pro, an acrobat of sorts who, grinding against the metal pole on the main stage, mimicking masturbation, fellatio, and, with her fingers, sodomy, and taking the offered ten-dollar bills with her toes, her thighs, and, even better, her buttocks, had just driven crazy the group of Chinese men I had noticed a few hours earlier at the Bellagio's gambling tables.

'And,' she goes on, 'do you see Tony and Frank at the bar?'

There are, in fact, two gorillas there, very Men in Black, whom I'd spotted in the main room.

'They're here for us. The new girls. To make sure the rules are followed.'

'What rules?'

'No personal relations… all professional…'

She says this very briskly, in a shrill, overacted voice, as if she were being pinched. Then, mechanical once again, a little talkative robot giving me her spiel, she elaborates on the 'professionalism' the house expects of her. No kissing, no unzipping, don't let the client grope breasts, and as to the foot (the foot is very important), contact is allowed with her leg, but not with her foot…. The fact is that, having got used to the darkness, I can now make out a guy at the table just next to ours, his legs spread apart, his mouth open, with the long, gaunt face of a dying tubercular, next to whom two dancers are at work in a very odd way. Undulating without touching, turning around to present their asses, taking turns sitting on his lap, sliding up to his stomach, crushing him, undulating some more, bringing their breasts close to his face and whisking them away as soon as he tries to grab them, one girl getting down on her knees to rub her cheeks against his closed fly, then suddenly moving back, getting up, placing her vulva at the level of his lips, drawing back again and doing another frenzied and frigid dance. The minutes pass. Linda sips her champagne, gazing elsewhere. And I remain struck by this accomplished and simultaneous art, this almost exact science, of the libido and its nonsatisfaction.

'Doesn't it drive the clients crazy, being treated like frustrated kids?' She glances at me without replying, with that same puzzled, robotic look.

'What happens when the guy gets too hard and you think he's about to ejaculate?'

Once again she acts the part of someone who doesn't get paid to answer that kind of question, and looks conspicuously at a client a few tables down who's visibly engaged in an acrimonious discussion with a brunette in a kilt and ankle socks, with whom he doesn't seem to be reaching an agreement.

'Then there's also the case, I'd imagine, where the client asks you to go to his hotel with him. I'm sure that happens, and—'

Does she take this as a pickup line? Is she afraid of the two bouncers? Is it true that everything at the Spearmint is filmed, then reviewed by members of the Clark County vice squad? Or is it simply that the allotted half hour is over? Whatever the case, she gets up, gives me her automatic, pointless smile, and as she walks away with the same swaying gait to bestow her calculated delights on other prey, leaves me to my thoughts about the mystery of a sexual practice that in the end is so different. Virtual sensuality. Not coitus interruptus but desire interrupted. Body bereft of flesh. Coy prurience. The wretchedness of Eros in the land of the Puritans.

The Law of the Brothels

FOR BROTHELS YOU have to leave Las Vegas and Clark County.

You have to head west toward Death Valley. Leave Blue

Diamond and its mines on your right. Go to Pahrump. Pass Pahrump's castle-shaped Kingdom Gentlemen's Club and Madam Butterfly's Bath and Massage Parlor. Leave the town. Get lost. Come back. Ask your way from a bunch of kids playing in front of a billboard, in the middle of the desert, that's advertising an edition of the Bible. Ask your way again further on, opposite the Green Valley Grocery, from a group of mothers stocking up on Coca-Cola and not the least bit surprised at having to provide a stranger with directions to the nearest brothel. Take a left. Pass a bar that seems to cater to war veterans, a motel, an antique shop, all perched on loose gravel. Look for the 'guns and supplies' store the moms happened to mention.

Then the South Valley Baptist Church, near a horse pen. Emerging from a steep slope, a rocky moonscape bleached by the sun, arrive at a crossroads where I'd swear no one ever passes but where a man is standing, holding a sign: VIETNAM VET, NO WORK, NO FOOD, GOD BLESS! With his long gray hair, his emaciated face, his dusty T-shirt, he has the eerie, almost alien look of a survivor from another world that poor and homeless people in these youth-elixir-drugged lands of California and Nevada end up acquiring. And finally, about five hundred feet further on, in the middle of nowhere but firmly within Nye County (which of all the counties in Nevada that tolerate prostitution is the closest to Las Vegas), you come upon a pink-and-blue kiosk marked TOURIST INFORMATION, SHIRTS, HATS, SOUVENIRS; a bill-board boasting the inevitable WORLD FAMOUS HISTORIC BROTHEL; and then—as incongruous as the Eiffel Tower in the middle of a savannah—a house like Snow White's, divided into a saloon on the right, with the sign LONGHORN BAR, and a bizarre facade on the left, decorated above with windows in pastel colours and at ground level with three garishly painted murals. The murals reproduce lifelike scenes supposedly taking place on this very site. A John Wayne double pushing open in a manly way the door that I myself am about to push. Another man leaning imposingly on the counter of the bar I'm about to enter. And a cowgirl, daydreaming, very much an icon of the Eternal Great West, posing on a fence identical to the one I'm passing through.

Walk through the Longhorn Bar, where a sign informs you that LADIES ARE ALWAYS WELCOME.

Pause in front of a TV that's showcasing *The Best Little Whorehouse in Texas* whose message is that whores are good little girls, too.

Express surprise to the manager that no one's here, and get told that the bar, like the brothel, has its peak hours later on, when customers arrive from Las Vegas.

And, finally, step into the brothel itself, the Chicken Ranch—thus named because during the nineteenth century the neighbouring ranchers paid with chickens at its original location in Texas. It has a concealed door, falsely secretive, in an imitation of a hotel hallway—a ghost of Nabokov's 'lush' Duk Duk Ranch where Quilty takes Lolita and has her perform 'filthy, fancy' deeds. Through the door is a seedy lounge, uphol-stered in burgundy velvet, where a wheezing electric system is triggered whenever a client enters, and a theatre curtain is raised, revealing a mirrored wall.

There are four of them—not as young as the lap dancers I saw in Vegas, not as sexy. A touch of the country girl, with permed hair, rosy rustic features, flesh squeezed into corsets you can make out beneath the flounced dresses. One after another they curtsy, pull in their stomachs, wriggle, and smile.

Of the four I choose the least pathetic one. Follow her to the end of another hallway, to a bedroom hung with makeshift drapes, which she proudly tells me is decorated 'like a harem.' Notice surprise in her eyes, a glint of fleeting fear, and then indifference when she understands that I have come not for that but for a magazine—Tocqueville, sex in America, and so forth.

And still, in the meantime, store up impressions and information.

Next to the bed is a message board, like the temperature charts in hospital rooms, where every other week the results of venereal-disease and AIDS tests are written. The brothel is a sanitary place.

On the bedside table, conspicuously displayed, a choice of condoms, the use of which is required at all levels of service, down to and including, she gravely explains, a mere striptease. This brothel is a place of safe sex. Higher up, hidden in the ceiling moulding, but not very well, the eyepiece of a camera that is there to ascertain that no violence is committed and that the prostitute, whatever the client's whims may be, will continue to be treated as a sex worker, duly unionised, in conformity with labour laws and the rights of men and women. This brothel is a politically correct place.

A bit lower down, just at the head of the bed and of the client, a statuette of the Statue of Liberty, in homage to the dear, suffering America honoured here by screwing as it is honoured elsewhere by intelligence, business, arts, weapons—'Is that why I saw a flag flying at the entrance?' 'Yes, sir, that's why.' 'So high?' 'So high.' 'So big?' 'So big.' 'Because…?' Because whores are first and foremost American patriots.

And then, finally, her catalogue of services and prices, which she announces to me with the same pride showed by the matchmaker in the Mall of America when she displayed her menu of weddings. I suddenly remember that in the lounge there is an ATM, along with brochures certifying that credit-card payments are accepted. I think of the business cards with mail and Internet addresses, the maps, the cards for twenty-four-hour-a-day limousine service next to a box of mints. I remember, to the left of the entrance gate and its few steps, the ramp designed for handicapped access—brothel or no brothel, business is business.

Protestant ethic and price list for love.

New sexual order, tests, performances.

Another face of the same puritanism and its obscene nether side.

The Prison Business

DEATH ROW IN the Southern Nevada Women's Correctional Center, in North Las Vegas, has only one inmate when I visit: Priscilla Ford, a seventy-five-year-old black woman found guilty of having deliberately run over twenty-nine pedestrians twenty-four years ago in Reno, killing seven, as she drove her Lincoln at full speed.

Be careful, the state's director of prisons told me. She is sick. Very sick. Emphysema. Can't get up or talk to you.

Actually, that's not how it is. She is tired, of course. Short of breath. Wearing a dirty jogging suit. Shaggy gray hair, with a bald spot at the back of her skull. But she is standing up, pretty straight. Welcomes me gravely into her tiny cell, plastered with photos of Prince William, Lady Di, President Bush, Pope John Paul II, Mel Gibson. A book on children's education near her bed. *The Da Vinci Code* and a Bible on a shelf. A television set. A sign that says GOD FIRST. Family photos she doesn't appear in, except by means of a rough and clumsy paste-up.

'I hope my friends didn't scare you too much,' she begins, alluding to the hundred or so women, almost all of them black, in the 'segregation' section you need to go through to get to her cell—veritable raging beasts, all dressed in the same brightly collared jumpers and shouting behind their bars that they haven't done anything, that they can't bear it anymore, that they want to be allowed to exercise, that they screw visitors, that I should go to hell.

Then, shaken by strange bursts of laughter, a hiccupping of sorts that doubles her over every time, cuts off her breath, and makes me think that the expert psychiatric opinion given at her trial that she was suffering from paranoid schizophrenia wasn't completely without foundation, Priscilla continues: 'I was wrong to confess. I didn't do anything. I was charged because I had a terrible lawyer who couldn't convince the jury that I'm the reincarnation of Christ himself. The real guilty one, here she is.' She shows me a photo pinned upside down, all by itself on a gold-painted corkboard. 'She's the real guilty one. She's my sister. She's still on the run, and that's why there are still crimes being committed in Reno.'

And then, finally, in response to my questions about the ordeal it must be to wake up every morning for twenty years and tell yourself that this could be the last day, she makes a remark whose sudden brilliance settles the debate on the 'merits' of the network of private prisons that this penitentiary has belonged to since its creation—as opposed to the 'normal' public system that it has just joined in the past few days after a controversy that inflamed passions throughout the state: 'For me, there's a before and an after; before, I was living like a dog, no one cared about me, but the advantage was that they no longer thought about executing me; today the food is better, the cell is cleaner, but I think they're going to come looking for me.'

Yes, in a few words she expressed the core idea.

Priscilla Ford is cut off from everything and, in the twenty years since she was condemned, has received almost no visits. But she has summarised one of the crucial issues that divide the country today, about which the Nobel Prize-winning economist Joseph Stiglitz talked with me at length in New York—she has expressed the advantages and inconveniences of the privatisation of American prisons as I had been able to glimpse them myself in a visit that preceded my meeting with her.

The positive side: an apathy in the behaviour of the prison

guards, which I imagine is an offspring of this culture of private enterprise that was the rule until last month. A certain casualness, almost freedom, in the way the prisoners (except, of course, the ones in solitary) walk around dressed as they please, talking, pausing if they want. Mini stereo systems in some cells, and sometimes television sets. Beauty parlours with posters of different hairstyles, just as in provincial hair salons. Even the colour on the walls of the common rooms—pink or mauve or blue—whose affected cheerfulness could be that of a kindergarten. Behind all this you can imagine the shareholders of Corrections Corporation of America, which had run the prison, coolly calculating that feeding and entertaining the human animal, loosening the bit a little, offering a less sinister environment than the punitive cells of a state prison, is an affordable way—less costly, at any rate, than armies of prison guards—to keep a prisoner quiet and tame.

The negative side: the abandonment, when the state withdraws and the law of profit reigns, of any kind of reform project. These outcast men—or in this case, women—whom the body politic, and thus the community of citizens, may forget to punish but with whom, at the same time, they have utterly lost contact. This is the height of abandonment. The most absolute dereliction. The docile bodies and sad souls described by Michel Foucault becoming half subjects, stupefied by medications that unlicensed doctors or prison guards, distribute to anyone who asks or even, for the rebellious ones, to the ones who don't ask. Bodies are fed but morally beaten. Souls are suspended and literally lost in the bright shadows of these sweetish dungeons. Snuffing out of human light. Residual subhumanity. Fundamentally, the completion of the gesture of exclusion and elimination that began at Rikers Island, that I sensed again at Alcatraz, but that finds here its most complete form, in this withdrawal of public authority, in this programmed indifference of the community to its delinquents and monsters.

Between the plague and cholera it's never easy to choose. And it's clear that when we contemplate the horror of Priscilla Ford's case, when we're faced with this hopeless scandal—the fact that thirty-eight states, including Nevada, maintain the death penalty—all other debates over the American prison system seem almost frivolous. Still, there are, at times, degrees of evil. And I fear that with this debate about privatisation, with the very existence of prisons subject only to the logic of money, we have taken one more decisive step on the path to civilised barbarism.

Creationism. They Say…

'THERE ARE TWO theories,' the helicopter pilot shouts when I ask him about the geological formation of the formidable Grand Canyon, which we're beginning to glimpse after an hour of flight over a landscape of deserts and dormant volcanoes, dried-up lakes and the Hoover Dam, on Lake Mead.

'There are two theories,' he repeats, louder, to overcome the noise of the helicopter's rotors and engine. One claims it emerged little by little, during millions or even billions of years, as it became eroded. The other claims that all this, all these wonders, these monuments as magnificent as the temples of Angkor Wat, these red and pink rocks you see below you, that formation on your left that looks like a Roman temple, this other one here, look, right here, that looks like a ruined fortress—that all of this can't be the result of chance, that it needed an artist, and that this artist is God.

And then, a few minutes later, when we're higher than the rim itself and above the dizzying chasm: 'And there are two theories here, too.' One says it's the Colorado River that carved the rift over the course of millennia. The other says no, that's impossible. Such a ravine, such a colossal gorge, such a clear-cut, perfect canyon, where geologists have found so many amazingly preserved fossils, this scar that runs in one stroke without deviating for three hundred miles—all of this could only have been produced all at once. Maybe not in one day, but in a year, maybe two, after a cataclysm like the flood in the Bible.

The pilot isn't yet thirty. He is modern. Thin and bright. With his Ray-Bans, his longish hair, his handsome young face and ruddy complexion, he doesn't bear much resemblance to the people I saw at Willow Creek, in the church with video screens, where Lee Strobel spoke against Darwin. And soon, when we return to Vegas, he'll confess that he's a Democrat, that he's getting ready to vote for John Kerry, and that he's a fan of R&B and 'dance-floor technopop.' But he has just drawn an exact sketch of this phenomenon called creationism, whose importance to the new American conservative thinking regardless of political party is one of the strangest, most excessive things ever catching the eye of a foreign traveller.

There was a time when creationists were pure ideologues, content to take up the old arguments of Darwin's contemporaries. How if man is descended from an animal is it possible to endow him with a soul and to bestow upon that soul the immortality postulated by different religions? This was the time, 1925, of the famous 'monkey trial,' when a court in Tennessee found a high school teacher guilty of daring to teach that man and monkey were genetic cousins. It was the era, throughout the 1920s and 1930s, when a number of American states instituted amendments forbidding the teaching of Darwinism in schools. It was the time, in other words, of the battle between faith and science—and the latter was often ordered to give in to the former.

Today, as says French author Dominique Lecourt, the strategy has been refined. It has even been reversed. Instead of opposing science; instead of making a stand against the scientific spirit and its methods; instead, in short, of contrasting a soulless science with the eternal human soul and natural theology, the creationist camp has had the clever idea of fitting itself into the adversary's mould, borrowing science's procedures and effects, and also starting to speak in the name of science.

That's the story of the scholar Jonathan Wells, recipient of Ph.D.s from both Yale and Berkeley, who under the influence of the Moonies developed a teleology of the history of species, demonstrating that their succession corresponds to an 'intelligent design.' That's the story of the Moonies in general, who, thirty years ago, with the support of the Nobel Prize winner and spiritualist John Eccles, established a series of International Conferences for the Unity of the Sciences—one object of which was to undermine the theoretical foundations of Darwinism. It's an array of organisations that use a vast arsenal of diplomas, validations, scholarly communications, and scientific commissions for the purpose of their crusade worthy of a great modern scientific institution. It's a plethora, in fact, of paleontologists, geologists, gemologists—or people who claim to be such—who, in seemingly scholarly journals, are writing articles aiming to call into question the theory of the primeval soup, to recalculate the age of Earth and the solar system, to discover the remains of Noah's ark, to date with carbon 14 the fossil-bearing layers, and to discover the 'actual date' of the Flood. In the end it's none other than our young pilot, who, having returned to the Vegas heliport, explains with the same self-assurance that there are two theories, too, about the origin of Earth.

This neocreationism no longer presses to exclude Darwinism from textbooks and schools altogether.

It no longer tries to dismiss it in the name of a divine knowledge that is imposed on the knowledge of scholars with the authority of fanaticism or revealed truth.

On the contrary, it accepts Darwinism, or in any case pretends to accept it—but only while asserting the right, the mere right, to oppose its 'hypotheses' with the contrary hypotheses, placed on the same level and equal in worth, of 'scientific creationism.' The invention of scientific creationism—this elevation to the rank of 'science' of what is patently superstition and pretence—can only be called inspired.

There are two theories, and you have a choice: that's the formula of an enlightened obscurantism; that's the principle of revisionism with a liberal and tolerant face; that's the act of faith of a dogmatism reconciled with freedom of speech and thought; that's the subtlest, most underhanded, most cunning, and at bottom most dangerous ideological manoeuvre of the American right in years.

The Mormon Masterstroke

ABOUT THE SIGNIFICANCE of religion in American democratic life; about the peculiarity of systematically placing public debate and plebiscite under the blessing of God Almighty; about the mystery of a people who are at once the most materialistic and the most spiritual, the 'greediest,' in Jim Harrison's view, and the most intensely religious; about the paradox of a taste for freedom that, far from having been wrested from the murky shadows of faith as in Europe, is, on the contrary, right in step with it, freedom feeding on faith, faith supporting itself on freedom, and so on, ad infinitum—about all of this, I don't think the traveller today can have anything to add to the prophetic pages of the second volume of Tocqueville's *Democracy in America*.

Salt Lake City, though, is an exception.

Case in point: the Church of Jesus Christ of Latter-day Saints, otherwise known as the Mormon Church, which has its spiritual centre here and which, I must confess, looks like nothing I've ever seen before.

I'm not talking about Salt Lake City itself, surreal and artificial, orthogonal and rigid, built in the nineteenth century in the middle of the desert by a Mormon colony fleeing persecution.

I'm not talking this Sunday morning, as I visit the Tabernacle and then the Mormon temple in Temple Square, about this uneasy mixture of the prophetic and the mundane, the intensity of fervour and the triviality of rites, which after all is not so different from what you can see in any of the big new non-denominational churches in America.

I'm not talking about the sectarian obsession—the Golden Section or the five-branched cross engraved on the temple walls, the rationalised occultism, the spiritualist puritanism (and, at its most extreme, the apocalyptic fantasies compelling believers to stock freezers with loads of provisions in expectation of the Last Day); this is not so exceptional, and in any case the Mormon Church maintains that it has put much of this behind it.

I'm not even thinking of the living prophet—yes, 'living prophet' which is what in Salt Lake City they call the spiritual head of the community, the man who rules over the Quorum of the Twelve Apostles as well as the millions of Mormons in Utah and throughout the world. I'm not even thinking, then, of my astonishment when at the noontime service, in what looks like a luxurious hotel lobby (velvets, gilding, chandeliers, brocades) transformed into a place of worship—another sign of the same confusion of the profane with the sacred—I was finally shown the prophet. And instead of the holy man I was expecting, instead of a dignified heir to Joseph Smith, the church's founder, whom I had imagined as an apostolic figure come to reestablish the plenitude of the Gospel on earth, I discovered a little ninety-four-year-old man, cautious and dapper, dressed in a double-breasted navy-blue suit with gold buttons, closer to a Cinzano drinker than to a WASP Dalai Lama.

No. The real story here is at 35 North West Temple Street— the Family History Library.

What's genuinely interesting, in my eyes, about this Mormon

Church is a procedure unique in history, not just among American churches but among all churches, which consists in travelling all over the world in order to assemble and store up the names of human beings from throughout the centuries.

'We take everything,' the librarian tells me. Everything. Birth certificates. Marriage and death certificates. Newspapers. Old letters. Photos. Civil and parish registers. Military papers. Ancestral diagrams. Family trees. Censuses. Land registries. Immigration and emigration lists. Court reports. We have emissaries who travel the planet. We have 'microfilm teams' who go sign deals and collect material. The result is a unique data bank. It's a supply of billions of names entered in our International Genealogical Index and preserved here in the library as well as for security purposes in a place twenty-five miles southeast of the city in the heart of Granite Mountain, in fortified rooms hollowed out of the mountainside, guaranteed earthquake-proof. Someday the dead from every era will be entered into the computer. Someday the entire history of humanity, from Adam and Eve, will be indexed and available for any living person who wants it. Come look. You'll understand.

He takes me to the second floor, to a room where a few dozen men and women, of every age and condition, are typing away on individual computers.

'There you are. This belongs to everyone.' These resources have no other purpose than to be put back into the hands of their legitimate owners, the people. They can do one of two things with them. If they're Mormon and if they believe in the definitive sanctity of family relations, for this life and the next, they can tighten the link with their ancestors and even, in some cases, if they think ancestors might have died without having had the occasion or the time to accept the tenets of Mormonism, offer them a remedial session and baptise them by proxy. Or if they're not Mormon, if they don't believe in baptizing the dead, if this blessing of the dead isn't part of their theology, they still have the possibility, so relevant in a world where more and more people are losing track of their roots, of knowing where they come from, who made them, and who they are. 'Would you like to try?'

The experiment, for me, isn't that conclusive.

In vain do I type, and retype, the names of the few ancestors I can recall. It must be that my family background lies in one of those terrae incognitae yet to yield to Mormon inspection, since the computer remains exasperatingly silent.

But I glance at the faces around me. I look at these people, dreamy or puzzled as if drugged, sometimes the hint of a smile on their lips, journeying through the mysteries of their ancestral past. And I hesitate between two sentiments. One is a certain respect owed to this relentless interest in one's ancestors, homage to the dead, wish to be, as the poet says, the living tomb of one's forefathers. But then there's also the idea that these Mormons are peculiarly cunning. In the struggle of all against all that the history of religions has been, and in this battle for power that I see American churches waging today, the Mormons have found the absolute weapon. How can you possibly fight a church that reigns not just over the living but also over the dead? Who can compete with people who, not content with taking possession of bodies and souls, place the memory of the world under seal?

Twenty thousand victims of the Shoah have been baptised, a non–Mormon in Salt Lake confides, by the companions of the living prophet… Some court proceedings have been started by institutions or churches that, after all is said and done, regret having lost their own….Yes, it's all out war!

Social Security or Social Insecurity?

TRACY IS A bartender in a hotel restaurant in Grand junction, Colorado, just over the Utah border, where I've stopped for the night. She's about forty.

She looks like a fine, solid, happy American, trouble-free, and keeps insisting, 'My life is my customers. I'm happy when they're happy.'

Except, when you dig down a little. When you ask her, after the last customer has left, about her work, her family, her life; when you ask her what she's doing here in this godforsaken hole, with her automatic smiles, her 'Did you enjoy your meal?' or 'Are you still working on it?,' you discover a far less cheerful story.

A father who worked in the Utah coal mines. One day, when he was fifty, he couldn't stop coughing. He had a heart attack and never fully recovered.

A brother, also a miner, but a specialist in mine safety. 'That's a cooler kind of work,' she admits, 'since there's the whole inspection aspect, which takes place mostly above ground. But if a fire breaks out, or if there's an explosion, or if the roof caves in, he's the one who has to go down to bring back his men, dead or alive. Last time there were eighty dead. He had to walk through all the corpses, and we were so afraid he wouldn't come back up!'

Three other brothers, also miners. But since the coal mines are dying out, they had to move on to soda-ash mining. 'And that,' she goes on, 'is worse. My father says you can't call it worse. But I think you can. I've seen them, my brothers, in Wyoming and Utah, working in all the soda-ash mines of the Green River basin. And I think it's much more exhausting than coal.'

And then, finally, her ex-husband, a miner too, the most damaged of the lot, with chronic depression, unable to work at all. They are divorced. But she remembers—in the beginning, when she was pregnant with their first child—those strikes that lasted for months, when no money was coming in. She remembers those mornings when she would wake up crying, unable to get up.

'What is the system in America when you're sick like your husband?' I ask her. 'In France they think Americans don't have real social security. Tell me what it's like in his case.'

Tracy reflects. Concentrates. And, adopting the expression of someone who is about to embark on a long, complex explanation, borrows my notepad and begins to write down some numbers.

The husband. He benefits from the federal Medicare program for his medical needs, and also from the supplementary Medicaid program, which I understand is state funded. He lives on $2,000 a month, or 60 percent of his last salary, which comes, in differing proportions that she's not aware of, from the federal government, the state government, and the mining company. He is also entitled to food stamps, but she doesn't know the amount. Finally, he has a subsidised apartment that he rents for about $250 instead of the $600 or $700 it's worth.

The father. Same thing for the medical care—same coverage by Medicare and Medicaid. Plus a retirement pension that in his case comes to 75 percent of his last salary. Why three-quarters and not 60 percent? And why, in the same profession, two different systems? She doesn't know this either. Maybe because one is drawing money from the retirement system in Colorado and the other in Wyoming, and it changes from state to state. Or maybe because her father also subscribed to a private fund. She doesn't know.

The brothers. They're still working. During periods of unemployment they continue to be paid for fifteen or twenty weeks, but if these periods last longer than that, a private fund, provided by a church, has to take over. As to health and retirement benefits, her brothers aren't so secure; they realise that the government system is on the verge of bankruptcy and that there are plans to dismantle it, so they have signed up for savings accounts run by their mining company.

And what about her? Oh, her! she laughs. She never would have thought she'd ever get a divorce. So until these past few years she didn't worry about it. But oh, well. She's started saving a little. She also has private health insurance. Once, when she had a minor health problem, she was treated for free by a hospital run by Methodists. The fact that there's an invalid and someone with a major illness in her family also makes her eligible for a special subsidy. And then she has a young son, and that entitles her to an allowance of $800 a month. Despite Clinton's reduction of Aid to Families with Dependent Children? Yes, that has nothing to do with it, since she's speaking here, she says, of a program run by the state of Utah.

In short, I don't know how much I can generalise. And I am well aware that none of the people Tracy talked to me about are among the tens of millions who constitute America's poorest and most marginal—the truly problematic category. But in the end I draw three lessons from her story.

First, an American social-welfare system of sorts exists. It may be threatened, it is insufficient, but it does exist.

Second, the American social-welfare system is bewilderingly complex. Despite what we say in Europe, it covers the main part of the active population, but it is complicated, varies from state to state, profession to profession, person to person.

Third, the main source of complexity, and thus of misunderstanding—the profound and almost philosophical reason for such a variety of situations—stems from the mistrust of the very idea of a government's centralizing all the tools of distribution in its own hands as in France. It stems from the methodical 'individualism' that, Tocqueville clearly showed, aims to leave with each individual, or to associations chosen by each individual, the responsibility for his fate.

I read in a book by Guy Sorman that social-welfare expenses per U.S. inhabitant are roughly equal to those in most European countries, including France. But this is true only if you add to the government share the contributions made by private institutions and private philanthropies.

Ghost of the Gold Miners

NOW, ON THE road again.

Early in the morning, taking not the road that goes most quickly from Grand Junction to Colorado Springs but, because I have a little time and my meeting at the military academy isn't until tomorrow, another route, which goes by Grand Mesa and then Aspen and is probably more scenic.

Heat.

Blinding, glorious light.

Rust-collared ravines, scorched by the sun. Giant rocks, sprawling wherever they please, sometimes crumbling with loose stones, sometimes reaching so high that their jagged outlines seem to overlap one another in the sky.

Even higher the structures are so perfect, and so perfectly overwhelming, that they seem purposely made to exclude and humiliate human beings—a barrier of rock, a Great Wall of China in the middle of America. Not one village, by the way. For dozens of miles on the highway not a living soul. Not a whiff of human presence. Nature stripped bare. Desert isn't the right word, since we're in the mountains, but it's a kind of desert. It has the same feeling of spareness, desolation, and infinity as the California scrubland had a few weeks ago— nothing but cattle guards, ditches hollowed out in the middle of the road and covered with metal grilles, their bars far apart, so that livestock don't try to cross.

Then I arrive in Hotchkiss—scarcely a village, more like an encampment, built on both sides of the road in a makeshift way. Ugly, precarious-looking houses that must be temporary, homes of lumbermen who thought they were in transit but ended up settling here, storage sheds, a fleet of trucks transporting timber, a museum of who knows what (maybe the lumbering trade?), a seller of wooden horses, a restaurant called the Elk, more storage sheds.

Then Paonia. Then Bowie. And then, on the outskirts of Carbondale—which on the map looks like the area's main hub—a change of landscape, from the world of the forest to that of the mine. Enormous disused coal ovens, completely round, that make me think of the atomic-bomb shelters you used to see on the road from the airport as you drove into Tiranë. Lower down, at the very bottom of a valley, far away, an immense black train with two hundred cars, perhaps three hundred, which looks like a giant caterpillar and is being filled with ore. Miners' houses. Cottages. A few Indian-style tepees. By the side of the road a line of galvanised half-moon mailboxes that look like they're for general delivery. Is this the world of Tracy's brothers? The road they followed from one mine to another, according to opportunity, mine closings, relocations?

The rock has gone from red to pink.

A wind has risen, making the crowns of the flowering cottonwoods and aspens rustle.

In a few minutes the temperature must have dropped a dozen or so degrees, and I'm beginning to see more and more snow by the side of the road.

I drive alongside a river, which reminds me of the rapids of the Panjshir.

In Carbondale itself, another fake town, shapeless and borderless, where the houses look like barns and the barns like houses; in Carbondale, which seems to me like the prototype of an unplanned town, where everyone lives in the same hideous wooden buildings mounted on metal frameworks that the first storm that comes along, the first major landslide, the first mudslide, will be enough to carry away; in Carbondale, then, I stop for a few minutes in Garcia's. Four tables, a kitchen in the middle of the room, Mexican specialties all day long—the worst kind of junk food.

We are at an altitude of eight thousand feet, close to the McClure Pass. In the distance I can see snow-covered mountains. And then, as I approach Aspen, a tiny sign, almost illegible, reads ASHCROFT, GHOST TOWN, 11 MILES.

I take the little road. I climb up into a landscape that's even colder. Strangely, although the weather was fine on the main road, here a misty rain begins to fall.

Even more strangely, since there isn't a living soul in sight, I encounter—climbing up, like I am, to the ghost town, but completely empty and thus ghostlike—a big yellow schoolbus. After mile eleven, finally, I'm there. A sign indicates the inevitable NATIONAL HISTORIC SITE. Another warns that what I am about to discover is placed, as it should be, under the protection of archaeological authorities. A third: MY NAME IS DEXTER. I'M AN ARTIST. AS YOU CAN SEE, I'M KING OF THE MOUNTAIN, AND ALTHOUGH I'M NOT MEAN, I'D BE GRATEFUL IF YOU KEPT YOUR DOG LEASHED. After which I cover the last little stretch on foot on a grass path strewn with pebbles. And here, in the middle of a superb forest with a vigorousness all the more brazen in its contrasts with the desolation of the place, the ghost town of Ashcroft.

I picture this town of silver prospectors.

This was one of those boomtowns from the end of the nineteenth century, born in a few months, sometimes a few weeks, like Chinese towns today.

One day a villager came back and said, 'There's no more silver.' Another repeated, 'No more silver! No more silver!'

And as the rumour spread, the town emptied as quickly as it had been built.

Only these blackened clapboards remain, this two-story building that must have been the saloon, this other one that was a hotel, these haunted houses, cracked stones, this main street that has returned to the great obscurity of American space, and then this thick, supernatural, almost solid silence in which the least breeze in the treetops, the least rustle in the undergrowth, the smallest noise of a broken branch, is enough to make you jump.

Poetry of these ruins. Beauty of these stranded wrecks from the past.

And beauty, especially, of this people so slenderly attached to their roots—beauty, once again, of the prodigious freedom with which they treat their places.

The Myth of the American Empire

I REMEMBER THE way we used to demonise the American army when I was young.

I remember the image we had of the My Lai kind of GI— all the makings of a brute and a fascist.

And I remember the fervour with which a few months ago Europeans in general and the French in particular seized on the revelation of the despicable crimes committed in the Iraqi prison of Abu Ghraib.

I know, of course, that in all countries in the world, and necessarily in America as well, an army has contradictory faces.

And I'm sure that the United States Air Force Academy in Colorado Springs, which trains officers for one branch of the armed services, is not the ideal observation post from which to judge the recent evolution of the military as a whole.

But when you come down to it: these boys with chubby, sensible faces... this girl from St. Louis, Roslyn Schulte, who went to one of the best high schools in the country, long brown hair pulled back in a bun, beautiful, gentle, deep gaze... this other cadet, who doesn't know the name Clausewitz but who has over his bedside table a printed-out quotation from Rabbi Harold Kushner on the meaning of life, death, suffering... this table at lunchtime where eight cadets out of twelve confess, in the heat of a surprisingly free debate, that they weren't in favour of the war in Iraq because, according to them, the chances of a 'police option' weren't fully explored....The class, finally, which I am allowed to attend, where the questions under considera-tion, the weighty and highly strategic problems that will be debated for an hour by a dozen future knights of the sky as they all sit calmly behind desks arranged in a semicircle, are these. First, 'How many times in the morning do you push the snooze button on your alarm clock? In what circumstances? Why? And how can you get rid of this annoying habit?' and, second, 'How can you stop this other pathological behaviour, much more serious for a future pilot and officer—the smoking habit? Do you think the right method is to use chewing gum? To slip the money you've saved from every unbought pack into a piggy bank and see how much you end up with after a certain period of time? If you're married or dating, should you get a gentle massage every time you don't smoke? Or should you be punished if you smoke, and be made to eat your cigarette?'

Why did you enlist? I ask them.

Why, at the beginning of the twenty-first century, does one decide to become an air force officer?

Some (whose decisions, they tell me, date from the shock of 9/11): to defend my country.

Others (who, evidently, are aware of the major historical debates over whether or not the United States has the right to meddle in the affairs of other nations): to defend the Constitution.

Others still (supporters of a neoconservative foreign policy—which is to say, plainly, a more active, more aggressive foreign policy): beyond even our own Constitution, to defend the values of freedom on which it is based, and to defend them everywhere, yes, everywhere, wherever they're scorned.

And last is Roslyn Schulte, from St. Louis: 'Do you really

want to know what brought me here? I wanted to fly the most exciting airplanes—the small, fast jets they only fly in the military. I was thinking of flying; I was thinking of fun.'

I don't meet a single one, in fact, who mentions the greatness of the military profession as such.

Nor do I meet anyone who really seems to take into account the increased risk of death today, given the Iraq War, inherent in the simple fact of choosing a military career.

The response of Brigadier General Johnny Weida, the commandant of cadets at the academy, is all the more clear-cut: very little military background in his family, not the least hint of fascination with war or the army. His first motivation was not planes but sports. What? I ask. He guffaws. Yes, he did say 'sports.' It was 1974; he was twenty; he had a friend who told him that the Air Force Academy was a great place to develop one's athletic skills. The vocation, of course, followed. It came to him, as it often does to others, at the controls of his first F16. But in the beginning that was it. In the beginning it was 'Integrity first, service before self, excellence in all we do'—the motto of the U.S. Air Force as well as the values of sport.

I repeat that his may be an exceptional case.

And I'll take care not to judge the broader mentality of the U.S. military (or, above all, of those reserve troops who dishonoured themselves at Abu Ghraib) on the basis of this academy where they train officers who make it a point of honour not to be 'mere' soldiers.

But I should confess that I return to my hotel somewhat confused.

And I decide, this very evening, that from now on I will think twice before allowing myself to talk glibly, like too many of my fellow citizens, about the imperial American military—or, beyond the military, about the imperial calling of the country itself.

'Involuntary Romans,' the French writer Paul Morand said.

'Incompetent imperialism,' added the British historian Niall Ferguson, whose thesis is that the United States doesn't have, and never did have, sufficient military will for its ambitions.

'Incoherent empire,' Michael Mann, on the other end of the ideological spectrum, asserts, denouncing the 'untidy militarism' of a country that never knew, and knows increasingly less, how to control the territories it has conquered.

And once again, Tocqueville long ago lent us a key to the riddle when he wrote that Americans have even less inclination for war than for politics.

To be continued...

A Gilded Apartheid for the Old

IN SUN CITY, Arizona, the rule is simple. Unyielding. No home without at least one resident above fifty-five. Children and teenagers admitted only to visit. A city of the old. A private city, reserved for retired people, cut off from the rest of the world. In this mock urban space with perfectly straight, almost deserted streets where once in a while a few granddads in golf carts pass by, an optimist will see an oasis of prosperity in a society plagued by crisis, a bourgeois utopia dreamed up by some grand developer. In this he'll recognise a strange variation, but a variation all the same, on the good old 'pastoralism'— inherited from eighteenth-century English landscape architecture—that played such a large role in the formation of American ideology. He'll perceive in it a meeting—not at all dishonourable in itself—of the spirit of Virgil and that of the Enlightenment. An intermingling of back-to-nature dreams, dating from the first American colonists, with the residential progressivism that I discovered in Lakewood, near Los Angeles, which had already shown me what sort of landscape such a combination can give rise to, and what kind of egalitarian pioneer philosophy it stems from. Emerson's self-reliance on a backdrop of ghettoised old age. Thoreau's Walden Pond in an imaginary version of a fortress under siege.

In planned cities of this kind, in citadels emerging in the middle of nowhere (in this case in the desert), perhaps our optimist will even discern a final manifestation, in the twenty-first century, of that pioneering spirit, that capacity to shape oneself 'by solemn and mutual consent' into a 'body politic' that Tocqueville writes of in the opening pages of *Democracy in America* (where, quoting Nathaniel Morton, he discusses the creation of Plymouth and the first New England colonies and describes them as the very essence of the democratic aim). And I confess, as an aside, that I didn't find the little dance organised by a few of these senior-citizen settlers at the Westerners Square Dance Club, in Sun City West, completely ridiculous. I confess to finding a certain charm in the spectacle of fifteen or twenty old ladies dressed like Scarlett O'Hara in ruffled skirts and other alluring apparel dancing to the point of breathless-ness, whirling with Rhett Butlers the youngest of whom is eighty years old.

The problem, obviously, is the rest. Everything else. The problem is all the black people you can't see. The Hispanics who, I am told, are here but whose presence I am not aware of either. Poor people in general, a huge population left out of this suburban dream. The problem, in fact, is the feeling of having reached, with this tribe of the old, the very last stage of a process of social segregation, a few premises of which I was able to observe in Los Angeles. Because they couldn't keep the poor in their ghettos or banish them to the city's outskirts, because they couldn't (as was done once in Phoenix) poison restaurant trash bins to keep tramps from stocking up, they resolved to make the best of things and move the rich.

The problem, in other words, is that all this implies a pro-found break with the very tradition of civic-mindedness and civility—I won't even say of compassion—that was responsible, and continues to be responsible, for this country's greatness. And this experiment in privatizing a public space at the expense of a community cannot fail to create a terrible precedent. No longer depending on either Phoenix or any municipal or government authority (the 'nation-state,' the 'station,' scorned by Emerson) for its taxes, its road maintenance, its police or administrative tasks, Sun City seems like a little satellite freed from the laws of social and national gravity.

If we accept this, I say to one of my Scarletts, if we ratify the principle of this gilded ghetto based on membership in a certain age and income bracket, then by what right can we tomorrow prevent the development of cities forbidden to the old? Or to gay men and women? Or to Jews? In whose name can we resist the definitive Balkanisation of American space that could well result? But that's completely different! my indignant square dancer exclaims. You can't compare such horrific plans to an organisation whose sole aim is to make life easier for old people who were suffocating in the big cities.

Maybe. I am in fact well aware of the little arrangements for everyday life in such old-age communities. Electrical sockets that are higher up so you don't have to bend down too far. Carefully calibrated lighting so as not to tire your eyes. Golf courses. Swimming pools heated both summer and winter. The alarm systems, connecting houses to hospitals, that save precious minutes in case of sickness, since delay is often fatal at this age. All that, obviously, is not trivial. But at the same time… this impression of dismal coldness… these artificial fires in the fireplaces, and these fake-looking lawns… this plastic-coated life… these dying people exuding health… this dead-end time, bereft of noteworthy events except dances, garbage collection that the community insists on doing itself, just like the volunteer police rounds, and, last but not least, the source of inexhaustible excitement: deaths and burials… I leave Sun City with a feeling of unease, no longer knowing if you come here to save or to damn yourself, to banish death or savour a foretaste of it.

Back in Phoenix, I learn that Del Webb, the inventor of this frozen miracle, this paradise laden with all the attractions of purgatory, kindergarten for senior citizens where life seems to have morphed into a pathology, learned his profession by building casinos, military installations, and internment camps for the Japanese.

On the Peculiar Electoral System in America

TEMPE, ARIZONA. THIRD and last debate in the Presidential campaign. Enormous building, transformed into a fortified camp, at Arizona State University. Journalists. Police officers. Groups of advisers. All these troupes of campaign aides who are all the more active, feverish, almost frantic, since they know that in a few days they'll fade back into the underbrush (whereas in France, as Tocqueville already noted, politics is a profession that gets ever more active after the election). I am struck by the relatively high quality of the discussion (here, too, far from the reputed vacuity of American debate), and the meticulousness of the event's organisation (allotted speaking time, lecterns, physical arrangement of the cameras). At the very end, after they've torn each other's guts out, the strange-and in France, unthinkable—spectacle of the wives of the debaters climbing onto the stage with their daughters, kissing their husbands, kissing and congratulating one another, and, especially, getting the candidates themselves to embrace and fraternise. I am struck, yes, by the complete inversion of the European model. In private they hate each other with a passion, feel entitled to use every kind of dirty trick, while in public, facing the audience, they play at being good American guys who have the same values and belong to one large family. The exact opposite is true in Paris, where everyone knows that adversaries are on familiar terms with one another, dine in the same restaurants, may even this morning have had a drink together at the canteen in the Assemblée Nationale—whereas in public every measure is taken to mask these complicities and present the image of merciless foes.

During the debate itself, each time one of the debaters slips up, utters an untruth, or dodges a troublesome question, I am struck by the sudden leaping up in the press room—quick as lightning, like acrobats of democratic virtue—of a horde of interns in jeans and sneakers, who distribute Xeroxed handouts, titled, for instance (in the case of the Democrats), 'Bush Versus Reality' and indicating (1) what 'Bush claims,' (2) the 'reality,' and (3) 'the truth about Kerry's record.' (Again, what a difference from France and its labourious, late-breaking clarifications, which always arrive after the battle is over and the bluffer has drawn all the benefits from his first blow! What efficiency at counterattack in the real grinding work of truth!)

I am also struck by Bush's body language. The I'm-not-such-a-tough-guy smile he must have worked on with his advisers. I'm struck by the way—when he suddenly strikes a pose, chin raised, eyes looking heavenward—he tries to suggest his elevation of spirit and his faith. I'm struck by the little deposit of spittle in the right corner of his mouth, the equivalent of Al Gore's heaving sighs in 2000, which is, above all, proof that some portion of the game is still uncontrollable. I'm struck by the fact that Kerry is so good and yet so enigmatically disappointing. And last I'm struck by the explanation that one of the president's campaign advisers (who asks not to be named) gives me after the debate.

'Why should he be good?' he says. 'This debate has absolutely no importance! None! It's important for you Europeans who are attached to these rituals that are high points in your campaigns. It's important for CNN, which makes money on these shows. But it sure isn't here that the real battle is fought. It's won county by county, city by city, over issues that concern not the country but the swing states; and I'll tell you something—'

He is interrupted by an intern who brings him the results of a Gallup poll confirming that Kerry won the debate hands down, throughout the entire country.

'These debates—we have to do them,' he continues. 'But I'm going to tell you something. It's not advisable in the end to be too good at them. You know what happens if you're good? You get eloquent, you get carried away, you let words out you don't have any control over later on. So, to please the intellectuals on the East and West Coasts (which already belong to the Democrats anyway), or the Wisconsin farmers (who have already been won over by the Republicans), you take the risk of saying something you'll be blamed for later, when you have to go fishing for the thousand votes you need in Virginia or Louisiana.'

I'll make allowances, of course, for paradox and bravado. But I can still see how this theory agrees with the oddity of an electoral system in which victory goes to the one who wins the majority not of votes in the country but of state electoral votes and in which, since the die is already cast in four states out of five or six, what is at stake in the remaining states is persuading the minority of voters who will make the difference and who will inevitably choose based on local, irrelevant, and, especially, contradictory questions.

How can you talk to the faithful souls in North Carolina without cutting yourself off from the secular folk in Minnesota? How can you speak in favour of affirmative action to blacks in Arkansas without being heard too clearly in Washington State, where many Asians are against it? How can you win over the thousands of Cubans who will change everything in Florida without being seen in Iowa, a state that's more than 90 percent white, as grovelling to Hispanics? How can you speak out against unemployment in Ohio and for prosperity in New

Hampshire? How, if you're Kerry, can you secure the Jewish vote in Cleveland without angering the Arabs in Detroit? How, if you're Bush, can you promise a constitutional amendment against gay marriage (essential in Oklahoma) without definitively alienating the last gay Republicans (numerous in Pennsylvania)? How can you pacify the doves in Philadelphia without upsetting the hawks of rural western Pennsylvania?

Those are the real problems of this election. You can deplore them or rejoice in them. You can deem the paradox antidemocratic or, on the contrary, in keeping with a democracy that has always mistrusted what Tocqueville called 'tradition and formalities.' You can judge improper the way a minority of states takes the election hostage by imposing their issues and their concerns on the country. Or you can see it, again in Tocqueville's words, as a fortunate antidote to the 'tyranny of the majority.' Last, you can be surprised by the contradiction in the return to ideology, of which I see so many signs, culminating in this localism.

In any case, the fact is there. This worldwide election par excellence functions as a local election. The mega-vote on which the peoples of the world rightly have their eyes fixed, the result on which, whether you're European, Chinese, Palestinian, Israeli, or Iraqi, the fate of the planet depends, itself depends on a series of decisions over which a debate like tonight's will, when all is said and done, have almost no influence.

A Frenchman in the Kerry Camp

I WAS HAVING a fine time on a two-day trip with the press corps accompanying John Kerry, but it almost ended badly.

The first night, for the Tempe–Las Vegas leg, right after Kerry's third debate with President Bush, they started by putting me in the second plane, the wrong one, the one without the candidate, the one carrying the luggage, the sound system, the staff.

Then, the next day, for the second leg—the one that, after a night in Vegas and a speech early the next morning to ten thousand AARP members, will take us to Des Moines, Iowa, for the great outdoor rally for which the Fort Hotel receptionist had been so intensely preparing this past summer—I was invited to plane No. 1. But, despite my pleas and repeated explanations that I was a writer, that I was following in the footsteps of Tocqueville, and that it was essential, for this project, for me to interview the senator-candidate, even if only for ten minutes, I still wasn't allowed to come near him.

There were about fifteen of us actually. Twenty or so Secret Service agents, an equal number of PR assistants flitting from the main cabin to the front cabin, which had been fitted out for the candidate—and fifteen or so journalists. And they all got their one-on-one at some time or another. Depending on his degree of importance and that of his newspaper, each was entitled to have a press attaché either discreetly signal that his turn had come or search him out in his seat to lead him by the hand into the holy of holies. But not me. I am the only one, oddly, who upon asking whether the candidate is available yet is systematically answered with a vague and annoyed 'In a little while.' And each time I present myself, I get embarrassed but negative replies. After a while they don't even bother to invent plausible excuses, and the automatic answer becomes 'The candidate is sleeping'... 'The candidate is still sleeping'... 'It's still not the right time yet, because the candidate is tired and he's sleeping.'

'Don't you think that's a bit strange?' my seat neighbour, a journalist for a television network who has been observing this treatment from the beginning without comment, asks sarcastically.

'Yes, I do. And I must say, I'm beginning to wonder—'

'And do you want an explanation—the real one, the one none of these bozos would ever dare tell you right out?'

'Yes, of course I do!'

Well, it's quite simple, he says. It's like the story of the Hermes ties Kerry replaced with Vineyard Vines ties, made in the U.S.A., out of fear that Bush's handlers would leap at the chance to support their 'Kerry as agent of the French' business. Or it's like the affair of the Evian bottle he had taken away in a hurry the other day from the Santa Monica hotel room where he was being interviewed by Matt Bai of *The New York Times Magazine*. You're French. You're as French as a bottle of Evian or an Hermes tie. And their real fear, the real reason you're the only one of us not to have any contact with Kerry, is that a Frenchman might suddenly claim eight days before the election that the candidate picked him to confide his secrets to....

I am astonished, of course.

Not just astonished—I feel slightly aggravated at the idea of this ludicrous fallacy.

And since, in any case, I've had enough by now and thus have nothing to lose, I charge one last time toward the watchdog standing guard by the bar in the middle of the plane and I say, 'Listen, I get the picture. Let's make a deal: if I get to see the candidate and if he talks to me, I agree not to publish anything before the election or even till the summer after, when my article will appear. But I also swear that if you keep up your idiotic arrangement, and if your anti-French fixation keeps me from seeing him at all, then when the time comes you'll get a portrayal revealing that the ex-candidate, who could by then be the forty-fourth president of the United States, is a guy who spends most of his time sleeping.'

Amused smile of the aide.

Laughter, in front of us, from the group of young women around their friend Alexandra Kerry, the candidate's daughter, who have been following the scene.

So it is that at long last, just before our descent into Des Moines, I'm granted the little one-on-one.

My impressions? A nice man, in shirtsleeves, joking with his staff; a man I have seen looking for volunteers to toss a football around with him on the tarmac so he can stretch his legs. A European at heart. He is interested to hear that this whole story of Francophobia is just bullshit made up by the Washington press corps, and that, in all the months I've been travelling through the heartland of America, I've never met any ordinary citizens who are angry with me for being French. A good candidate. A courageous activist, fully involved in the battle that's under way, absorbed in his role and his mission, inspired, passionate. A rationalist, above all. A genuine rationalist, a man of the Enlightenment and of his word. Not doubting for a single instant that truth—even if it takes a while to come to light, even if the professional masters of deceit and disinformation appear to be gaining the upper hand—will always win out. That's why he took so long to react to the scurrilous campaign of the Swift Boat Veterans that cast aspersions on his past as a Vietnam hero. That's also why he himself is always ill at ease with that terse style of argument, and why he prefers long, drawn-out explanations that are reasonable, articulate, sensible. Is he naïve? Optimistic? Does he fatally underestimate the irrational factors that can decide an election? Just a few more days, and we'll find out.

V

Gone with the South
FROM AUSTIN TO LITTLE ROCK

Tocqueville in Texas

'I'M LOOKING FOR Paul Burka. Professor Paul Burka. He's teaching a class on Tocqueville that must have begun about twenty minutes ago, and I can't seem to find his classroom.'

The man I'm talking to is a giant with a gray moustache, clad in jeans, T-shirt moist with perspiration, taking the fresh air with a dozen or so youngsters sitting like him on wicker chairs in a sunny, comfortable lobby in the immense University of Texas at Austin.

'Paul Burka?' he replies, raising his enormous and fragile carcass in a sign of welcome. 'I'm the one you're looking for. I'm Professor Paul Burka.' Then, pointing at the group of young people sitting around him, similarly languid, carefree, without notes or notebooks, just one book on their knees: 'And here's my class. Yes, that's right, we're in class now. We've been talking about the opening lines of Chapter Eight from the first part of Volume One, on the federal Constitution, as we were waiting for you. But now it's your turn, since you're here. You know as much as I do—so I'll give you the floor.'

What? This is actually a class? This is a professor—this amiable colossus, with no rostrum or lectern, who looks like he's having a drink with a few former students, and who explains briefly that he was once a lawyer and is now the executive editor of *Texas Monthly*? Yes, a class. It's rather bewildering for someone who's accustomed to the rigidities and ceremonies of the French classroom, but it really is a class. And if I'm to believe Burka, it seems I've happened upon a freshman honours class—in other words, unusually bright students who began the year with Thucydides, continued with Ibsen, went on to Eliot's *Murder in the Cathedral*, and are now immersed in Tocqueville's *Democracy in America*.

'What do you know about this book?' I ask them, having pulled my chair into a narrow band of shadow against a wall between two bay windows. 'I'll tell you what I think about it. But you go first. What does it mean to you? What does it tell you about your country, your times?'

The 'tyranny of the majority,' one student tells me, tracking an enormous butterfly. 'The idea that tyranny exists when one single party holds all power in its hands.'

The place of religion, a second student continues, bare arms in the afternoon warmth. 'The necessity, for democracy to function, of keeping church separate from state: is that actually the case everywhere these days?'

And a third student, shirt open down to his navel, ebullient, cheerful: 'But look, Tocqueville isn't Montesquieu—the principle of separation isn't exactly a Tocquevillean principle!'

And another, talking off-handedly, through his teeth: 'Look at the country's Founding Fathers—weren't they super religious? Wasn't religion the very foundation, in their eyes, of a politics that was faithful to morality?'

And yet another: 'Kerry lost because of abortion; you can't say at the same time that you are conscientiously opposed to abortion and that you want a law authorizing it.'

And finally a pretty redhead, with long tousled hair, sunburnt nose, and the bashful look the sun's glare lends her: 'On the contrary—that was his honour. To believe one thing but refuse to impose it on other people; to have your convictions but leave other people free to act the way they want—isn't that a good policy? Isn't that the definition of democracy, in Tocqueville's sense?'

For of course we have begun to talk about current events—which is to say (quoting Tocqueville again), about the re-election of the president yesterday.

Then, when I ask the question straight out, I am surprised to find that a majority of the small group is in favour of gay marriage, and that the same majority thinks Bush overdid the flaunting of his religious values. Only a minority, if properly registered, would have voted for him. In short, in this class here in Austin, the capital of Texas, a state that is supposed to be a conservative stronghold, the trend seems to be in the other direction.

Since yesterday everyone has been harping on the same story of 'triumphant moral values.' Everyone, myself included, has described this society's profound evolution toward the far right, definitively turning its back on its European heritage. Some intellectuals (last night, for instance, in New York, Jason Epstein) have brooded over the so-called tidal wave that's risen up from the Deep South to inundate American lands, down to the coasts.

But what if that is not the case? What if the fundamental movement, the one that these youths embody even if they don't yet express it, is going in the direction of freedom of behaviour, of conduct, of mind? What if, in the living forces of this country, there is an unredeemable desire to preserve the great achievements of the democratic revolution of the 1960s and 1970s? What if the election—far from being the expression of a sinister trend or a reversal, far from heralding the future face of an America denying the heritage, say, of Kennedy or Roosevelt and giving shape once again to the ghosts of McCarthyism—is, on the contrary, a last stand? What if it is the last fight of a majority that—furious but desperate, determined but devoid of illusions—knows it won't always be the majority, knows that America has already changed so much that it will be increasingly difficult to advertise one's hatred of blacks, Jews, Indians, or women? I ask myself. Here in Austin, on the edge of the South I'm about to dive into, I think up this conjecture.

Christians Lost and Found

I MEET ROD Dreher farther north, in Dallas, in a funky organic restaurant where you eat breakfast in the middle of a kitchen garden. He is the archetypal trendy journalist.

He has that collected intellectual look, an easy casual bearing. At *The Dallas Morning News* and the *National Review*, and, earlier, at the *New York Post*, he's been focusing on literature, cinema, and the most up-to-date issues. He isn't afraid of any subject. Doesn't shrink from a scandal. At *the New York Post* he was the one who consistently seized on the most controversial movies. And he's the one who, at the beginning of 2002, with a thundering article in the *National Review* titled 'Sins of the Fathers,' helped bring attention to the enormous scandal about paedophilia in the Catholic Church.

But here's the thing—he's Catholic.

Intensely, deeply Catholic.

And he just has this feeling that life in the big cities is difficult for a Catholic. He thinks you can't raise your children properly there; he thinks public school, in a city like New York, is just a diabolical system designed to produce and reproduce illiterate kids. And that's why he's moved here, to Dallas—which is a city too, that's true, and an enormous city at that, but it's actually one of the places in the United States where the rules on home schooling have been stretched the most.

Do I know what home schooling is, by the way? Do we have anything like it in France?

Here, in the United States, it goes without saying. Since the right to educate your kids yourself, in your own home, is an unalienable right. Even in New York there is a Home School Education Association, to which he belonged when he lived there.

But New York was still New York. The whole culture was dominated by the ideology of shopping and fucking, which cannot but corrupt and wreck your kids. And then there were the rules. If the State of New York allows home schooling (like every other state); if it allows families who so desire to remove their kids from the wretched public school system, that has to be straitjacketed in a stranglehold of rules. Whereas here, in Texas, there's no structure. No limit. You raise your kids however you please. And that's why he's here.

His oldest child's name is Matthew.

Four days a week, four hours a day, he takes him to the neighbourhood church school in Junius Heights where there are about fifteen students per class, who are taught the basics.

In the afternoon he and his wife, alone at home, take charge of Matthew for two or three hours, at times four, and, alone, dispense the main part of the teaching that will make him not just a Christian but a free man.

In the evenings, no TV allowed. Unlike Rod's own home when he was a kid, unlike all the American homes where TV has become the epicentre of family life, young Matthew lives in a world where the set is turned on exclusively on rare occasions, and where in the evening they read.

Result: he's five years old and reads like a twelve-year-old.

Result: he's practically a baby, but he's already broken with that evil, utilitarian, idiotic, debauched culture that produces nothing but slaves.

Isn't this method, I interrupt, a resounding defeat for society? Yes, of course, Dreher replies. I'm not saying it's a success. But too bad. That's really not my problem. For a long time now the problems of society haven't been my problems, and I never even vote.

What will happen when Matthew is twenty years old? Thirty? Won't he be ill-adapted to a world from which you've cut him off? Perhaps he will, yes. The risk is there, obviously. Even before that, when he goes to college, there'll be the problem of exams and adaptation. But all in all, it's a less serious problem than the one posed by the encroaching vulgarity of society, by pornography, radical Islam, terrorism.

What does he teach his child? What kind of culture? What books? Does he censor the material? Control its contents? What about Darwinism, for instance? When the time comes, will he teach Matthew Darwinism? Of course, he replies in a burst of laughter. You're talking like my old friends from New York who thought my family and I entered a new Middle Ages! I'll teach everything to Matthew. Nabokov. The French Revolution. The history of the Industrial Age. Dostoyevsky. Kierkegaard. Everything. With no qualms. Don't confuse me, if you please, with those absurd fundamentalists; I don't have any problem at all with Darwinism. I'll tell Matthew that the Bible is true on a certain level but that science is also true, albeit a different kind of truth, on another level.

Baffling story. Singular situation. Nothing in common, in fact, with the fundamentalists of the mega-churches.

The opposite, I can tell, of those neo-Christian born-agains whose sole aim was to join the mainstream, mass culture, modernity—all things he wants to break away from.

I am essentially confronted with an altogether different phenomenon, one that obeys a completely different logic. I wonder if—allowing for a few minor variations, with mysticism lapsing not just into politics but into farce and with Dallas suddenly substituting itself for the Syriac cities of the first century—this phenomenon isn't closer to the flight from the world, the retreat to the deserts, of the original Christians.

Yearning for secession.

Logic of the enclave and the monastery within the great city itself.

Times of decline. Times of misery. Generalisation of a corruption in which it's the Church itself, as in the era of Thomas More, that is crumbling around its faithful. You need to hang tight, say people like Rod Dreher. Waiting for the renaissance, you need to save what you can and patiently stand by. The scene takes place in Texas—that is to say, in the heart of darkness. In Texas, Dreher wants to be a new Christian of the catacombs.

Do Americans Believe in Their Own Myths? (The Kennedy Question)

DALLAS, STILL.

The genuine Kennedy mystery is here.

It's not about knowing whether Oswald acted alone or not.

It's not about the endless discussions whether there were three bullets or more, whether the shots came from the rear or the front.

It's not about the interlacing theories that blame the loading of the most famous 6.5mm Mannlicher-Carcano rifle in history on Castroites or anti-Castroites, on the Mafia or the CIA, on the Russians, on Johnson, on the far left, on the far right, on the military-industrial complex and the casino lobbies, on China or Israel, on the Jews or the Protestants, on rich Texans, on the FBI, on the Vietnamese, on J. Edgar Hoover, on Howard Hughes.

It's not even, and far less so, about the pathetic and tireless 'JFK assassination researchers' I see this morning opposite the Texas School

Book Depository, in Dealey Plaza, on the very site of the

crime, haranguing their meagre public, desperate to sell paraphernalia. One has his 'Real JFK Facts,' proving the existence of the second shooter. Another his 'Never Seen World Exclusive Interview' demonstrating that the president's wounds were faked at the autopsy. A third offers a new 'Eyewitness Video,' whose dramatised freeze-frames, paranoid zoom-ins, blurred faces circled in red, are supposed to shatter to pieces the Warren Commission's conclusions. The last has 'the missing thirteen seconds' that Abraham Zapruder didn't film, which establish without the least possible doubt that his film was doctored.

No. The mystery, if there is one, is lodged here, on the sixth floor of the book depository, in this emotion that overwhelms me (and I see it overwhelming nearly everyone around me as well) as I face these black-and-white images, these films and stills that we all know so well.

It is, more precisely, contained in this rare—perhaps unique—emotional reaction, whose equivalent I have experienced in no other situation or museum or memorial in the world, and the paradox of which I can only describe this way:

1. These images are clichés. We've seen them over and over. In all these photos of Kennedy's life and in the short films that are featured in endless loops and that show for the nth time either the assassination or the funeral, nowhere does there appear the slightest original or even mildly surprising piece of information. It's no longer the comedy of repetition but the tragedy of repetition, and the Americans who are here, all the devotees of the myth who came, as I did, into the small projection room to see, indefinitely repeated, the scene of the last turn, or the one of the motorcade leaving, sirens wailing, for Trauma Room No. 1 at Parkland Hospital, know these sequences by heart.

2. The Kennedy myth itself. For a long time now the Kennedy myth has ceased to be a myth. Or, to put it another way, few myths have for forty years been the subject of a demys-

tifying rage so radical, so unbridled, and in the end—scandal after scandal, bestseller after bestseller—so overwhelmingly effective. I question the people around me. I talk to these fetishists of memory and legend who have come from all over the United States. Nearly every one of them knows that the spectacle of family happiness with Jackie was a made-up publicity representation. Nearly every one of them knows that the tanned young hero, exuding optimism and health, was a sick man, heavily drugged with testosterone and cortisone, whose air of vitality was an illusion. All of them have at least heard of 'the sins of the father'—Joseph P. Kennedy's anti-Semitic or pro-Nazi leanings, the suspicious origins of the family fortune, even the shabby tricks that got JFK into the White House. No one, in other words, can manage to completely ignore that this 'great president,' this 'visionary,' this official incarnation of an America that wins and dictates right and wrong, still had the time, in a thousand days, to send the first military advisers to Vietnam, to launch the disastrous invasion of the Bay of Pigs, and, one year prior to the beautiful '*Ich bin ein Berliner*' speech, to let the shameful Berlin Wall be raised.

3. Despite all that, despite the stock of information available to anyone who wants it, despite the concealed face that is no longer concealed from most people, despite the methodical disenchantment the Kennedy myth has been subjected to for more than forty years, one single image of this man in his glory is enough. One of his photos as a young, beaming Prince Charming, American tabloid, from Washington to the moon, opulence, happiness, New Frontier, insouciance. One image of Jackie, in an Oleg Cassini gown during their great media-driven lie, is enough. Another one, on the day of the tragedy: pink suit stained with blood, legs splayed, on all fours, all care for her image forgotten, leaning over the rear seat of the Lincoln, gathering together the pieces of her husband's brain. Yet another one: Jackie again, in the same bloody suit she didn't want to

change out of, next to Lyndon Johnson as he takes the oath of office. Or another: black crepe veil over her face, next to Bobby in tails, or with her two children climbing, with their slightly too short legs, the steps of the Capitol for a final farewell to their father. That's all that's needed, just one of those vignettes, and you are overcome with a malaise I'm not sure there's an equivalent to—not even in the images of September 11.

What is a cliché that makes you cry?

What is a myth you no longer believe in but that still functions? That's it. It's the question asked by lovers of antiquity when they wonder if the Greeks believed in their myths or not—to which they reply, as did André Gide, that the problem is less a matter of belief than of assent.

And the fact is that in the great, simple sentiments that the Kennedy saga mobilises; in this live death we are given to witness over and over again without ever tiring of it; in this proximity of suffering and love; in this nexus of power and misfortune, fall and redemption; in this story of youth struck down; in this true story of a glamorous and cursed family, blessed by the gods and pursued by a fate perceived as both inconceivable and necessary, it is the eternal form of the Tragedy—'terror and pity,' Aristotle said—that is played out and makes us shiver.

The Kennedys are not, as is often alleged, an American royal family. They are the brothers in fate of Oedipus, Achilles, Theseus, Narcissus, Prometheus. They are the tragic lining of a nation who thought it could do without tragedy. They are America's Greeks.

Armed Like Nazis

'YOU WON'T UNDERSTAND anything about this country if you choose to overlook the question of weapons,' the vivacious Carole Keeton Strayhorn, the Texas comptroller of public accounts, warned me in her Austin office. Here, carrying a weapon is a right, she insisted. This right is inspired by the English Bill of Rights of 1689, which was explicitly linked with the right to resist tyranny. And what you Europeans don't want to see is that it is guaranteed as such by the Second Amendment of the Constitution. Are you driving to Dallas from here? Yes? In that case you should head to Fort Worth, where there's a major gun fair. You'll see what the mood's like. You'll see all the people there. And you'll understand that it's the heart of Texas, and of America, that's beating in that kind of place.

No sooner said than done. Just after reaching Dallas, I take Route 30, the Tom Landry Highway, named after the former coach of the Dallas Cowboys football team. And here I am, in the midst of a most puzzling city, all parks, deserted hotels, highway overpasses with very few cars—here I am at the centre of this empty city where neither the admirable Kimball Art Museum, by Louis Kahn, nor the Hotel Texas, where John and Jackie Kennedy spent their last night together, seem to attract anyone, and where everything looks as if it's actually been constructed around the Mussolini-style building and its white-washed façade the comptroller had told me about, where a sign reads GREAT WESTERN GUN SHOW. In the lobby I see an obese couple, man and wife each carrying a new rifle. I see a gray-haired fellow with pinched features transporting an oversize package in the shape of a machine gun. I flash my ID to a group of policemen who make sure—absurd, but true— that I'm unarmed. I pass a table covered with worn-out felt where the National Rifle Association is recruiting. And I enter the showroom.

Hundreds of stands. Thousands of buyers and window-shoppers wandering with concentrated gazes from stand to stand. Groups. Individuals. Families. Overexcited mothers pushing strollers. Old men, young men, with feverish eyes. Tattooed guys and middle-class folk. Phoney cowboys. Authentic southerners dressed as Confederate soldiers, looking for eighteenth-century guns. A stand displaying rifles from the Korean War. Another, where clients come to caress daggers whose certificates of origin bluntly specify how many 'Viets' they've stabbed. Competition Bushmaster AR-15s like the one used by the snipers who killed thirteen people near Washington, D.C., in 2002. A guy who says his name is Yoda—*Star Wars* fans beware—selling a 'sport version' of the Barrett 82A1 .50-caliber rifle. Price? Eight thousand dollars. Requirements? Hold an American passport and carry a valid driver's license. That's it? That's it. No need for authorisation from the FBI? Yeah—a phone call. The agent at the other end takes note; he doesn't jot down the serial number, he just takes note. Still, don't you sometimes have to turn someone down? Sometimes, sure. Suppose someone comes to you saying, 'I've just been robbed. I want a weapon to take revenge.' In that case, well, I'd hesitate; I wouldn't sell to some guy who's out of control. What about me, for instance? If I weren't French, would you sell me one of your marvels? He hesitates, looks me up and down. Dunno. I don't sell to just anyone, and you look like you know nothing about it, that's pretty obvious….

And then, next to Yoda's stand, another one I did not see at first. The fellow's name is Michael Morris. He's about sixty, brick-red complexion, white hairpiece. A sign says COLLECTOR PAYING TOP PRICES. And I notice that the objects of his 'collection' are 'German war relics'—in other words, Nazi weapons and souvenirs. A jumble of pilots' badges. Goebbels dolls. Swastikas. Lugers priced at $18,000. Himmler's personal revolver. Göring's sword. A piece from the door to headquarters in Munich. A fragment of what is said to be the führer's own helmet. One of thirty-one armbands—'Limited series! Numbered!'—that belonged to his first bodyguards. And, exhibited like the most precious art book, a catalogue containing photographs of the rarest pieces of his collection: life-size wax statues of Nazi officers; helmets in a library; a silver bowl—

gift from Hitler to Eva Braun; dishes, engraved with a skull, from which the couple is supposed to have eaten; and the star attraction, an immense painting, almost a mural, showing Hitler in uniform—a coat draped over his shoulders, fist on his hip, quite feminine.

Doesn't it bother you to sell this stuff? Since there are people who want to buy it, someone's got to sell it. Are you aware that this is absolutely forbidden in Europe? Makes sense. You were occupied; we conquered them! No misgivings, then? No misgivings; the Reich killed fewer people than Genghis Khan. Would you sell objects that belonged to bin Laden? Oh, no! He is outraged. That's completely different! Those things sure wouldn't have the aesthetic quality of these Nazi artefacts.

As I burrow deeper into the show, I get to meet a half dozen other 'antique dealers' like Michael Morris, good Americans with a bent for the Nazi 'aesthetic.' But worse yet, I discover the shop of Lance and Judith Frickensmith, Ukrainians, who sell 'the most prejudicial, controversial films ever made'—cassettes of Leni Riefenstahl, Nazi marches and songs, an anti-Semitic film titled *The House of Rothschild*, another called *The Glory Years: Ruins of the Reich, Volume III*. Is this 'right to bear arms' really a constitutional right? A right linked, as the comptroller indicated, to the suggestion of 'community' comprised in the ideal of safeguarding order?

I take to the road again, toward Louisiana, more sceptical than ever—a part of me wondering if the crux of the issue isn't here in this monstrous and grotesque fascination. Of course, there are all the fine speeches and all the grandstanding. The campaign arguments. The pompous professions of faith of the NRA and its president, Wayne LaPierre, interviewed the other week in Virginia, defending the right to bear arms with the same energy Rod Dreher radiated when he spoke of his right to choose home schooling. But here could lie, in the end, the unexpressed thought of these gun-toting humanists; the possible horizon to their logorrhoea; perhaps its ultimate truth; the secret that, although usually unconscious, seems wordlessly active in their minds: the Hitlerian kitsch, the morbid flirtation with horror, the utterly idiotic wish to dress up openly as a Nazi....

The Splendour of New Orleans

I WILL REMEMBER New Orleans, Tocqueville's 'French' city.

I will remember the variegated quality of New Orleans and the impression I gleaned on this damp November day—much like Tocqueville's on the morning of January 1, 1832—of a city where they speak, think, feel, in several languages, influenced by France but also by Spain, Africa, India, the Cajun spirit, Creole, China.

I will remember this mixture of souls in New Orleans, and this mixture of bodies, and the many mixed-race people, minorities, that you see there. There aren't actually that many mixed-race people in America not as great an intermingling of community practices, symbolic systems, imaginations, as people seem to think. And it's here in New Orleans that I become aware of this methodical and, at heart, mutually agreed upon nonmixture of communities and of the low number of, for instance, mixed marriages.

I will remember jazz fever in New Orleans, its exuberance of living and dancing. I'll remember the impression you get, in the shabbiest bars of the French Quarter, of being present, every night, at the invention of blues and gospel.

I will remember the New Orleans dance halls, their lap dancers, so much bolder and more cheerful than the cloned dolls in the Las Vegas clubs. I'll remember having wondered about what in the world prim and proper America thinks of New Orleans. New Orleans the scandalous. New Orleans the libertine. Las Vegas, all right, but beware New Orleans and its accursed eroticism—Sodom and Gomorrah of the South. A bastion of licentiousness in a puritan land.

I'll remember one night in New Orleans, over a Bourbon Street restaurant smelling of beer and sweat, a very young woman, fifteen, maybe sixteen, years old, dancing on her balcony, taking off her shirt, hair barrette, bra, skirt, while a band of kids threw handfuls of beads at her from the street.

I'll remember another kid in Jackson Square, a fake street kid and real musician, the black double of John Kennedy Toole's Ignatius Reilly (and, since it's the same thing, of the filmmaker Michael Moore), re-enacting *A Confederacy of Dunces*, moaning 'I'm an ethnic white, I'm an ethnic white' between harmonica tunes.

I'll remember the slowness of New Orleans, its tropical languor, as well as its effervescence. I'll remember the city's strange time—doesn't each city have its own time, each place in the world its own quality of time, just as it has its own colour, landscape, history? Well, in New Orleans it's an awkward, forbearing, slow-to-anger time; it's a time that lingers and doesn't come to a decision; it's as if, Capote wrote, time had found a way in this city to stop passing, to take a rest.

I will remember the interminable card games of Stanley Kowalski in *A Streetcar Named Desire*—do these two guys who look like bums, slapping down cards past midnight on the stoop of a hovel on Constantinople Street know that they're repeating the gestures, almost the words, of Tennessee Williams?

I'll remember New Orleans as the city where I saw the greatest concentration of marginal people of all stripes: crackpots, eccentrics, guys playing vampire tricks on you, voodoo drunkards, girls offering you a frozen daiquiri on the sidewalk, and others, further on, who tell you in hushed tones the story of a drag queen beaten to death right here, a year ago, by an unhinged priest. The result, as in Chicago, of opening up the lunatic asylums and throwing their population out onto the street? No, nothing to do with these idiotics—nothing to do with the sad, controlled madness of the newly mad people in other American cities. There's Erskine Caldwell, Cormac McCarthy, in these strays. And when the violent people carry the day; when you understand that the Big Easy isn't far from holding the national record for blood crimes, often atrocious and unexplained; when they tell you there are red lights in certain neighbourhoods at which it isn't wise to stop, it's the shadow of Flannery O'Connor that assails you—literature again.

I will remember my arrival in New Orleans, at night, coming from Baton Rouge through stretches of swamp and bayou, through forests of ghostly trees with branches eaten by Spanish moss, itself eaten by fog.

I'll remember that New Orleans is, to the best of my knowledge, the only city in the world built not just on swampland but beneath the water, several feet below sea level, with a system of dikes, piles, pumps, and aspirators that are supposed to prevent the city from being drowned when the Mississippi overflows. Is that why the cemeteries in New Orleans are always on hills, the tombs almost always mausoleums, aboveground? Is that where the impression comes from of a haunted, slightly morbid city, which neither music nor dance manages completely to dispel? And this feeling of unfocused precariousness? And the certainty, which never leaves you, that someday the water will win out and New Orleans, a new Nineveh, will sink in a new Flood?

There's the dead, devouring water, the smells of humidity and mud, when you enter New Orleans, which I will remember.

There are the alligators that, they say, encircle New Orleans—are they watching and waiting for their time to come? No one knows; but I'll remember them too.

I'll also remember that French president of an oil company

who came to pick me up one morning to take me off the city's coast, out to the open sea, and onto an oil platform—very *Breaking the Waves*-ish. And I'll remember how we got there, flying over the suburbs of the radiant, spectral city and then over the Mississippi, getting progressively wider. I will remember its infinite delta, its dozens, then hundreds, of branches, some enormous, some spindly, like a web of clear threads thrown onto the silty earth. I will remember the lethal struggle between water and land, tatters of land saved from the water; after a while they seemed like rare islands lost in the ocean, increasingly narrow and long, with increasingly fragile, absurd houses. What the hell are these people doing? Why these slim barriers against the least peaceful of rivers? Don't they know that infinity, like death, always ends up winning the day?

The Venice of the South, they say. No, worse: New Orleans.

The capital of the South, the French think. But no—it's not the South. It's still not the South. Just New Orleans.

Hell Must Feel Like This

AT FIRST SIGHT it's a prison.

It's even, apparently, a decent-looking prison.

A wholesome life in the great outdoors, on this former plantation north of Baton Rouge, where you arrive via a sad and splendid road planted with trees covered in kudzu and, again, Spanish moss.

The bend in the Mississippi, the assistant warden, Cathy Fontenot—a young blonde, hair pulled back, pregnant—explains that it serves as a natural barrier on three sides and renders unnecessary the cumbersome apparatus of watchtowers, barbed wire, walls.

The 'trusties'—in other words, the eight hundred of the five thousand prisoners who have earned certain privileges through good behaviour—may walk without surveillance, almost free, on these eighteen thousand acres of greenery that they call 'the Farm.'

Carey Lassaigne, for instance, the trusty in charge of tile stables, who, with his well-polished boots, his immaculate white T-shirt, his handsome, honest blue eyes, his faithful dogs, looks more like a gentleman farmer than someone serving life.

The cell blocks themselves look all right.

They have birds' names: Raven, Hawk 1 and 2, Falcon 1, 2, and 3. The dormitories, showers, collective baths, are in an altogether different league from what I was allowed to see at Rikers Island or in Las Vegas (not to mention that veritable pigsty Tocqueville discovered when he visited New Orleans, where the prisoners, he wrote, lived chained up like animals in the midst of their excrement).

And then there's the rodeo season, which, every October, attracts thousands of tourists from all over Louisiana. The prisoners are so proud of it that none has ever taken advantage of the occasion, or of the relaxing of discipline it inevitably entails, to attempt an escape and, thus, risk having the administration retaliate by suppressing this 'social benefit.'

There's the volleyball court on the impeccable lawn at Falcon 3.

The boxing matches with referees, gloves, all the rules of fair play, as in any southern university a century ago.

Wood figurines at the entrance to the housing blocks, made by the prisoners themselves for Thanksgiving, represent a fairy, a dwarf, a piglet on a leash.

In short, an above-average prison.

A prison that from the outside looks almost like a model prison. Except for one detail.

One small detail, which has less to do with the prison itself than with the ruling legislation in the state, but which causes this landscape of green pastures to topple over into nightmare.

Since Angola is a prison reserved for the most part for people condemned to death or life in prison, and since Louisiana law has the distinctive feature of suppressing the very principle of parole, the men who enter here know that they'll never get out, that they're condemned to live without the vaguest prospect of release that is the prisoner's final hope in most other prisons.

How can you live when there's no hope for anything?

How do you bear with prison life when you know that, no matter what you do, you'll only exit by dying?

You think about your death, Cathy Fontenot replies unflinchingly.

Here in Angola we have a magnificent hearse, drawn by a horse and modelled by the prisoners themselves, like the piglets. We have a special prisoner, a robust black guy with a shaved head, who dresses in a tuxedo for the occasion and has made it his profession; he gives us grand funerals worthy of Princess Diana. So, as a detainee, you think about all of this. You prepare your funeral. You build your own coffin, with your own hands. When you no longer have a family or when your family has forgotten you, you go to our cemetery and choose where your future grave will be. You learn to read too—most of these people are illiterate, and they learn how to read so they'll be able to take comfort in the Bible or the Koran when their time comes to be led to the death chamber.

So I make my way to the cemetery, where those detainees for whom prison had become their entire universe are buried.

I visit the death zone, which includes, in addition to the execution chamber itself and the tiny adjoining room where the victims' representatives can watch the execution from behind glass, a dining room whose organisation Cathy Fontenot is proud to explain: separate men's and women's toilets; evacuation plan in case of fire; a chest full of T-shirts with ANGOLA or SNIFF SNIFF printed on them, which the people who come to watch the execution can purchase as souvenirs; an immense hope-inspiring fresco showing a man rising into the sky on a winged white horse; three tables (yes, three—they don't skimp on expenses at Angola) where the condemned can have his last meal served to him—good meat, foie gras, excellent side dishes, and even once, paid for out of his own pocket by the wardens' superchef, a deliciously stewed dish of crayfish. Just outside the prison gates is a museum and gift shop where visitors can buy T-shirts printed with ANGOLA: A GATED COMMUNITY.

I visit, finally, the weirdest place in this decidedly unreal place: the chapel where thirty or so prisoners sitting on wooden pews listen to three of their own sing gospel songs to the accompaniment of a Yamaha organ.

'What hope is there? Our hope is in here,' one of the three ministers, Audrey Fradieu, a serial killer condemned to life in prison, tells me, striking his own heart. 'It's been here, inside me, ever since I decided to give my life to the Lord. There's a seminary in Angola; there are a hundred of us ministers who were trained there. That's where the meaning of our life is: to go to all the prisons of America, spreading the Good Word that was taught to us here.'

The worst is that Cathy Fontenot, in a sense, might not be completely wrong.

These men could have become enraged or desperate.

They could have fomented revolts next to which the riots of the sixties would look like pale try-outs.

But that's not the case.

It's really a form of life that's been organised here.

A diminished life, a bloodless life, but a life all the same.

What can one think of this ersatz life? Is it really the worst, or only a lesser evil? Should we rejoice in the thought that life is stronger than death, or should we see Angola as a laboratory of the inhuman where it's an anti-life that is being invented, established under the rule of death, and possibly worse than death itself?

In case I had any doubts, Cathy Fontenot, as she walks me

back to the car, certainly crushes them. 'Hope,' she says to me, suddenly thoughtful. 'Hope is such a relative feeling, you know. Take, for instance, the condemned they unstrapped at the last second because the red telephone, the governor's, rang. True, they reattached him right away. True, after the governor said something to him—no one ever knew what—the governor asked to speak to the executioner and had the poor guy strapped down again and executed. But what is hope, if it isn't that? Isn't that proof that hope is still alive in Angola?'

The Glory of the South

ANYBODY WHO'S GOT his head full of literary clichés about the South of the post-Civil War era; who continues to see the new white man of these regions as an oaf in bib overalls out of Faulkner, Steinbeck, or Caldwell; who clings to the eternal myth of the dumb, silent, infantile southerner, speechless and, for that very reason, somewhat barbaric. All the lovers of folklore who keep seeing in these cotton and tobacco plantations a desolate landscape haunted by a God who is himself silent or, on the contrary, deafeningly omnipresent. All the Pavlovian anti-southerners for whom a white man from Louisiana or Alabama is at worst a killer in the making, and at best a degenerate destroyed by incestuous, alcoholic parents; manipulated by harlot-slaying ministers; simpleminded; inhabited by the spirit of evil; racist by tradition, segregationist by reflex and nature; criminal through resentment but also because he can't bring himself to accept the inevitable liberation of the blacks. All those fabricators of prejudice, I recommend, should meet two admirable men. Morris Seligman Dees, Jr., and Jim Carrier.

I was warned against Dees, a lawyer and the head of an organisation called the Southern Poverty Law Center, which specialises in hunting the 'bad guys' in the Ku Klux Klan. 'Be careful with Morris Dees,' a journalist from Dallas said to me when I expressed my intention of going to see, as soon as I got to Montgomery, the distant descendant of the lawyer Tocqueville met on January 6, 1832, as soon as he entered the capital of Alabama. 'Be careful with him. The guy's not straight. Many people don't think that much of him. Lots of money for fund-raising, not much for concrete action. Strong on publicity, weak when it comes to speaking out against the death penalty—which might expose him to a loss of popularity among contributors. And then there's the struggle against the Klan…. Isn't there something suspicious in his determination to bring the ghosts of a dying movement back to life, his desire to go all the way to hell to search them out and wake them up— and this, just to assure his own personal glory?'

The reality is a tall, elegant guy, a handsome Clint Eastwood of a face, a thin man in his sixties with gray eyes made pale by hardship and time, whose life was turned upside down one night in 1967 at the Cincinnati airport. Why that night? He couldn't say. But it was that night, after a semi-mystical illumination, that he understood that his existence no longer had meaning and that he had to change his soul. It was that night— and he doesn't care if he's ridiculed for this nightly Pascalian revelation in an American airport—that this ordinary son of Alabama farmers became aware of his responsibility as a white man confronted with the civil-rights movement. And it was that night that—like the founders of MoveOn.org I met in San Francisco, like so many young millionaires typical of an America that Tocqueville noted wasn't finished with oscillating between the frantic pursuit of wealth and a certain idea of redemption through philanthropy—he decided to sell his mail-order book business and create the centre, which he did, with Joe Levin, in 1971. Since then he has hunted down fascist activists throughout America.

Here, on six floors of the glass-and-steel building that now houses the offices and archives of the centre, he accumulates all possible evidence on each case of racist violence he can get hold of. And then he follows up. On more than ten occasions the 'bad guys' have condemned him to death. Each time he laughed at their threats and kept going. Is the Klan finished? Is the struggle against those nostalgic for white supremacy a battle of the rear guard? He shrugs his shoulders. I don't want to discuss that, he seems to be saying. It's just the heart of my existence. And the honour of Alabama.

With his white beard and laughing blue eyes, his handsome square face, his athlete's build, his yellow raincoat, Jim Carrier, a writer and journalist, looks like a young-old sailor. We have dinner with Dees in the oyster bar of a working-class neighbourhood, seemingly 100 percent black. We spend the night talking about the fulfilling hours of the struggle for civil rights—a struggle that, people seem to forget, managed in a very short span of time to reverse an order that had appeared unchangeable. And we spend the morning walking up and down the deserted city in the rain, looking for the places where this struggle was actually played out. The Dexter Avenue King Memorial Baptist Church, where King preached. The Rosa Parks Library and Museum, named after the black woman who in 1955 refused to give up her seat in the section of a bus reserved for whites. The stop where she got on the bus. The Civil Rights Memorial, where a marble clock is engraved with the names of forty heroes and martyrs of the cause. And then the more modest sites: a bridge, an intersection, the place where an old market once existed, a neighbourhood chapel, a grave—a succession of nondescript little sites that no plaque announces or, worse, that are pointed out only because of the place they occupy in the other memory of the city, its Confederate memory.

For the entire difficulty is right there, Carrier explains. The complexity lies in this superimposition, this overlay, this confusion and rivalry of memories. The whole problem here, for instance, on this avenue where, three hundred feet apart, Jefferson Davis declared war and Rosa Parks waited for her bus, is that the two memories are woven into each other and that one can't appear without the other yielding to it. That's why his role, Carrier's, is less to celebrate than to wage war. That's why, in the end, he acts not as a pilgrim but as an activist of a memory that for now exists only in palimpsests. To persuade the blacks of Montgomery that it isn't enough to be elected to the town council and that they have to take over the local historiography: that's his job. To persuade white people that this historiographical reversal is their business as much as their black brothers': that's his obsession. To raise awareness, in blacks and whites alike, of how this memory, when it's written down, will seem to be full of glory as well as of infamy; to help them understand that Alabama was indeed a land of racism and crime, but that it's also the place where antiracism triumphed, and that it is thus legitimate to be proud: that is his ultimate goal.

It's the first time in months that a matter of memory has managed to grip me. In this country where everything—that is to say, anything at all—ends up as a memorial, it's the first time I feel, in the developing museum and in the language of its promoter, an act of truth. Battle for memory and for the path to freedom. The will of memory—cornerstone in a strategy whose stakes appear as no less, suddenly, than the southern accomplishment of democracy in America. Let us now praise this famous man.

Those Who Believe in the South and Those Who Don't

REGARDING QUAIL HUNTING and its importance in southern folklore and culture, I knew only what Tom Wolfe wrote in the opening scene of *A Man in Full*. In a way, that was plenty. Once again, the merit—the miracle?—of literature is that this actual hunting party on the outskirts of Montgomery, this hunt for real quail I've been invited to by Rex Pritchett, tallies surprisingly well with its paper version. Same naïve warrior ritual. Same way, after lunch in a lodge decorated with stag and elk heads, photos of hunters and ads for smokeless cartridges, of starting out for the hunt. Same khaki outfits. The hats—in this case orange—that accentuate the impression of a uniform. The rifles, both archaic and sophisticated, that the hunters carry cradled in their arms like babies. The wagons, which haven't changed for a century and where, beside the ladies, the guests take their places and form the little audience without which Wolfe's hero, Charlie Croker, couldn't imagine a successful party. The guides (ours is named Adam Smith; no, it's not a joke—Adam Smith) in charge of tracking and handling the dogs. Their inimitable manner, when the dogs stop, sniffing the air, tails erect, of producing from far down in the throat, half whispered, half hissed, the same 'Sssstop' that has the same power of provoking the same surge of adrenaline, not just in the hunters but in all of us. Same dogs, what's more. Yes, looking at them, you'd say they were the same hunting dogs, standing identically at attention, except that—progress oblige—these dogs are wearing invisible collars that allow Adam Smith to send them an electric shock, should they stray too far, and bring them back to the pack. And then the same racket, same extraordinary din of wings and underbrush when the dogs have stopped for real, and Smith, too, and the flock is finally flushed and flies skyward. Wolfe writes of a flurry of birds exploding like rockets and dispersing in all directions to confuse predators; and it's true that even for a non-hunter, even for someone who, like me, has never felt any affinity with this type of scene, there's something aesthetically pleasing in the suddenness of the upsurge.

The difference, which changes everything, is that Rex Pritchett and his guests don't actually seem to believe in it.

They're southerners. True to life. Unlike Wolfe's hero, a rich real estate developer from Atlanta in whose eyes the acquisition of a hunting reserve was the most spectacular sign of wealth and success, Pritchett is heir to a long line of planters, probably ruined during the weevil epidemic but able to keep their land and turn it into a hunting reserve. But unlike Croker; unlike Inman, his guest; unlike the Tom Wolfe kind of company who (women included, even if they feigned indifference) played the game and appreciated the rules, Pritchett—though he carries out the gestures, plays along with the rituals, shivers with the same apparent delight when his servants go into the grass to collect and retrieve the quail he's killed—has in all his actions a slight distance, a hint of listlessness and almost coarseness, that wasn't in the novel and that suddenly alters the nature of the scene completely.

I ask him about the origin of this tradition he's perpetuating. He replies by listing the celebrities to whom in the last few years he has rented his property for the weekend. I ask him if he can elucidate the connection between this form of conviviality I see him practicing with his friends and the values of the Deep South, whose traces I'm looking for. He retorts, as if he didn't understand anything of what I said, that the great regret of his life is not having welcomed John Lennon, who was—nobody's perfect—an opponent of firearms and hunting. Worrying about his relations with environmental movements, I want to know if he respects the dates that begin and end hunting season: I do better than that, he snaps; I do something neither my grandparents nor my great-grandparents would ever have done, but it's my contribution to the ecological spirit—every year I introduce new quail, I import and introduce farm-bred quail, which we then go on to hunt.

When the hunting party is over and I'm tired of waiting for Adam Smith and his dogs to flush their last covert, I find Hal Hepburn, Pritchett's nephew, in the guest wagon and ply him with questions. His reaction is even more revealing. Does he suspect my disapproval? Does he, because he's younger, sense the European in me who is critical of the values of the Old South? Or has he himself privately broken with this world and its principles? Whatever the case, he answers in a tone that sounds incredibly revealing. 'Yeah, I like this sport.... What? Yeah, that's right, I did say "sport"... I know it was more than a sport for my ancestors.... But times change. What can you do?... And as for me—I come here only on weekends—it's a sporting activity, like any other.'

I observe his round face, a bit too red, and his rueful smiles. I listen to him tell me, as if he were justifying himself, about his attachment to this region and his reasons for choosing the MBA program at Auburn, which people don't know is ranked nineteenth among American law schools. I notice his timid looks when he explains that he understands very well 'why some people are against quail hunting' (he repeats this five times), but still, he doesn't believe you should see it as a manifestation of a white macho reactionary assassin culture, as the enemies of his family do. The least one can say is that here we are far from the legendary southern pride and arrogance. We're many times removed from those country aristocrats obsessed, according to Tocqueville, with their sense of honour and the honour of their race. Hepburn is unquestionably a southerner. He has preserved all the reflexes of southern culture, as well as that mixture in his voice of drawl, studied nonchalance, and black and peasant tonalities that are so characteristic of the region. But this old culture suddenly seems implausible. In this boy the culture appears at once bitter, discouraged, ashamed of itself, and exhausted. Could this be the victory of Morris Dees and Jim Carrier? The disappearance of the 'adventurer' with 'brutal mores' in whom Tocqueville saw the distillation of the southern spirit? America is changing.

On Slavery in America and Its Suppression

ATLANTA. THE GREAT black city of the American South. The city where the mayor, most of the politicians, and much of the upper class is black. The city of Morehouse College, the magnificent university that was the pride of Benjamin Elijah Mays and later the alma mater of his disciple Martin Luther King, Jr., where there is hardly a white person to be seen.

The city of King himself, devoted to the cult of King as Memphis is to the cult of yet another king. The sacred city, the Mecca, where people keep coming to visit the house where the hero was born, in the heart of Sweet Auburn; or the Ebenezer Baptist Church, where, they say, he began to preach; or, in the middle of an ornamental lake, the white marble tomb that holds his remains.

Atlanta, city of *Gone with the Wind*, which you can walk through for miles, at least in its southern and western neigh-bourhoods, without seeing the slightest trace of Rhett Butler or anyone resembling him—except in the Road to Tara Museum, where they have preserved his supposed cane.

Atlanta, city of CNN. Atlanta, city of Coca-Cola. Atlanta, which, apart from any ethnic consideration, remains the head-quarters of twelve of the five hundred largest businesses listed by *Fortune.*

The Atlanta airport—I don't like the Atlanta airport. From the first glance I hated its endless underground passageways, its ghost trains that don't go anywhere, its escalators that plunge straight into hell. But it's Atlanta's symbol of prosperity; it's the mark, to talk like the economists, of the extraordinary 'attrac-tiveness' of Atlanta. 'Too busy to hate,' the first black mayor of Atlanta said of his city, and it's true that this is how it feels. It's true that as soon as I land at Hartsfield-Jackson Atlanta International Airport, I sense a real-life prosperity that I didn't feel in Montgomery or, this morning, in Birmingham.

Here I am in Atlanta, then, showcase of peaceful desegregation. Here I am in Atlanta, symbol of an emancipation completed without tragedy.

Here I am in the city that has proved that racism, stupidity, crime, are soluble in capitalism, and where more than the 'ghetto look' displayed by middle-class high school students attests to the fact that a page has actually been turned. And then, all of a sudden, in a suburb north of the city, in this bar, Manuel's Tavern (named after Manuel Maloof, an old local Democrat who has recently died), in this room walled floor to ceiling with coarse exposed bricks, where Budweiser ads hang next to photos of the late owner with McGovern, Humphrey, Clinton, Gore—here, sitting at a table among journalists and politicians of the county who all express nostalgia for the Kennedy, Carter, or Clinton eras, depending on their generation, is the young bureau chief of *The Wall Street Journal*, Douglas A. Blackmon, who approaches me and starts a conversation.

When Blackmon was still just a local reporter and Pearl worked for *The Wall Street Journal* here in Atlanta, he knew Daniel Pearl.

He can still see the memorial to Pearl that was held here, right where I'm standing, when music was played in his honour.

But here is the point: he's writing a book on the South and, more generally, on America, which he'll probably call *Slavery by Another Name*—and he'd like to talk to me about it.

Did you know, he asks me, that there's an entire section of the history of slavery that remains completely unknown?

Did you know, for instance, that in the beginning of the nineteenth century there were Baptists who searched through the Bible to find texts they could use to explain how a slave should be treated and also to provide theological justification for this despicable practice?

Did you know that there was a 'non-racist' period in this history of appropriation of man by man?

Did you know that there was an entire prehistory, when Darwinism hadn't yet arrived in America and racism hadn't formulated its theorems, when it wasn't unusual to find Africans—do you understand? black people—owning other Africans, white people owning other white people?

Did you know that slavery continued in other forms after its abolition?

Did you ever hear any rumour—this is the starting point of my *Slavery by Another Name*—of this new three-way commerce that took root in America after the Civil War? It worked, in effect, this way: a sheriff in Alabama or Georgia was paid by the number of arrests he made; blacks were ordered, for some trifle, to pay fines they couldn't afford; some friends of the sheriff would appear out of nowhere, like saviours, and offer the poor guy a job that would allow him to pay off his debt; so the former slave all of a sudden found himself chained again to forced labour, paid a wretched wage, and—if he slacked off or complained—subject to the threat of going to prison.

And did you know that all this—this whole mechanism I'm describing to you, which didn't really end until 1945, with the great return of blacks from European battlefields—all this prehistory or posthistory of traffic in human beings, the dark, rejected face, the deformed mirror of the country, is hushed up by both white and black America, who have agreed not to learn anything about it?

Another example, he insists.

One last example, which says everything.

During the New Deal a noble initiative aimed to gather the testimony of survivors of actual slavery, before it was too late.

But the undertaking was carried out in such a way that the people involved said nothing, or almost nothing, about their immeasurable suffering. The method used was such that in all the states except one—Florida—it was white people who were asked to gather the interviews. The result, except in Florida, was that the interviewees said precisely what the whites hoped they'd say; the result of the chosen method was that these 'slave narratives' that were so eagerly awaited were often aseptic, watered-down documents, very 'Oh, how good life was in the days of the Deep South.'

Listening to him, I remember those Holocaust survivors who dared not bear witness or speak.

I try to imagine—even if the situations are completely different—the Jews' not reclaiming the right to tell their stories and be heard, as they finally did.

Is that the situation with American blacks?

Are they a community without memory? And this whole happy façade, this representation of a black city without bitterness or complexes—is it really just a façade with, in the middle of it, an enormous gap in memory?

Gospel and Company

THEY ARE EVERYWHERE.

For the forty-eight hours I've been in Memphis, Tennessee, following in the footsteps of my youth and of rock-and-roll nostalgia—for the forty-eight hours I've been going from the ultrakitsch house of Elvis to the bars on Beale Street where they're still singing his songs; from B.B. King's club to Sun Studio, on Union Avenue; and from the Rum Boogie Café to the Music Hall of Fame, where I wanted to see Booker T. Jones's organ—I haven't been able to take a step without bumping into them.

The men are in tails, shirts with starched collars, soft hats or top hats, patent-leather shoes, gloves, carrying canes—black men of all ages, sometimes very old, sometimes fat, sweating under fur coats too hot for the season, puffing, all dressed up as if they were dandies from the Roaring Twenties.

The women, also black and of all ages, all grades of corpulence, some quite gorgeous, others enormous, in evening dresses, moiré taffeta cloaks, brocades, pearls and earrings, an entire jewellery shop around their necks and on their wrists, iridescent or embroidered silk blouses, gloves reaching beyond the elbows, high heels, hats like hanging gardens, tiaras, veils and fans, gauze and organdy parasols, mink coats reaching to their feet.

In the beginning, I thought they were actors for some grand reconstitution of Tennessee's good old days.

Then, since they were arriving from all over and coalescing in the lobby of my hotel, since they were beginning to be too numerous for me to even count them—hundreds, no, thousands, maybe tens of thousands; it seemed like a joke, a hallucination, a dream—I told myself that the whole city must have dressed up for a carnival, like in Venice or Rio.

Is there a carnival in Memphis? I finally end up asking one of these ladies, in a long, shimmering, bronze-collared outfit, pearl belt and golden tiara, royally awaiting the elevator next to me.

Of course not, she replies. Why a carnival? We're just followers of the Church of God in Christ, and we're having its ninety-seventh annual convention here in Memphis, where it was founded. There are fifty thousand of us delegates from all over America, and today is women's day. I'm going. Would you like to come along?

I leap at the chance.

I follow her, and some of her friends, to the minibus that's shuttling back and forth between the hotel and the convention centre.

On the way, I learn that the most beautiful of these women, the ones most richly adorned, are often the wives of bishops.

'We're elegant for Him,' the lady tells me. 'Beauties of our Lord. Fiancées of God. For a long time black people went to church in rags. Those days are gone. The day of glory has come. It begins like this, in splendour, in the way we dress....'

And so I find myself across the city, in the middle of a secure area where the traffic is directed by police officers, in one of those huge auditoriums I got a taste of at Willow Creek, where thousands of delegates converge, formal, deadly serious, walking as if in a procession, at once rivals and accomplices in their admirable wish to offer the Almighty the spectacle of their gold and finery.

Same blaring public-address system as in the auditorium at Willow Creek.

Same giant screens, on both sides of the stage.

Same atmosphere of merchandised faith in the wings, with—even worse than Willow Creek—stacks of flyers advertising cosmetics; hat stores; communion tables; a manufacturer of 'First Lady Eve' (Barbie-style dolls that look like the Virgin Mary); and a preacher, Cody Vernon Marshall of Illinois, campaigning for a board position in his church and distributing on glossy paper a profession of faith, the main focus of which seems to be, aside from testaments to 'fairness' and 'proven commitment' printed in gold letters, a photo of himself posing handsomely with a stern look, finger placed pensively on his mouth, dressed in the purple robe of the high dignitaries of his church.

The real difference from Willow Creek is in the women.

The newness, the shock, is in these thousands of women, now seated, each more ostentatious than the next, whose eccentricity and extravagance are a fine challenge to American puritanism.

There are those in their Sunday best (I recognise them from the streets of Memphis) and others, dressed all in white, whom I hadn't seen before.

There are the wives of bishops but also the young, virginal-looking adepts of what is, I am told, the fastest-growing Pentecostal church in the country.

There are the meditative ones and the ecstatic ones.

The ones humming quietly, eyes shut, and the ones singing at the tops of their lungs.

There are women who, when Mother Willie Mae Rivers, 'international supervisor' of the 'department of women,' intones her gospel, just have tears in their eyes and women who get up, begin to dance, and shout, pointing up to the sky, eyes rolling upward: 'Thank you, Lord, for being there! Thank you, Lord, for your mercy!'

But the dominating trait, the trait that surprises and, after a while, moves me, is this joy, this fervour, this spirit of communion I haven't seen in any white church.

How much comedy is there in this spectacle, and how much faith?

In the heart of Vanessa, a delegate from Nebraska, how much is civic religion, whose task it is to prohibit gay marriage, and how much is authentic enthusiasm?

And at the Mason Temple, in that concrete building, half mall, half bunker, where the church's headquarters are located and where I'll have the opportunity, a few hours later, to interview the international presiding bishop, Gilbert E. Patterson; in this Vatican of Pentecostalism, which resembles the centre of operations for a holding company more than a house of God, and where all the ministers I meet look like lawyers and all the lawyers look like bodyguards, and where Patterson himself, with his heavy bracelets, silver chains and rings, looks more like a prince of the church than a humble preacher—how can you, in all the bustling activity of this place, disentangle what is ostentatious display and calculating stagecraft from what has to do with the legitimate manage-ment of the interests of a church with six or seven million members?

I don't know. In all truth, I'm quite incapable of deciding.

But that there exists another kind of religiousness; that there is in this church and perhaps beyond it, in the big black churches of the South, a quality of bliss that you don't find elsewhere; that there is, at the root, in the population of the faithful themselves, an intensity of piety that has nothing to do with what can be observed in the megachurches of the North—of that I am convinced.

Tragic Ball in Lillie Rock

THEY'VE BEEN TALKING about it for months. It's been weeks that attending or not was the ultimate question for the glamorous crowds of New York and Washington. Bono and Barbra Streisand announced they'd be there. Dozens of government officials let it be known that they'd be present or, at the very least, represented. Thousands, tens of thousands, of ordinary citizens, from all corners of the country, invaded the city's hotels the day before. It sometimes seems that in America the sole purpose of history is to end up in a vast museum; I even saw a group of Democrats from Tennessee explaining that the very night of his election, in November 1992, William Jefferson Clinton sent out the first solicitations for contributions toward the building of his monument and that they began themselves to reserve their places three years ago, just to make sure. In short, this was his day. It was the moment, so eagerly awaited, when former presidents, inaugurating their libraries, called the world to witness the glory of their rule.

And in this case, everything, truly everything—the beauty of the building and its futurism; its purpose as a boon for Arkansas and a link between generations; its $165 million budget; its 80 million presidential papers exhibited or stored; the scale of the production; the siting of the reviewing stands out in the open, facing the glass-and-steel building; the live telecast of the entire ceremony on giant screens—everything was planned to transform this dedication into an apotheosis of the Clinton years and what they represent. Alas, that didn't take into account three meagre grains of sand that would be enough to throw everything off.

The former president's health, first of all. That wretched heart operation he had to undergo two months back, from which you can sense immediately, whatever they say, he hasn't completely recovered. His voice is good, certainly. It's the voice of the perennial Clinton, cheeky and firm, tinged with a southern lilt and full of authority. But in his thinness, in the slight awkwardness of his step when he gets up to walk to the podium, in his rather childlike way of squeezing Hillary's hand very hard in moments of intense emotion, in his melancholy gaze when the simple people of Little Rock come to tell him how his presidency truly changed their lives, there is a new frailty, something slightly absurd, a look that doesn't become him.

Then the elections. John Kerry's historic defeat, still recent, the extent of which no one would have imagined a few days ago. It's not Clinton's defeat, of course. Maybe a part of him even obscurely wished for it. But finally, there it is, present in everyone's mind, lending the gathering an undertone that's inevitably sepulchral. And it has one little consequence that I'm convinced neither he nor any of his advisers foresaw. Since protocol calls for the presence at his side of the sitting president and all other ex-presidents still living, the said sitting president being named George W. Bush and another George Bush being among the ex-presidents, here is the hero of the day framed by two Bushes; worse, since each of the two Bushes is himself flanked by a Mrs. Bush, Clinton is boxed in not by two but by four Bushes, whose rude health, seemingly modest but actually triumphant smiles, thick brown or navy-blue wool coats belted carefully at the waist, upturned at the throat, only emphasise his new fragility.

And then, to top it all off, the weather. Weather is so ridiculous. It's the uncontrollable, hence neutral, parameter par excellence. But there's weather and weather, and since I've been in

the United States I haven't seen a storm as violent as the one
that's been beating down on Arkansas since morning. So,
because the ceremony was planned to take place outdoors, now
the whole population of Clintonians, journalists, ambassadors,
guests of honour, heads of state, and orators find themselves,
heads bare, under icy rain and doomsday lightning. 'Welcome to
my rainy library dedication,' Clinton says, attempting a joke. 'If
my beloved mother were here, she'd try to remind me that rain
is liquid sunshine.' But you can feel that his heart isn't in it. You
can see that the dimness of the sky only adds to his own sadness.
'Thanks for coming,' he says to Bush, in a humble tone I'm not
sure he's feigning. 'Welcome to the realm of ex-presidents, that's
to say of the future deceased,' he emphasises, trying to be
humorous but not quite getting there. And you only have to
observe the Bushes, you only have to take note of their smug
smiles when the cameras frame and project them onto the giant
screen, you only have to hear George W. explaining, not without
ferocity, that the greatest success of the man we've come to
honour is 'his daughter,' in order to understand that the affair,
from their point of view, leaves no room for doubt: heaven, as
usual, has cast its vote—and it has voted Republican.

The stands, which we were told had been overbooked, begin
to thin out. Hillary, who planned a long speech, makes do with
a few words. Chelsea looks bored. Jimmy Carter looks cold. The
noteworthy Democrats, who came to be seen, hide under
umbrellas and are so wet that when the camera zooms in, you
can barely recognise them. There's Al Gore, his face swollen.
Kerry—or, rather, his shadow, almost his ghost, glimpsed for half
a second and given timid applause. It's not an apotheosis; it's a
debacle. It's not a glorification; it's one more step in the descent
to hell that began in Boston fifteen days ago, when Kerry
conceded—or maybe, who knows, five years ago, with the
Lewinsky affair. It's not even that cosy family reunion the
Democrats had hoped for. It's not even 'time recaptured,' when

different generations come to greet one another before starting in again on their conquest of power. Or else it is, but in the Proustian sense, like the terrible ball at the Guermantes' where the guests suddenly look twenty years older and appear like caricatures of themselves. For that's the ultimate effect of this lugubrious ballet, that it seems somehow to recoil on the scene it should have been celebrating—a bit like in those anamorphoses, where all you need is a mirror, or a change in the angle of your gaze, to deform the whole tableau; it's the whole Clinton era, his 'legacy,' which suddenly seems altered by the reflected light of this gloomy, twilit, graceless day. What are the end results of the Clinton years, after all? The Balkans, true. The Near East, if you like. The memory, already faded, of prosperity, sure. But from now on, this eclipse too, this disaster.

VI

Eye of the Hurricane
FROM MIAMI TO PITTSBURGH

James Ellroy in Miami

BALD SKULL. TALL frame, at once powerful and awkward. He conveys the impression of an owl that keeps bumping into the bars of an invisible window. That's probably unfair. But James Ellroy has what we call '*une sale tete*'—an evil look. He's like a murderer in one of his own novels. Like the perverts in early Polanski films. But also like a guy who couldn't care less what kind of impression he makes.

Obviously, the important thing isn't his looks but his books. The main thing, the only thing that seems to count for him now, is this crowd of a hundred or so spectators in shorts, sandals, and loud shirts who are watching him here, in this auditorium at the Miami Book Fair, as he reads the opening pages of his latest novel. But he's not reading, he's speaking. And he's not speaking, he's acting. Never before have I seen a writer put so much passion, rhythmical gesticulation, vehemence, ferocity, into the way he declaims. Artaud, perhaps, in his famous lecture at the Vieux Colombier. Guyotat, in the 1960s, belching out his

Tomb for 500,000 Soldiers. But neither had this way of shouting, braying, whispering, beating the air with his arms, turning suddenly stiff, howling, boxing the void, laughing, recoiling with a colossal scream, swaggering, yelping, sweating, dancing, inhaling and exhaling like someone who was suffocating but then miraculously regains his breath—in short, dizzily embodying the words he has written and, through these words, each one of his characters. Pollock, maybe. Yes, his authentic counterpart, the name that flashes in my mind, is not a writer but a painter: Jackson Pollock. Ellroy performs Action Reading as Pollock performed Action Painting. He acts out his text, toys with it, rolls it under his tongue or between his teeth, bites into it, swallows it, squeezes it out, just as Pollock skipped around his drip paintings, circled around them, spat and pissed on them, eviscerated his canvas or feigned eviscerating himself.

That, Ellroy tells me later—already yawning from boredom in the private room where we meet to talk, supposedly, about prisons and the death penalty in America—is the only thing that interests him. To write and then spit out the sentences he's written, and by spitting them out, by ejaculating them, surprise his readers, pick the locks of their minds and pretty much of their bodies, throw sound and fury into them, set them on fire—yes, to him that's all that seems worth experiencing in this life. And the rest?

Oh, the rest… He doesn't look at newspapers. Doesn't watch TV. Doesn't know about anything that's happening on the planet. Doesn't even read much. Usually writers read one another's work, at least a bit. Not Ellroy. It's been years since he's read a classic, let alone a contemporary novel. Years since he started thinking of himself as the Dostoyevsky of American crime and stopped seeing the point of studying anyone else's books. The only pages he reads, he confides with an attempt at a smile, are police records. The only events that interest him are the unsolved crimes of those dreadful years in the 1950s and

1960s when he was mourning for his murdered mother. Here, for instance, in this Miami he hates, the only prospect that sustains him is the idea that in a few hours he'll be back home, in Kansas City, and see his cop buddies, who are his only friends. The one idea that gets him through this ridiculous book fair, where he's forced to give one interview after another and has to make moronic comments on purpose to keep from falling asleep—the only saving grace is knowing they'll meet again very soon, the novelist and the policemen, over one of those good old crime files, a nice vile, disgusting case, which is the only contact he has with people in real life.

Because it's not human beings that turn him on, he adds in such an exaggeratedly wicked tone that the contrary effect is produced and he conveys the fleeting impression of a little boy—it's crimes. Not even crimes in general, he insists (as if to show he has no interest at all in my talk of prisons in America today), but those from the 1950s and 1960s that he's been fixated on ever since that horrific morning in June 1958 when, as a child, he saw them bring back the half-naked corpse of his strangled mother, her gaze forever startled. What was life like as she was dying? What did this accursed America look like? He remembers the day, two or three years ago, when he was with one of his cop friends at the Los Angeles Police Department and a guy came up to them saying, 'My brother died in 1963 in South Central L.A. I've always wanted to know what happened. Please help me.' So his buddy gets out the file and together they lean over it as if over a sacred text, and they realise what no one in 1963 or since ever understood: namely, that this mysterious crime was a homophobic crime. He remembers another day, around the same time, when, visiting Lyon and leafing through an old issue of *Paris Match*, he discovered what happened on October 17, 1961, when General de Gaulle's cops killed two hundred Arabs and threw their corpses into the Seine. When he got back home, he rushed to the Los Angeles Sheriff's

Department Homicide Files and relayed the story to his cop friends, who could not believe at first that in a country as civilised as France their colleagues might be capable of such grisly murders. Then they got their heads together and for days waded through this river of blood; kept going over this insane, succulent slaughter. 'I go back, I get hooked on old murders, I get to relive them. Give me an old sex murder file to read and I'm just as happy as a pig in shit.'

James Ellroy is alone. Alone in literature and alone in the world. Alone with these crimes he keeps resuscitating, his memory's bouquet of black dahlias, whiffs of polluted air that are the only oxygen he breathes—and alone with the novels he draws from them. In a country where everyone wants to be connected to everyone else, in an America where the height of earthly wretchedness has become the 'bowling alone' of the postmodern dissocialised subject, he offers us the unique case of a man alone, desperately and resolutely alone, locked up in his territory of books and graves, cut off from everyone—but happy.

Is It All Over for Miami?

THE CUBANS AREN'T happy. In principle they're the lords of this city. And—at least in Miami–Dade County, where they and other Latin Americans represent the overwhelming majority—they're in control of political, economic, and cultural power.

But all the same…

There are those who have never got over the Elián González affair, and who, like Juan Clark, a professor of sociology at Miami Dade College, live surrounded by pictures of the little boy martyr who was sanctified and canonised after the American police ignominiously delivered him back to Castro.

There's Jose Basulto, a combatant, who, in the living room of his home in Coral Gables, south of downtown, tells me about the day in 1996 when Cuban pilots took off from Havana to shoot down two of the planes belonging to Brothers to the Rescue, the organisation Basulto founded to guide, from the air, struggling *balseros* on their makeshift rafts through the dangerous waters of the Florida Straits. The Americans didn't lift a finger.

There's Jaime Suchlicki, the head of the Institute for Cuban and Cuban-American Studies, who explains to me, in a more academic tone, how the death of Soviet communism, and then the end of the Cold War, and then the declaration of war on a terrorism that now dons the mask of Islamic fundamentalism— how all these have demoted Cuba, the Cuban question, and, consequently, the Cubans of Miami from the eminent place that was theirs in yesterday's world and its Great Game.

And the fact is that, for these reasons and several others, a cloak of sorrow and acrimony seems to have settled on a community of men and women who had long been described as the salt of the earth, who in times past—as soon as they set foot on American soil, even as they boarded the plane that would carry them to freedom—heard the president of the United States announce that they were the vanguard of the free world in its war against dictatorship. And now, forty years later, with the collapse of communism and the laser pointer of universal history directed at other countries, they discover that they serve no purpose, no longer play the slightest role in the geostrategy of an America struggling against a new empire of evil, and that when this very America chooses Guantánamo to imprison its enemies, Fidel figures nearly as an ally, while they, the former heroes of antitotalitarian struggle, figure as trouble-makers and intruders.

So when you're a Cuban from Miami and you feel swindled in this way, the victim of such a sudden and spectacular reversal of history, there are two solutions.

You can let things be, renounce your former exceptional

status, go back to business as usual, bid farewell to the old Washington-Havana axis, to the most-favoured-immigrant status from which you've benefited for so long, and say hello to becoming an actual, ordinary American.

Or you can persevere in the mirage, deny reality, dream on— and that's the spectacle one catches glimpses of in the heart of Little Havana, in this Calle Ocho that since the first exiles started arriving, I'm told, has never before indulged its taste for burrowing into its own past, its clichés, and its folklore, as much as it does now, to a dizzying degree.

The hat stores that now sell only models copied from the 1940s and 1950s... the cigar makers who have rediscovered the prerevolutionary techniques for making *puros*... the Cuban newspapers from way back when, reprinted and sold as facsimiles... these bars where the phone books are from 1959... this Versailles Restaurant, where frail gentlemen who all look like Batista go on playing dominoes, just as in the old days.... It's the James Ellroy syndrome on the scale of an entire society. It's nostalgia for a fixed time in almost a million souls.

After lunch at the Versailles I pay a visit to Commander Huber Matos, whom I'd met in Washington in 1982, not long after he was released from a twenty-year sentence in Castro's jails. I want to see where this former figurehead of dissidence, pin-up of my youth, has ended up. If only from the difficulty I have in just finding his address, I sense that this new Miami is scarcely aware of his existence. But what strikes me in the man who welcomes me, some two decades later, to his too large and too empty house, too full of posters and flyers dating back to his age of glory; what astonishes me in this transparent old man who seems to wander around in his haunted office, absurdly shuttered and encircled by ostensibly needless bodyguards; what stuns me in this spectre, this revenant, agitated by a tic that compels him to constantly chase imaginary fireflies away from his eyes, is that by some ruse of time whose meaning isn't clear to me right away, he seems both terribly aged and, like the domino players at the Versailles, paradoxically rejuvenated.

True, he gives the impression of a phantom. He has these sullen gray-blue eyes that keep tearing up. He has the exceedingly fixed look of people who can no longer hear. But as soon as he starts talking, and especially when he talks about his distant past, before the jails—the years as a young revolutionary leader, veteran of the combats of the Sierra Maestra, rival and comrade of Fidel Castro himself—he conjures a tone of phenomenal youthfulness, which betrays that history and life have stopped for him, too. 'Two fingers on one handy' he shouts, his eyes suddenly livelier, evoking the early kinship. 'We were two commanders, like two fingers on the same hand, entering insurgent Havana in the same tank.' Then, noticing how surprised I am at the disproportionately stringent security with which he has equipped his house: 'He's like Stalin, the *cabrón*, the old goat. He just has one idea in his head ever since I've come to the United States, and this idea, morning and night, this obsession that my agents assure me will never leave him, is to send me a Ramon Mercader who, by murdering me, would rid Castro of the one person in the world who has caused him the most trouble and harm.'

And then, with another vague smile, feigned weariness, but a flash of victory, joy, and, it should be said, gentle madness in his eyes: 'Unless it's the opposite; unless it's him, Fidel, who's already dead. Do you know, there's a rumour over there that he died in secret and was buried in three different cemeteries between Cienfuegos and Sierra del Escambray. Then I, Matos, would be the survivor....'

For a long time now I've heard talk not just about Miami vice but about Miami madness... but all of a sudden, I touch upon a different style of madness. A different style of irrationality. That, too, is Miami.

On Feelings About Nature in America

FOR A EUROPEAN, one of the most enigmatic characteristics of the American ethos is its relationship with nature.

There's the wildness of nature here, first of all. The proximity of this wild nature that, we tend to think, has been domesticated by technology—when in fact it's just been pushed back a little, moved farther away.

Here, for instance, in the Everglades, in this national park scarcely fifteen miles from Miami, it's been contained within an immense reservation right at the edge of I believe, they would have exterminated the wildlife that here continues to paddle around in the swamp's deep waters. I am convinced that these pythons, giant iguanas, piranhas from the Amazon, rabid raccoons, these cottonmouth moccasins with their deadly poison, these potent blue herons that feed on baby alligators—and the alligators themselves, presented to us as the 'guardians of the Everglades' and carefully observed by the old nature buffs of the county—would doubtless have been victims of the great prophylactic cleanup demanded by European civilisation, whose dream ever since Descartes has been to turn us into masters and possessors of nature. Not here. Here there is no real mastery. No possession. The Floridians don't tame nature; they push it back. Instead of subjugating it, they drive it away. Florida is so vast, and space is of so much less importance than in Europe, that there's room for both city and nature. And the same goes for California, where, my friend Charlie Lyons tells me, some nights he hears wolves and coyotes howling in the hills behind his house.

There is the violence of nature. There is the extreme brutality, also unimaginable in Europe, not just of certain species of animals but of the elements, especially hurricanes and tornadoes. I heard them talked about at every stage of my journey, and I ended up realizing that they are more numerous and, in a sense, more devastating in the United States than anywhere else among so-called developed countries. 'Florida under attack!' a dishevelled, livid journalist shouted on CNN the other day, live from some coastal town buffeted by a storm in this paradise for retirees. Attack from what? I wondered. Who was attacking? Which bin Laden or Saddam Hussein emulator? But it was just Jeanne. It was the nascent Hurricane Jeanne, coming from the Bahamas and briskly swooping down on the southeastern American coast.

It would be so easy in this case to wax ironic. One could detect in this journalist's anxiety an additional symptom of the American taste for grand spectacles and exaggeration. But you might snigger a little less if you tried to imagine behind Jeanne—and also, in recent months, behind the familiar names Alex, Frances, Ivan, Charley, Karl, Lisa, and Bonnie; or, last year, Kate, Larry, Isabel, Erika, Ana, and Claudette—the mudslides, the torrential floods, the walls of furious water beating down on the beaches, the houses with their roofs blown off, the rain of frogs and lizards, the trees uprooted; in short, the landscapes of desolation that we have no actual concept of in France and that three weeks ago in Puma Gorda, for instance, resulted in the trifling sum of sixteen dead. People in the United States don't need to imagine; they know. (And this knowledge feeds their extreme sensitivity to this type of cataclysm when it takes the form of a tsunami and devastates a destitute country.)

Finally, the most striking aspect for a European when faced with this implacable recurrence of natural catastrophes, some of which (Hurricane Andrew, the Mississippi floods of 1927) have gone down in history and have shaped the construction of the American landscape, the most incomprehensible thing, is the relatively passive roles of politicians and citizens. Oh, I'm well aware of how television carries on about the weather. I know that Florida has the most effective meteorological forecasting stations in the world. And in New Orleans I noticed the ingenuity deployed to avoid a repetition of the 1927 scenario. But let me tell you about Homestead. I'll take the example of this town on the road to the Everglades, in a landscape of fake trees painted yellow, orange, blue, and red to liven things up, this town devastated twelve years ago by Hurricane Andrew, and hit by most of the ensuing hurricanes. What takes you by surprise in Homestead is the vulnerability of the houses. What bewilders and stuns you is that everything has been rebuilt just as it was before, with the same prefab kits and the same kinds of trailers, which look as if they've been set down ready-made, patched together, somewhat rickety. You wonder what will keep them from flying apart in exactly the same way when the next Lili, Isidore, or Allison comes along.

Yet America has the means to protect Homestead. The America that hasn't ceased to dream of the Star Wars space-defence shield has the most effective warning and prevention systems in the world. Yet, strangely enough, it doesn't use even a tenth of its capacity to put the inhabitants of Homestead out of danger. Just as I've never seen a European airport as profoundly paralysed as the major American airports can be by a snowstorm, for instance, so I can't imagine the principle of precaution so poorly applied in my country as it is here in Homestead.

Why?

There's the culture of risk, stronger than the culture of security and the inclination to self-protection.

There are the remains of a pioneering spirit that for centuries has accommodated itself to a sense of temporary habitat, perched, as it were, on the side of the road, pressing forward with the frontier, and by definition precarious.

But there is also, anchored deep in the mentality of the country, a slightly supernatural, almost superstitious relationship to what Americans, even the secular ones, are prone to call Mother Nature. As if omnipotence found its limits there, reached its rational confines. As if the Promethean will to get the better of all things and all people imposed on itself a limit of principle and wisdom in this relationship to the elements. No pity for our enemies, the American of the twenty-first century seems to be saying; no mercy for terrorists, certainly, or even for opponents of the country's economic supremacy. But let Nature take her best shot.

My Own Phantom in Savannah

ALL RIGHT, I'VE changed my mind. If I had to take up residence in one city in this country—if I had to choose one town, and only one, to live in—it might not be Seattle after all, but Savannah. Savannah's allure. Its striking, Old South beauty. The pastel houses—water-gray, pale mauve, sea-blue, sepia—of Savannah. The mixture of Italianate and Hellenic architecture, Victorian and Doric, Second Empire and Regency, witnesses to bygone eras when rich shipowners from London, settling in Savannah, vied with one another for style and splendour. The foam-collared stucco, imitating cut stone. The rare marble, the columns, that lend the town an air of triumphant grace. The wide avenues lined with trees enveloped in moss—giant magnolias, sycamores, myrtles—where, more than in Atlanta, you expect to see the ghosts of Rhett Butler and his Scarlett appearing on a stoop. The squares—there are twenty-two of them—with huge oak trees, around which the town was built. The deliberate, thought-out quality of the city. (Didn't its founder, James Edward Oglethorpe, mean to create a model city, a utopia, cleansed of the sins of crime, alcohol, prostitution, and—even more unusual in the South—slavery?) At the same time, there is the absence of that hysterical, levelling modernism that swallows up the past and all shades of difference, which almost always goes along with programmed urban growth in America. Here is a city that is as methodically marked out in grids, as perfectly geometrical, as the city-camps of the West but that has managed to preserve its past, cultivate it, enhance it, with the same conscientious care of Venice, Amsterdam, or any other European museum-city. This cemetery over here, for instance, this old cemetery with just a few graves scattered among the wild grasses, all, or almost all, dating back to the Civil War or earlier. This necropolis in the middle of the town is not a museum, since anyone can wander through it without aim or itinerary, ticket or guided tour. These lopsided obelisks and crypts, these slabs and tombs of cracked or crumbling stone, these monuments, these uneven flagstones, which anywhere else would be either destroyed or museumified like the Cardiff Giant and the dinosaur teeth of South Dakota, but which here, in Savannah, just form part of the landscape as objects of a discreet but passionate piety.

And it's here that I come to realise the importance that the memory of their wars possesses for the men and women of the American South—not so much the World Wars but the other wars. Wars that we Europeans barely think about but that southerners, in one way or another, in shame or glory, bitterness or exaltation, never seem to tire of commemorating. The Indian wars, obviously. The Civil War, which here they call the War of Secession and which, I begin to understand, remains an open wound in the side of this refined Savannah, infused with aristocratic value, where, I am convinced, this very aristocracy, this art of living and this taste for art in life, more so than slavery itself, inspired northern resentment. And then the War of Independence. Here, in this cemetery, in the intricate shadows of two-hundred-year-old trees, are half-effaced plaques from this first American war on which one can still, with great difficulty, make out the names of young men from England, France, and Poland, caught in obscure affairs of duels, honour offended or avenged, heroic deeds, who now have only these humble inscriptions in great books of stone to recall them to the memory of the living.

In a word, I love Savannah. I love the way the inhabitants are fond of their town. I love the gesture, for example, of those officers who in 1864 wanted to surrender to General Sherman rather than see Yankee troops sack the city. And I love the story of those citizens who a century later mounted guard in front of the Davenport House to prevent it from being demolished and thus founded the Historic Savannah Foundation that watches over the memory and integrity of the city to this day. I have seen so many unloved cities in America since this journey started. In my mind's eye there are so many cities half destroyed, or simply disfigured, by vandalism and the indifference of their inhabitants. Buffalo... Detroit... Cleveland... Lackawanna... the cities die off, the great shattered cities of the American North and also the northern-style cities in the South.

Savannah is the antimodel, then. Savannah—a rare but all the more precious case of metrophilia, or city love, in America. The love in Savannah of this portion of intelligence and beauty that dies when cities die. The way time passes slowly in Savannah. The extraordinarily special, almost enclosed, space of Savannah. This feeling you have of drifting in a greenhouse, almost a bubble, a minuscule and fragile island protected from barbarian invasions. And also the enchantment of Savannah. And this other feeling that overwhelms you soon enough: that this unostentatious town is no less subtly poisonous, decadent. And then Savannah at night, still more enigmatic than it seems, less pure, bathed in a twofold light and exhaling the two habitually opposite flavours of flaunted austerity and secret liberty, of the most extreme puritanism and the most concealed criminal licentiousness: moral bewilderment, noxious spells, gardens of good and evil. Isn't that right, John Berendt? For all these reasons my mind is made up. For these reasons and a few others it's Savannah I choose. Especially since...

One last element in my story. I am at John Duncan's place, on East Taylor Street, facing Monterey Square and the famous Mercer House, which is the centre, if ever there was one, of the actual event that gave rise to Berendt's fiction. On the mezzanine, I visit Duncan's 'antique maps and prints' store. Then I visit the several floors of his private apartments, whose wood panelling, costly mirrors, rare books scattered about on polished inlaid tables, offer a concentrated dose of Savannah's elegance. And impishly he tells me that Savannah has, in a way, already chosen me. Do you know who the first known owner of this house was? he asks, and then corrects himself. Do you know to whom we owe its most drastic renovations? Well, it was a Frenchman… an Alsatian, in fact… He had a store not far from here, on Bryan Street, and then another one on Jefferson, and then, at the end, on Congress and West Broughton….And guess what this Alsatian's name was—this Frenchman whose ghost haunts this house? B.-H. Lévy! He had a brother, his partner, whose name was Henry Lévy. But his name was B.-H. Lévy, Benjamin-Hirsch Lévy—BHL.

Elegy for F. Scott Fitzgerald

IMAGINE F. SCOTT Fitzgerald in Asheville.

Imagine Zelda, first of all. Imagine her in the asylum, Highland Hospital, which I was, at last, able to locate. Highland? you ask. Zelda? Asheville has its excuses, given that the asylum burnt, together with Zelda, the night of March 10, 1948, and nothing remains. But I would have no excuse had I not set out this morning in search of some trifle, some ruin, some ashes, maybe a museum, at least a plaque. America makes museums of everything; why shouldn't it have erected a Zelda museum in Asheville? So I looked. And I eventually discovered the spot, after wandering for several hours along Elizabeth, Magnolia, and Cumberland streets. But no plaque. Not a word. Not the least shadow of a memory, whether in passersby or neighbours. And for the oblivion to be complete and the obliteration thorough, another clinic, the Fine Psychiatric Clinic, built—without even mentioning it—on the exact site of Zelda's burnt-down death trap: the perfect crime.

So I have to imagine Zelda here, on the fifth floor, on a foggy morning like this Tuesday's—yellow foliage through her barred window. Cries of insanity, convulsions. I imagine her paintings, her exasperated drawings, her severe self-portrait, the sketch of the young Scott in which he appears like an old Baudelaire, the letters reproaching him for plagiarizing her, sterilizing her, killing her slowly, having her locked up—that was convenient, wasn't it! Disposing of a real madwoman to inspire the madwomen in his novels! Never does her memory become clouded; never does she loosen her grasp; it's 1936, but she hasn't turned in her weapons…. And you have to imagine him, Scott—a good boy, really, a good husband, unless she's right and he really can write only when he's near her—raiding her inner depths, drawing from her diaries and her letters. You have to imagine him settling down here, in contact with his despoiled muse, a few hundred feet away on Macon Avenue in this frightful Grove Park Inn, half hotel, half hunting lodge, which still exists. If the memory of Zelda has been lost, the memory of Scott has been reinforced. Scott? Of course, a guy at reception says to me. Everything's here. Nothing's been changed: the fake panelling in the lounges, the stuffed buffalo heads, the immense terrace looking out onto the void. And then, at the entrance to room 441-43, the brass plaque indicating that this was a 'place of solace' for the ruined Scott from 1936 to 1938. And the obscene insistence with which I am asked to believe that the author of *The Great Gatsby* came here just to look after his mad wife. He had come here by himself in 1935, one year before Zelda, to cure his lung disease. Asheville is a pretty town; Asheville is a radiant town; he came from Baltimore to Asheville because Asheville is a town that does writers good—that was his idea.

What is he really doing at the Grove Park Inn?

Since Dr. Philps and Dr. Slocum have told him it isn't healthy, either for him or her, to see Zelda too often, what does he do to fill those long days in the summer of '36, and in the winter, and in the following summer?

He sees the young Pauline Brownell, whom the biographers don't mention but who is looking after his shoulder, dislocated in an absurd diving accident in June. He is playing Pygmalion to Dorothy Richardson, his other nurse, whose presence the hotel required after his most recent suicide threat and whose main mission is to prevent him from drinking.

He is flirting with Laura Guthrie, his typist, to whom he dictates the first drafts of scripts that his new slave drivers in Hollywood have ordered and that he hopes will give him one more shot at glory.

He spends long afternoons locked up in one of his two rooms with Beatrice Dance, a rich Texan. According to Asheville rumours, he seduced her.

He reads psychiatric manuals.

He goes to his friend Tony Buttita's place, the best bookstore in town, and purchases all kinds of psychiatric books. Schizophrenia? Manic depression? Is it iron she needs? Salt? Is it merely a fluke that her remissions have always coincided with her asthma attacks? For a long time now he's been trying to understand…

And then he goes to see her.

Whatever the doctors say, he can't prevent himself from travelling the few hundred feet. I am Francis Scott Fitzgerald, the ex-famous writer; I'm coming to visit my wife.

I imagine him then, as in the Carl Van Vechten photo, his knitted tie a little short, wide-lapelled jacket a little long, handkerchief in pocket like an aging dandy, cheerless gaze, hair still carefully slicked back but with the part on the side. The charm has gone flat.

I imagine him in Zelda's room. Endless arguments. Bitter memory of happier times: Antibes; Murphy; charades in towels; grant me this waltz; the day when, to please her, he ate an orchid; the night in Saint Paul de Vence when Isadora Duncan gave him the address of her hotel on the sly, so to punish him Zelda threw herself down the steps of the Colombe d'Or restaurant.

And then I imagine him just outside Asheville, prowling around the Vanderbilts' mansion at Biltmore, which was already being touted as the most beautiful house in America. He loved the rich so much! There are writers who write to seduce women; he wrote to get closer to the rich and to live a bit like them. These rich here, then—this combination, in one place, of the Loire chateaux and the Villa Borghese. This intersection, in one family, of the Vanderbilt side and the Gatsby side.

I visit this mansion. I look at the portrait, in the tidy ground-floor living room, of Cornelius Vanderbilt, the first offspring of that name. And I can't imagine Fitzgerald's not being irresistibly drawn to this blending of pomp and style, easy money and austere rectitude. And I can't imagine that living here, in Asheville, he didn't do everything—really everything, as he used to in his prime—to get himself invited. At the same time, I know—and it was from him that I learned it— that there's never a second chance for American heroes. And I know that they most likely ignored him, even rejected him outright. Who? F. Scott Fitzgerald? Oh… the failed writer. The former dandy. The husband of the mad woman. The outcast. Get lost!

Forgive me, Asheville. Forgive me, all you in Asheville who welcomed me so warmly. Those days, in my eyes, will have the lasting perfume of a wretched past. This town will remain linked with the image of this great writer destroyed, reduced to obscurity, disowned. Poor Belgium, uttered Baudelaire toward the end. Poor North Carolina, the F. Scott Fitzgerald of the last days might have said in turn. In his name, and in the name, too, of so many writers that America has humiliated or driven mad, I dare say it.

Home with the Wind

HE IS ONE of the major figures of New York.

He moves in the same circles as movie stars, tycoons, think-tank intellectuals, ex- and future presidents, the ones who were almost made president and those who might conceivably be president someday.

He can be in Baghdad in the morning to see the Iraqi prime minister, in Tehran at night to interview a dissident. The next day he can meet a filmmaker, a banker, an administration official in D.C., an advertising executive in Paris, the city closest to his heart. (I've noticed that a lot of people feel this way; from Bobby Shriver in Los Angeles to Adam Gopnik and Felix Rohatyn in New York, I keep meeting Americans who say to me, 'Paris... ah! Paris. Is there any other city in the world more desirable or more civilised than Paris?')

In a nutshell, he is the modern, informed city dweller, the embodiment of these perfectly uprooted mutants. The planet is my home, I'm at ease everywhere. Where do you live? Air France, seat 1A.

But what few people know, what the television viewers to whom his face is familiar can't quite imagine, what I'm not even sure some of his own friends are aware of, is that there is another Charlie Rose who is revealed here, in his native town of Henderson, North Carolina, in Vance County, not far from Raleigh.

Typical landscape of a southern small town ruined by the collapse of the cotton and tobacco industries, closed-down mills, torpor, city hall, firehouse, clock tower.

Same spectacle—paradoxical in a country that is, once again, a country of triumphant science—of these basic, almost coarse houses that seem set down on the ground itself, fragile, temporary, like trailers, bivouacs.

Eternal image—but one that I still can't seem to get over, it's so odd for someone used to countries where the humblest house is still built out of stone and is meant to last, from generation to generation, through the centuries and ages—yes, eternal but disturbing image of these frail houses, in suspense, on borrowed time. You have the feeling, as Jean-Paul Sartre once wrote, they're just waiting to be torn down, or that they're already headed toward their ghost town fate.

Here, at 1644 Oakdale Street, is Rose's childhood home.

Here, in this redbrick school, he spent his pocket money with the sons of neighbourhood farmers.

In this minuscule church, on this pew, he received Communion—he remembers singing 'Onward, Christian Soldiers.'

And here's the family grocery store, Rose Gin and Supply Co. And here, at 903 Hargrove Street, his parents' second house, purchased later on, after he'd left home for college, a more prosperous, comfortable house; Rose's father had been in the Battle of the Bulge, he deserved it. And here, behind Main Street, Rose's Discount Store—another Rose, he insists, nothing to do with his family, but one of the last stores still standing. And there… and here…

Hi, Mr. Rose!

Happy to see you back, Mr. Rose!

What an honour, Mr. Rose! What a pleasure, and what an honour! They are in high spirits, the inhabitants of Henderson.

They are proud of the local boy who became somebody and who still comes back to visit.

But the happiest one, the proudest one, the one most visibly moved, is Mr. Rose himself, in this role of prodigal son, a pilgrim to his own memory.

Rose in front of his parents' very last house, same street, but on the other side, even whiter, with a pretty veranda; this is where they spent the end of their lives.

Rose in front of the post office; it, too, just the same as it was before, fixed in time—he has only to close his eyes to see his father again, toddling along to get his mail.

Rose in Norlina, twenty miles away, hometown of the family on his father's side, another world, another culture; and Rose, three miles farther on, in Warren Plains, where his mother's family comes from. Yet another story, another humble saga, the disused railroad station that the Raleigh and Gaston Railway ended up selling to the family when the line was done away with, the wooden building just like in the westerns, where he would pass so many hours, a kid looking out the window, projecting himself into far-off places: Raleigh, Richmond, maybe Baltimore someday, New York, the good life.

And then, outside of town, on a hill in the woods, this last house. It was the most striking house in the town. It belonged to Jack Watkins, who stopped by the store everyday to see Rose's father. Watkins's wife's name was Nora. And he, little Rose, spent his childhood dreaming about this place that seemed to him the height of elegance, the embodiment of the 'shining house up on the hill.' Now it's his. He's in the process of restoring it. It's his anchor in this world, his special place. He is so thrilled to be here again; so pleased to mount and descend the polished wooden staircases, just like that, for no reason, as if he wanted to get the house used to his human presence, his tall form reflected in the windows, which themselves reflect the snowy white of the garden.

Rose is obviously not the first city dweller to restore a second home, or to take root in it.

Nor is he the first to have tears in his eyes when he meets the people and places of his early memories.

But the point is that he contradicts the conventional scenario of the landless, rootless American going from city to city, his house on his back or in his head, driven by a tireless conquest of the new frontiers of his life.

His case says something more intricate about the relationship of Americans with their space. It hints that America is the place both of the most extreme uprooting and of the most single-minded territoriality; that it's the one country in the world where you move, change places, change your home most often, and the one where, at the same time, you remain the most strongly attached to your point of origin and childhood. What these hours in North Carolina suggest (and what the Cleveland philanthropists who returned to save their city while they made a living elsewhere had already taught me) is that this is the link—dialectic but impossible to sever—between cosmopolitanism and nostalgia.

Mars Versus Venus, and Vice Versa

HEADED FOR VIRGINIA, and for Norfolk, which is, if I'm not mistaken, one of the oldest towns in a state that was one of the original thirteen in the Union.

It's the stopover town, halfway between Florida and New York, where, after Tocqueville had decided to skip Charleston for lack of time, he arrived on January 10, and boarded the vessel that would take him to Washington.

Today, along with San Diego, it's one of the largest naval bases in the country, and the headquarters of the United States Joint Forces Command, from which the coordination of American forces throughout the world is directed. It's also—which is almost more important—the heart of the new Allied Command Transformation, the strategic structure that since the Prague summit of 2002 has been in charge of research and development geared toward the transformation of NATO.

When you think of the American army, you think of GIs and land forces.

When you think of American power, or the so-called American empire, you think of the human—all too human—troops of the expeditionary corps in Iraq. Or, if you are a European, you think of the Portuguese, Italian, or Belgian NATO bases that, it should be stressed, no longer frighten anybody very much.

Well, here in Norfolk it is hard to be so blasé.

The power at work is palpable.

It is in this research centre of Norfolk, ultra high-tech, almost ethereal, that the strategic plans for the future are worked out.

It is in this science-fiction port, tacked on to the old town of traditional southern houses, where cruisers, battleships, colossal airplane carriers, SSN attack submarines, and SSBN strategic submarines all lie at anchor.

And it is in this particular submarine, the USS *Scranton* (SSN 756), 360 feet long, 7,000 tons, one of the most modern submarines in the fleet, that I have the opportunity to spend half a day—escorted by a young ensign with shoulder-length blond hair, so surprisingly charming that if not for the military cap cleverly tilted over her ear, nothing would give her away as a sailor on assignment.

It's a fragile power, of course.

I can't prevent myself from thinking, while the ensign showcases this concentrated intelligence at the heart of the submarine, that so little is needed (consider the *Kursk*, but also the *Thresher* and the *Scorpio*, which were American) to transform this admirably buoyant capsule into a coffin.

And when I visit the microscopic cabins into which they've managed to cram as many as twelve bunk beds, when I see the hundreds of cans of food that, for lack of space, have been lined up on the floor, on which people are standing and which, in some places, cause the tallest men to walk bent over, I can't prevent myself, as I imagine this closed world, so perfectly silent, where soon no daylight will penetrate, from realizing that of all the prisons I've visited, this one may be the most terrifying.

But when it comes down to it, there really is immense power here.

The wonder of high technology, of precision, of force.

These nuclear-powered turbines and reactors.

The engine room in the stern, which looks like the tip of a rocket. The diving controls fore and aft, incredibly complex, which govern the trim or the immersion of the submarine.

Ballast tanks that, depending on whether they're filled with seawater or air, allow for the apparatus to dive or stay on the surface. Diabolical thermal pressures that make the walls of the ship expand, contract, or, at worst, break apart, depending on the location. Heating and cooling systems.

Radars and sonars.

These antennae that are both passive (able to capture the slightest noise, the least vibration outside) and active (emitting a pulse radar that, by measuring the time it takes for the echo to bounce back, enables one to calculate the distance from a target or a reef).

Ultrasonic devices that gauge the depth of ice or water.

Consoles and instrument panels—I'm not sure if they're used to control the reactors or the guns (perhaps both).

Missile-launch tubes and these jamming systems capable of tricking the enemy's torpedoes by causing them to explode in the open sea.

And then the missiles themselves—tools of death, some of which, like those on the Trident II, are equipped with twelve nuclear warheads and give just one submarine a firepower one thousand times greater than that used on Hiroshima.

Torpedoes with magnetic sensors—summit of the art of destruction—that explode not on contact but beneath the targeted ship and thus give off an energy from the blast comparable to a tidal wave, the result being that the hull, regardless of the solidity of its steel cover, is inevitably torn in half.

The extreme sophistication of all this. Dizzying strategy, technology, logic. Conjoined dread and admiration which I feel when faced with these manifestations of American power.

I leave Norfolk wondering if such a visit might be possible in my country.

Probably not, since it's hard to imagine a foreign visitor offered such a comprehensive tour on a French nuclear-submarine base. So I wonder about the motivations of my guides.

American democracy again? The taste for transparency that Tocqueville, before many others, noted as a basic component of its ethos?

A different relationship with secrecy? An open-society characteristic even in these zones that tend to be closed everywhere else?

But this other hypothesis crosses my mind when I think I can detect a fleeting gleam of irony in the eyes of the pretty ensign, who is telling me for the umpteenth time about the force of a cumulative strike of the MK-48 torpedoes, Tomahawk missiles, and MK-67 and MK-60 mines stored in the ship. Maybe this open-door operation is in its way a demonstration of force. Maybe this kind of guided tour is an integral part of the program of the largest army in the world when it has to deal with the representative (and, moreover, a French one) of a country that is in principle an ally. Maybe it's just a case of Mars parading before Venus and telling her, off-handedly, in the good-natured, frank tone suitable to friendly relationships, 'This is who we are and what we are capable of. Take note of the force of your ally before you claim to be its rival, or even its partner. In the era of a multilateralist ideal that has reached an impasse, that, dear Frenchmen, would be wise policy....'

A Conversation with Richard Perle

STYLISH FURNITURE.

A picture of Arthur Rimbaud on the wall.

A large, rustic kitchen that appears to be one of his favourite rooms—perhaps a discreet homage to Albert Wohlstetter, his intellectual master, whose fiercest passions, they say, included the culinary arts as well as math and strategic planning.

Numerous books, numerous objects and knickknacks, some of them brought back from the south of France, from Gordes, where this hawk known for his Francophobia, a man who declared at the height of the tension between Presidents Bush and Chirac that the French were a 'greedy' people and that America should 'stop spoiling' them, actually has a second home.

As he prepares coffee, we begin talking about another famous resident of Gordes, the Marxist philosopher Louis Althusser, whose work he appears to know.

I ask Perle if it is true that his first calling was literature and that his dream as a young man was to teach a course not on international strategy but on Joyce and the genesis of *Finnegans Wake*. He shrugs his shoulders a little sadly but doesn't answer.

We talk about Tocqueville, and he points out, annoyed, that we shouldn't exaggerate. My compatriot certainly didn't foresee everything that has happened to the United States in the past century, and he overlooked America's belief in its exceptional status, its quasi-religious belief in a mission—which, according to Perle, the Founding Fathers clearly supported.

And here we are, facing each other in the garden, teeming with dead leaves and bathed in sunlight, of his quaint Virginia home where he's been spending most of his time ever since the suspicion of a conflict of interest forced him to resign from the Pentagon's Defence Policy Board. Here, sitting on a simple wooden bench, his face sagging and tired, his eyes terribly wrinkled, wearing one of those gray shirts with white collars that I've noticed in most of his photos but that he put on this morning without a tie—here is the great architect of American policy in Iraq, out of a job.

Where does he stand now? What does he say two years later about this war that he and his friend Paul Wolfowitz contributed to charting, and which is creating condemnation and debate throughout the world?

To my great surprise, Perle begins by giving vent to reservations about the manner in which the operation has been conducted.

He denies, by the way, having been the architect I call him; he insists that he has never, alas, been in a position to decide anything. And he tells me, imitating 'our friend Althusser,' about all the things that 'cannot last any longer'—not, this time, in the Communist Party but in America's war policy in Iraq.

He regrets, for instance, that they declined to place more troops on the ground.

He still has confidence in Chalabi, who was also a disciple of Wohlstetter's, and he maintains that Chalabi refuses to transform himself into a manipulative, unscrupulous, venal politician like everyone else in Washington now.

Worse, he grumbles, fiddling with his shirt collar as if the mere idea of it were suffocating him—worse, he believes today that the administration committed a major mistake, and that this mistake was neglecting to enlist the support of the local armed forces from the beginning as was done in Afghanistan. 'We needed scouts,' he says angrily. 'Iraqi scouts, like in the westerns, and that's why, even though we started out as liberators, we're turning into an occupying force.'

About the basic principle, though, of the validity of the war itself; about the appropriateness of the choice that, right after September 11, consisted in targeting Saddam Hussein and bringing him down; about the political aim, then and now, of establishing the seeds of democracy in this country martyred and abandoned by the West, in this land of suffering and of methodically ignored mass graves, Perle hasn't changed one iota. And I even have the feeling that his recovered freedom of speech only makes him more eloquent in hammering home his conviction that no source of disorder or insecurity in this world is worse than the existence of dictatorships and our indulgence of them.

This conversation has the effect of reviving my old questions not about the war itself—of which I disapproved from the first day, and of which my analysis hasn't varied at all—but about these peculiar characters whom we, in France, stubbornly persist in demonizing ('princes of darkness') or ridiculing with simplistic epithets ('neocons,' which can also mean, in French, 'neo-dummies'), but who aren't quite as unidimensional as they seem.

Sometimes, listening to this Bush follower who has, among other peculiarities, remained a Democrat and boasts about it, I say to myself, of course he's right. How can one be against the overthrow of such a tyrant? How can one spend a lifetime, as I have done, deploring the inaction of rich countries, their pusillanimity, their recurrent Munichism, when faced with enemies bent on destroying them and willing to try anything to acquire the means of doing so, and not be delighted when in the most powerful democracy in the world there finally appears a generation of intellectuals who arrive close to the top and can concretely work for the universalisation of human rights and freedom?

But then, at other times, I catch a word, an intonation, an off-hand phrase, implying that the actual presence or absence in Baghdad of weapons of mass destruction isn't so important after all. Or I hear a dismissal of people who, like me, recoil from the idea of a preventive war. I hear them bluntly compared to a man who 'waits till he's sick to sign up for health insurance.' Or I hear something that I interpret as a condemnation of the Geneva road map advocating a division of land between Israelis and Palestinians, which I ardently support. It's a slight hint of populism, a sudden frivolity, a reaction like that of an outraged old conservative when he asks me if Althusser paid the penalty for strangling his wife and I tell him no, that a small cabal of people at the École Normale Superieure—where he taught—managed to protect him and keep him from going to jail. Or I hear an unfair phrase about Kerry or his wife. So I swing over to the other side; I rear back internally; I tell myself that this man and I surely don't belong to the same family.

This is where I stand.

What Separates Me—Radically—from Bill Kristol

I HAVE BEEN looking forward to this meeting.

First and foremost because of his surname, associated in my mind with a whole legendary landscape in which the saga of the American extreme left, the secrets of Alcove One at CCNY, the memory of the ideological jousts of Irving Kristol, his father, with Daniel Bell, Irving Howe, Nathan Glazer, and Gertrude Himmelfarb, Irving Kristol's future wife, are inextricably meshed.

Also because of the idea that such a small magazine, *The Weekly Standard*—with a circulation that would seem somewhat ludicrous on even a European scale, nearly devoid of advertising, gray, printed on bad paper, never shying away from a long, sometimes indigestible text—can have such a significant influence, including, I am told, on the White House and the State Department.

And then, of course, because of the neoconservative ideology itself, this notorious neoconservative ideology, the mystery of these people whose intellectual journey increasingly fascinates me: I tell myself that, through his status as a journalist, through the autonomy of thought it grants him, through his family origins (although he himself doesn't come from the extreme left), Kristol is, more so than Perle, an archetype of the neoconservative. Are these neocons truly united? How are they followers of Bush? How does their thinking tally with Bush's? What is the extent of their influence? What should I think of David Brooks's analysis when he explained the other morning that the media were exaggerating the importance and the impact of this group? What should I think of his notion that this matter of intellectuals' taking Bush's brain by storm right after 9/11 is an invention of the extreme right in general and Pat Buchanan in particular and that we aren't very far here from the Jewish-conspiracy theory?

In a way I'm disappointed: with his big-boss suit, his impeccably combed hair, his overfriendly showman manners, his laughing blue eyes, his florid complexion, the man opposite me looks more like a leader of the American Enterprise Institute (based, perhaps not by chance, in the same building, one floor up) than Europe's idea of an intellectual.

On the other hand, my hopes are rewarded: the conversation is a long one, and as it progresses, in this modern, efficient office more reminiscent of the conference room in a commercial Manhattan bank than of the office of an editorialist or a man of ideas, I'll get, if not the answer, at least a part of the answer to the question of what it is that links me to, or separates me from, this man and others of his ilk.

What links us: history, genealogy, a certain number of formative experiences, the oldest and perhaps most essential of which seems to be his long rebellion against the way the West had consented to the enslavement of the countries of 'captive Europe.' When I hear Kristol talk about how his youth was formed by the great antitotalitarian thinkers of the twentieth century; when I see him get carried away about the cultural relativism and the historicism that were alibis for the most dreadful dictatorships; when I imagine him laying siege, as he did in the 1990s, to America's foreign policy decision makers in order to persuade them to intervene in Bosnia and then in Kosovo; and finally, when I imagine him pleading against the Taliban and, even more, against our silent assent to the iron rule it imposed on Afghanistan, it's my own history I find: these are the dates of my own intellectual biography I see quickly pass by. I mean to say that, though our positions diverge, our axioms are shared.

What separates us? The positions, the differing consequences that we draw from common premises in the Iraq affair. But certainly other subjects as well—indications, throughout our conversation, of attitudes far from mine: the death penalty, for instance. I find, to my great surprise, that Kristol supports the death penalty. I find, too, that on the questions of abortion, gay marriage, and the place of religion in American politics he isn't far from the most extreme positions of the leading players in the Bush administration. Then there's the copy of *The Weekly Standard* I found in the waiting room and had time to leaf through before our interview. It's the most recent issue, the one that talks about the inauguration of the Clinton Library, in Little Rock. I see that *The Weekly Standard* is a paper in which you can read, under the byline of Matt Labash, a text crammed with the vilest gossip about the private life of the former president. Paula, Gennifer, Monica, Connie, Sally, Dolly, Susan—they're all there, the 'WOCS,' the 'women of the Clinton scandals,' the Miss Arkansas, the women who aren't quite whores, the ex-cover girls turned into married women. They're all set down in ink, slammed, denounced, in this cartload of filth and accusation that presents itself as an article.

I sense that Kristol is annoyed when I mention it to him.

I sense that he thinks a European can't accept this mingling of politics with such trash, so he plays it down.

Don't jump to the conclusion that I believe in it, he seems to be saying. That's just the deal, you understand—supporting a crusade for moral values is just the price we have to pay for a foreign policy that we can defend as a whole.

Suppose it is.

Let's agree his annoyance isn't feigned.

In that case the question lies right there, and in my mind it's almost worse.

When you uphold one goal of a given policy, do you have to uphold all its goals?

Because you're in agreement about Iraq, do you have to force yourself to agree with the death penalty, creationism, the Moral Majority and its virulent practices?

When I have dinner with someone in a restaurant, do I have to order all the courses on the menu?

Or, on the contrary, isn't it the privilege of what we call an intellectual—isn't it his honour and, at core, his authentic strength as well as his duty—to continue to defend his own colours, including the shades of those colours, even and especially when he lends his support to the government on a specific point?

Bill Kristol is listening to me, but I sense I'm not convincing him. And I feel that here I grasp, at least for now, the essence of what separates us.

A neoconservative? No—he is a Platonist bereft of the ideals. An adviser to princes without detachment or reservations. An antitotalitarian who, at bottom, and whatever he may say, hasn't read enough Leo Strauss, Hannah Arendt, Julien Benda—and who, not having done so, deprives himself of the necessary freedom that the status of intellectual induces in France.

The End of History Is No Banquet

WASHINGTON, STILL.

A visit with Francis Fukuyama.

We met in Paris, a little over ten years ago, when he was

working on his book *The End of History and the Last Man.*

I had, at the time, taken a strong stand against his argument.

But I remember thinking—and saying—that whether one agreed with it or not, it was one of the boldest statements of the period. He is the prototype of an American intellectual.

More precisely, he, unlike Kristol, seems to come close to the idea we in France have of an intellectual.

And I must admit that I'm happy to see him again, here in his little office full of books and stacked-up files, at the Johns Hopkins School of Advanced International Studies. He is lucid and sardonic, as much at ease with complex conceptual gymnastics as he is with geostrategic considerations, as obviously fascinated by world-historical panoramas as by more down-to-earth political analysis. (One feature that strikes me about these major American intellectuals who are close to power and its think tanks: their ability to steer not exactly two careers but two different intellectual cultures at the same time. Wohlstetter is an outstanding mathematician; Harvey Mansfield is a translator of Machiavelli and Tocqueville; Donald Kagan, Gary Schmitt, and Victor Davis Hanson are specialists in ancient Greece; not to speak of Wolfowitz, an eminent neo-Straussian and also a leading Hebrew scholar.)

So we are talking, Fukuyama and I, about that first text, about the end of history.

I tell him—and this makes him laugh—that like Byron, he became famous in one night thanks to a conversation.

He tells me that he has read some of my texts on Islamic fundamentalism, but—and of course I'm not convinced by this—that he doesn't think Islamism is weighty enough to become the third totalitarianism that will set the great machinery of history back in motion.

Then we start talking about the war in Iraq, which, contrary to my expectations, he, unlike most neoconservatives, in fact condemned. We talk about another one of his texts, 'The

Neoconservative Moment,' which he wrote in reaction to a speech given by Charles Krauthammer at a conference at the American Enterprise Institute and which was published in the summer 2004 issue of the neoconservative journal *The National Interest.* This article unleashed one of those vigorous debates Fukuyama seems so good at provoking. Barely a dozen pages long, it has the same provocative, cold tonality and the same Zen-like ability to break everything in sight without touching it.

What's the reason behind his condemnation of the war?

What objection does he really have to this war waged by George Bush and by his ex-friends from the RAND Corporation?

No moral objection; for a Hegelian, such an argument would be nonsensical.

No objection from a strategic point of view. The apostle of the end of history, a man who keeps telling us how the provinces of the empire will be brought into line with the victorious world order, could scarcely disagree with the plan to democratise Iraq.

Certainly not the traditional conservative idea that some cultures are better adapted to freedom than others; I sense that Fukuyama isn't the least bit torn between his two great mentors, Irving Kristol and Samuel Huntington—between the ex-leftist who has on the whole remained faithful to the universalism of his youth and the postulator of a conflict of civilisations who has great difficulty ridding himself of the stumbling block of relativism—and that it's the former who remains closer than ever to his heart. No, his great subject, his chief and, indeed, only disagreement, has to do with the relationship to time—and hence with opportunity and political tactics—that he thinks he can sense in most of his friends who are unconditional supporters of this war. (There is also the argument that the pro-war stance is too close to the policies of Israel. But if that question is raised in *The National Interest* article—if he may have been reproached for his way of 'Likudizing' the opponent during his polemics with Krauthammer—it doesn't come up in our conversation.)

These people are strange, is the gist of what he says to me.

They've spent their entire lives preaching against lending too much power to the government. They told us to beware of the naïveté of the social-engineering specialists who purported to be able to eradicate American poverty with one wave of their political wand. And then they lost all perspective as soon as it was a question of going and eradicating such poverty, along with the roots of despotism, four thousand miles away. And they have complete faith in a political decision when it's an issue—as a nation and a government are being constructed—of winning not just the war but also the peace. And they adopt the same 'messianic' tone for which they've so often reproached their progressive adversaries as soon as it's a matter of building a Western-style democracy, ex nihilo, in a country that's never harboured such a concept!

Odd, this Hegelian who condemns the messianism of others.

Odd, this historicist who used to tell us that the absolute Spirit was about to emerge, and who starts stressing the delays and difficulties of posthistory.

Paradoxical, the spectacle of this disciple of Kojève, fed on Hegel's *The Phenomenology of the Spirit* and on the prosopopoeia of the Idea, reproaching others for their excessive idealism.

Captivating, nonetheless.

First of all because it's another sign, this time inside a single ideological family, of the intensity, the vigour, the quality, of debate that so struck me during the two conventions. Hegel plus Leo Strauss… Hegelian providentialism chilled, almost reduced, by the 'Greek' scepticism of the author of *The City and Man*… that is the Fukuyama equation. Those are the metaphysical—thus political—coordinates of this atheist-universalist, this pessimistic progressive. And it's more than a variation—it's actually a new stance on the American political chessboard.

But above all I get the impression of finding here the first serious—I mean theoretically articulated—objection to the war. Before that operation was launched, I had written that because it mistook the target, because it was aiming at Iraq instead of worrying, for instance, about Pakistan, it was morally right but politically wrong. Quietly, almost whispering, with that special smile whose very reserve oddly reveals a certain intensity, Fukuyama tells me that these people are to him—theoretician as he is of the inevitable triumph of democratic order—what Lenin was to Marx. By trying to act like angels, behaving as if time were not an issue, they condemn themselves to acting like idiots.

The problem with neoconservatives is not, as Europeans think, their lack of moral centre or their cynicism. On the contrary, it's an excess of morals. It's the victory of mysticism over politics. They're noble spirits who don't do enough concrete politics.

Two (at Least) Rights

FLASHBACK.

The scene occurs in Pittsburgh, three months ago, at the end of a fine autumn day.

Christopher Hitchens is the one who actually persuaded me to come.

We had taken opposite positions at a debate in New York about the war in Iraq (which he, like Kristol and Perle, ardently supports), and he just let slip in passing, in his very British way of mumbling important things, 'Kissinger lecture in Pittsburgh. I'm giving another one, an hour later and a few blocks away, after a screening of my film *The Trials of Henry Kissinger.* You should come. You might enjoy yourself.'

As soon as I get there I drive to the Gypsy Cafe, a trendy bar in the Cultural District, where the enfant terrible of the intelligentsia and a crack team of fellow conspirators (the curator of the Warhol museum, the editor of the alternative paper sponsoring Hitchens's rival lecture, a producer of independent documentaries, a professor) are putting the last touches on what is turning out to be something of a guerrilla operation.

From there I go to Heinz Hall, where, in front of a room filled with burgundy velvet armchairs that remind me more of a brothel in Maupassant than a lecture hall, the secretary of state under Nixon and Ford utters, in his gruff, stentorian voice, a litany of self-satisfied platitudes ('the dust of China and India'... the necessity to 'identify big problems and reduce them to little problems'... yes to the war, but a half-hearted yes, just for a short while, keeping in mind the perspective of 'perpetual peace' that was 'proclaimed by Immanuel Kant').

Suddenly Hitchens arrives; he has evidently made a switch in tactics and, using another journalist's pass, has been able without warning to sashay into the back of the auditorium. The conspirator turned provocateur arrives and hurls abuse at the audience near him ('Toads! You're all toads who've come to listen to a toad') before getting himself thrown out by security guards who, noticing me with him, throw me out as well and force me to erase from my camera, in front of them, the part of the lecture I have filmed.

So we walk into the night, with an obligatory stop at each of the bars still open on Penn Avenue, with a meagre escort of reporters thrilled by the incident and the excitement Hitchens is causing in their sleeping city: Death to toads! A kingdom of toads for a bottle of wine! On our way to the Harris Theatre, where his film must be almost over, a signal that the discussion can begin.

This film is Kissinger's nightmare, Hitchens says, delighted.
Wherever that bastard goes, my film precedes or follows him.
Wherever he talks, there's someone there, during the question-
and-answer session, who asks him about his war crimes in
Chile, in Indochina, in Timor. Do you realise that because of my
film he can't travel anywhere freely? Do you know that in Paris
a magistrate came looking for him, even to his suite at the Ritz?
That son of a bitch.... Leave that lowly toad to us.... You'll
see....

We've arrived at the theatre.

It's one of those independent art-house movie theatres, old-
fashioned and militant, that still exist in some ordinary
American towns. Black-and-white posters for *Grand Illusion*
and *Citizen Kane*. Ads for the workshops, festivals, and retro-
spectives that the Pittsburgh Filmmakers are organizing here.

In front of the ticket office are flyers saying KERRY OR
BUSH, IT DOESN'T MATTER, AS LONG AS WE GET
OUT OF IRAQ—which is, of course, the exact opposite of
Hitchens's stance. And the audience is, in keeping with the
place, made up of old leftists with salt-and-pepper ponytails,
political tattoos on their forearms, pierced ears. At first glance I
realise that they're in the uncomfortable position of having
come, at once, to applaud a cult film (this Kissinger trial, this
ultraleft charge against Richard Nixon's secretary of state, is
obviously all they care about) and to express their incompre-
hension about what the film's director has become. How can he,
without renouncing what he has said about Kissinger, agree on
the Iraq question with Bush, Rumsfeld, Cheney, Rice, and the
various others who, in their eyes, are the new embodiment of
the same old American right?

I'm watching Hitchens on the stage, behind his lectern.

I observe him suddenly energised, not drunk at all, fielding
questions, battling, making fun of his opponents, pleading,
insulting, explaining that yes, he is against Saddam just as he was

against Pinochet, it's the same fight that's going on, the same antitotalitarianism being replayed; democratic revolution (as Clemenceau said about the French Revolution) 'has to be taken as a whole'; jihad is just one more fascism. What a pity you didn't understand; you are the left wing of a big party of toads....

The scene has its appeal.

It always takes a kind of courage to run the risk of disappointing or alienating your own followers; and in this case it takes courage to stand firm on both fronts—to stand in front of these two hundred leftists for whom Hitchens used to be a hero, and who ask nothing more than to go on celebrating him as one, and tell them, 'I am and I am not one of you. There is Hitchens No. 1, who is responsible for this film and who, ten years later, wouldn't take one word or shot away from it. But there is Hitchens No. 2, who continues the fight without you by supporting the war in Iraq.'

That's not the essential point, though. The essential point is this: I see him active on both fronts at once, and not lowering his guard on either of them. I see him, unlike Kristol, not giving in about Vietnam on account of Iraq, and thus taking the risk, necessarily, of losing on both counts. I listen to him try Kissinger on two charges, because he reproaches him for his role in Indochina in the 1960s but also, like so many of the realpolitik people, for his far too flabby involvement in this war against Islamic fundamentalism. And I tell myself that here, between the two branches of what from afar appears to be the American conservative party, is a debate, even a gap, of which we have only the faintest conception in Europe.

You need to dig deeper, of course.

You need to acquire a better understanding of this conflict in the heart of the American right between the soft and the radical, the realists and the idealists.

You have to go far back into history and look for hidden

keys to this quarrel between those who, like Kissinger, wage war in order to strengthen dictatorships and those who, like Hitchens, think of war as a vector of democracy in the world.

For now, it's a new sign of the reorganisation of the political space that, I sense, has been coming for quite some time and that is causing the real divisions to emerge, not so much between the two parties but rather between other factions, not yet named, within each of the two historical parties.

VII

The Beautiful and the Damned

FROM WASHINGTON, D.C., BACK TO CAPE COD

The Democratic Party as a Black Hole

THE REAL SURPRISE on the other side—that is, on the political left in America—is that nothing is happening. Not that I claim to have seen everything in such a limited time. But I did meet former members of the Clinton, Gore, and Kerry teams. At the AFL–CIO (federation of American unions) headquarters I attended a 'joint conference' of three organisations designed to extract lessons from the defeat and prepare for battles yet to come. I saw union members and intellectuals, elected officials and strategists, the old and the young. For three days I hunted down the New Democrat, that supposedly developing breed of which, I was told, I could find as many specimens as I liked in Washington.

The results, I'm afraid, didn't measure up either to my hopes or—far more serious—to what anyone might reasonably expect given the quality, intensity, and strength of the ideological argument mounted by the right.

At the end of my inquiry I found:

1. Sixty-year-old 'young' Democrats whose arguments date back if not to the Kennedy years then at least to the centrist wave that elected Bill Clinton. Thus Al From (of the Democratic Leadership Council) and Will Marshall (of the Progressive Policy Institute) spent two hours selling me on the merits of a 'third way,' which I am convinced they would have described in exactly the same terms twenty years ago.

2. Very peculiar progressives whose only concern seemed to be to persuade the visitor—hence, I imagine, the voter—that they shouldn't accept lessons on patriotism, religion, or morality from anyone, least of all their opponents. 'The heartland of America is us' is basically what John Podesta, formerly the White House chief of staff, now the head of the Center for American Progress, told me. The Bible, religious faith, the crusade for family values—all of that is us, too, and letting others monopolise it is simply out of the question. When the Lewinsky affair was brought up, and the key role it played, in my opinion, in America's swerve to the right; when I told him that the founders of MoveOn held the same prejudices as their enemies on this question and almost condemned the former president, I beheld the extraordinary spectacle of the grand adviser blushing like a baby, laughing nervously like a maiden aunt, and replying that perhaps Clinton had committed a 'blunder.'

More radical left-wingers, people like Michael Moore, who at least understand that the only way the Democrats can break out of the mess they're in is to take the initiative, construct a worldview that's distinct from the Republicans', and stop all their whining that they're good guys, too, and that the lowest rates of extramarital birth and divorce are in the blue states. But here the problem is in the rhapsodic—or, worse, populist—flavour of a far too abstract radicalism. And when the question of Iraq is brought up, and—beyond Iraq—the role of America at large, the problem is also a certain pacifism that has a whiff of isolationism, difficult to distinguish from the isolationism of someone like Pat Buchanan.

People who supposedly fight for their ideas: activists who explain that they have only one objective, to regenerate the ideological substance of their party; heads of think tanks who, as genuine or feigned progressives, as people who are nostalgic for moral order or who advocate steering away from it, present themselves as ideologues and assure you that their aim is to vanquish the right, and especially the neoconservatives, on the battlefield of doctrine. But when you push them a little, when you ask them what their timeline is and, within this timeline, what their tactical or strategic priorities are, their only common ground is talk about… money!

During the presidential campaign, I had already observed this phenomenon. I had noticed the frequent press releases that informed us, day after day, like so many victory bulletins, about the status of the party's finances. I had seen how, here, money is the very sign and symptom of excellence, whereas in France money is What Must Above All Never Be Discussed.

But now the campaign is over. Now is the time for reconstruction. So let me take the instance of the AFL–CIO joint conference. I'll choose those three hours of debate in which the participants, myself included, were meant to question one another about the profound reasons for the increased 'electoral turnout' that occurred during Bush's re-election.

The fact is that two-thirds, maybe three-quarters, of the speeches were devoted to talking not about 'party lines,' not even about 'communication' or 'advocacy,' but about marketing, fund-raising, the relative merits of the ceremonies financed by the Republicans or the Democrats, the role of the Internet. The fact is that these brilliant pioneers who were supposed to set down the cornerstones for the people's house of tomorrow had only one idea, one obsession, and, fundamentally, one watchword: how, in four years, to fight the

Republicans on the battlefield of fund-raising....

I have nothing against money as such. And there's a part of me that doesn't hate the complex-free, off-hand manner Americans have of approaching the subject.

Yet that day, I wanted to hear about something else. I looked for speeches about why this money should be raised. I yearned for one voice, just one, to articulate the three or four major issues that, given the current debate and balance of power, might constitute the framework of a political agenda. A defence of the Enlightenment against the creationist offensive. A Tocquevillean revolution extolling certainly not atheism but secularism and upholding the separation of church and state. A new New Deal for the poorest of the poor. An uncompromising defence of human rights and a rejection of the 'exceptional' status of Abu Ghraib and Guantánamo.

No.

Money, and then money yet again. Money, the index and criterion of all things. The hypothesis, the axiom, according to which, in order to win the battle of ideas, you first have to win the battle of money.

An observer—someone who, like me, was struck by the vigour of the neoconservative awakening and was expecting to see at least its equivalent on the other side—senses a trap in the process of closing. For a long time the Republican Party was the party of money. For a long time the Democrats repeated, 'We have ideas but you have money, and that's why you win.'

Today a turnaround—or, rather, a ruse of history—has occurred, and all of a sudden the two camps are struggling on opposite fronts: a right wing of money but also of ideas, which in twenty years has renewed its ideological supplies; and a left wing that, by dint of wanting to compete on the minefield of money, is in the process of losing its footing on the ground of ideas, and thus of losing, period.

The Left According to Warren Beatty

I SAW HIM for the first time during the Kennedy Center Honors presentation ceremony, where, frankly, he didn't make a dazzling impression—tuxedo, wheedling look, his voice too unctuous, his children and wife too obviously on hand, the air of an old crooner who's subscribed to his own legend too early to have anything interesting to say about the future of his country.

I saw him in the vast, ultra-Hollywood-style auditorium, where Senator Ted Kennedy was chatting with Faye Dunaway, and where John Kerry wandered from table to table like a rejected phantom, murmuring to whoever would listen (ah! the cruelty of this country to its losers), 'If you hear anything about fifty thousand votes in Ohio, let me know.' I saw him among these rich and beautiful people who, as always in America when you catch them in real life, form a masquerade of the living dead, each one more face-lifted and mummified than the next, fierce, a little mutant-looking, inhuman, ultimately disappointing—and this was scarcely the ideal situation for having a discussion.

I see him again this morning.

To my great surprise, I find him in the conference room of the AFL–CIO, where, with his corduroy trousers and plain tweed jacket, he's no more than one activist among others, sitting in their midst without any particular consequence, without any favoured treatment or unusual aura, just listening, taking notes, not a word, not a gesture, humble.

After the conference, when we walk into the next room to begin a conversation, and I ask him what he thinks about those interminable arguments that never shake off the question of finances, and when he undertakes to decode what we have just heard, I discover another man, another Warren Beatty, before me—ebullient this time, intelligent and precise, extremely well informed, and, despite fatigue from an evening that must have ended quite late, in much better form than the night before.

Kerry. We start off talking about Kerry, whose voice I thought I'd overheard on Beatty's cell phone when it rang earlier, during the meeting. Kerry's a good guy, he tells me. A really good guy. His only problem is his superego. The 'parent within' taking over. And also, too many words. Too much knowledge and far too many words. 'Since you've asked me what time it is, would you like me to explain how my watch functions and how it's actually made? That's how Kerry was. That's one of the reasons he lost.'

The left. The state of this American left, about which we seem to have formulated more or less the same diagnosis. A fearful left, he says. A left that's afraid of itself and its own values and ideas. The Clinton left. The left of Al Gore, who waited until he lost to explain how far left he was. Obama? Sure, Obama. New face. New orator. But what does he really think? And what has he done in Illinois? No one has the least idea. The only thing they know is that now he's going to have to run after votes, and so he has to begin to commit himself.

Because that's the secret, he continues, suddenly regaining the mischievous, tormented, childlike look he still had in *Bugsy*. The whole problem is in the dictatorship of this new master, Opinion, which decrees to all politicians what their choices will be. We believe leaders are leaders. We are in the old panoptic prison mode, where the dominators survey the dominated and keep them under their eyes. But the opposite is true. The panopticon has been reversed. Now the dominated keep the dominators under their eyes, under surveillance; they dictate their analyses to them, and thus program their choices, their plans, even their desires.

The left again. The left not as it is but as it should be, if the system were not as he says it is, and if politicians, real politicians, could invent and compel destiny. Here again we're in agreement. Genuine harmony of viewpoints with this American of the Enlightenment, raised on European culture, for whom the values of secularism, rationality, and human rights are not just a creed but simply go without saying. Iraq? He is against the war in Iraq, of course, and said right from the start that Vietnam would soon seem like a picnic by comparison. But he wasn't against the war in Afghanistan. Or against intervention in Bosnia, ten years ago. Which means—and I appreciate this nuance, too—that he is for peace but, unlike the politically correct of Hollywood, still not a pacifist.

What about him as a candidate, then? What about Beatty, in this field of ruins that the Democratic camp is turning into? He hesitates. Stammers. Explains that he likes movies too much to take the risk of the journey from which there is no return, the journey that going into politics would inevitably entail. Mentions his children, who have become the centre of his life, and for whom he wants to reserve his time. Talks about his wife, Annette Bening, whom he loves so much, and who was pregnant when he toyed with the idea of running opposite Gore for nomination by the Democratic Party in 2000. But I sense he's not telling everything. I sense there's something bothering him, and that a reason more profound than the ones he outlined prevents him from taking the plunge. And then, I understand. Yes, I think I understand. The new panopticon, of course. The eyes of the slaves on their masters, of those below on those above. His private life, which would become the prey of tabloids…

I know I'm going to annoy my American friends. I know they're going to say, These Frenchmen are impossible. Leave it to them—after they've gained access to the most prominent figures the movement has produced, after they've been able to see and interview the mighty Al From, the pleasant Will Marshall, the admirable John Podesta, along with all the young hopes of a Democratic Party that's busy rebuilding itself—leave it to the French to wind up going into ludicrous ecstasies about one of those old movie stars who are exactly what the heartland of the country no longer wants.

But there it is.

I leave Warren Beatty with regret that he isn't another Schwarzenegger—an anti-Schwarzenegger.

Worse: coming to the end of this voyage and trying to figure out who, of all the men and women I've met over the year, lingers in my memory and isn't too far from the idea we might have of an enlightened, antitotalitarian, modern left, I see a few faces, a handful of isolated personalities not connected with one another, who represent, alas, only themselves. I see a journalist here; a union leader there; some activist in New Orleans from a civil-rights movement that can't bring itself to disarm; a filmmaker, Robert Greenwald, whom I met in Los Angeles; a mother of a soldier who died in Iraq; escapees from the Clinton era such as—in no particular order—Richard Holbrooke, Felix Rohatyn, or Sidney Blumenthal; a philosopher, whose case I will return to later; a trio of young women trying to prevent a Wal-Mart from being built in Englewood, California; the New York State attorney general, Eliot Spitzer; and, this morning, I see Warren Beatty.

Doing Away with Junk Politics

WE ARE ALWAYS a little ashamed, Baudelaire wrote, of mentioning names that won't mean anything to anyone in fifty years.

In the case of David Brock the shame is redoubled.

First, because you won't need fifty years, or twenty, or even ten to see this name disappear from American political memory. But also because the character himself is in many respects one of the most objectively loathsome I've met in the ten months I've been travelling through this country.

He is about forty years old. Dark brown hair, smug good looks, thin wire-rimmed glasses. The well-defined square jaw of a tennis pro. Yet in the corners of his mouth; in the self-satisfied bitterness of his smile; in his morose, fugitive glance; last, in his odd complacency in not sparing any detail of his shadowy past, there is something that makes me deeply uneasy.

Here is his story, as he tells it to me.

This is the guy that Republican officials connected with the special prosecutor Kenneth Starr came to see in 1994, to offer him, keys in hand, the so-called secrets of Bill Clinton's body-guards. He is the journalist who, based on these cobbled-together pieces of information, gave *The American Spectator* the article (titled 'His Cheatin' Heart') that launched the whole Lewinsky affair.

But after he'd done his dirty work and the president was crucified and his private life spread out on all the American networks and throughout the world; after the delayed-action bomb had been thrown that would poison the political life of the country for a decade, then he regretted what he had provoked and made it his new specialty—on all the airwaves, in the columns of all the newspapers, in interminable conceited memoirs that immediately became bestsellers, in a thundering letter of excuse to Clinton himself, published in *Esquire*, in which he asked forgiveness for wanting 'to pop [him] right between the eyes'—to declare his shame, his very great shame, and he went over to the Democratic Party, to which he had done so much harm but that he wanted thereafter, cross his heart, to serve with all his remaining strength.

Now, in this Washington office where he receives me and where, since his conversion, he has set up Media Matters for America, an agency that works against Republican disinforma-tion and which he created with the help of a handful of Democratic sponsors, here again is this theatrical way of covering his head with ashes: 'I am a forger... a faker.... I am an abominable bastard, I have no honour… In this affair, I did just what I did ten years earlier, to that poor Anita Hill…. I invented facts… rigged information… I didn't care about the rules of my profession but about fame… not even fame, but money… just money… the lure of a reward…. Now I regret it…. Oh! I so regret it…. There is not enough time left in my life to redeem myself, to ask for forgiveness, to grovel at the feet of my new friends, hoping they'll one day forgive me….'

Just think, say the bigwig Democrats who recommended that I see him, for whom the winning over of such an individual is obviously perceived, even today, as a godsend: An apostate! A renegade! Someone who comes to us with, in his beggar's bundle, the stuff, the secrets, the list of the enemy camp's dirty tricks! The ideal political spy! The most valuable of turned spies! He was in the heart of the machine, had close contact with the Beast, and he's just abandoned it all! You can't get much better than that, can you?

To me, this man is the embodiment of a manner of acting not just in journalism but in politics, a manner that has undeniably gained widespread acceptance and that, over time, has turned into one of the country's ways of life. In the beginning, Clinton; then the gossip about Gore's mental health; then the scurrilous rumours making Tom Daschle an agent of Saddam Hussein; then, more recently, the ads fabricated by a 527 group, the so-called Swift Boat Veterans, aiming to sully Kerry's military past. I won't go into all that; I'll also pass over the cases—for there were several—in which the Democrats, through their own 527s, tried their hands at this base game. But in the end, the example is there: each time, it's the same combination, expertly applied, of insinuation, gross lies, and media hype; each time, it's personal attacks and manhunts instead of the exchange or clash of ideas. Step by step, it's a degrading of public debate of which I know no equivalent in any other democracy and which, all in all, is deeply worrisome.

A modest suggestion, then, from a reader of Tocqueville who cannot forget and doesn't want to forget that this is the same America that invented modern democracy.

A humble proposition to the newspapers I see involved in the formidable task of self-criticism: I'd like to be able to convince them that David Brock deserves treatment at least as severe as that meted out to Jayson Blair, Stephen Glass, and Mike Barnicle (the falsifiers from, respectively, *The New York Times*, *The New Republic*, and *The Boston Globe*).

Of course, these publications aren't the only relevant players in the degradation of public life. We should not leave it to them, in place of politicians, to perform a postmortem on the corpse of calumnies. And certainly, we should not leave it to them to try to rehabilitate the public arena, without which a democracy wastes away.

But still…

Imagine the leading media reaching a decision on some kind of minimal ethical charter.

Imagine them agreeing on the absolute necessity of respecting the private lives of political leaders.

Imagine them proclaiming the inalienable character of this new human right: not, as Baudelaire proposed, the right to contradict yourself and the right to leave, but the right to secrecy.

Imagine a solemn declaration by which the papers, radios, and networks would prohibit one another from ever acting as the echo (whatever the form of this echo, whether underhanded or mock-hypothetical or warning-like or seemingly disinterested) of any ad hominem attack that hasn't passed the test of those rigorous fact-checking techniques at which they're experts.

Picture a journalist who has publicly confessed that he made up information with the sole aim of hitting a president 'between the eyes,' or else launched, without prior verification, the appalling accusation against a presidential candidate of having invented, exaggerated, or simulated his war wounds. Imagine this journalist, this rabble-rouser, being banned from his profession with the same vigour as would be a plagiarist or a fabricator of interviews in this country.

A different paradigm might ensue. Junk politics in its entirety might turn out less profitable. And for American democracy, this would be the most resounding way of reviving the legacy of Thoreau, Emerson, and, of course, Tocqueville.

When Security Breeds Madness

THIS IS A personal anecdote, but one that says so much about the security-related neurosis that reigns in this country that I can't resist the temptation to record it here.

I get a phone call informing me that my daughter has just given birth. Naturally, I decide to travel back to Paris to see mother and child.

The problem is that with a final meeting in Washington that same night and a dinner the next day in Baltimore that's difficult to cancel, I see I have exactly enough time to make the round-trip in its literal sense: takeoff from Dulles Airport on the last plane, at 11:00 p.m.; landing at Charles de Gaulle at noon the next day; a motorcycle that will take me to the clinic, wait for me, and take me back just in time, two hours later (my having, so to speak, fit myself into the regulation period for cleaning, inspecting, and refuelling the aircraft), to take the same plane back and be in Washington for dinner.

It's tight, but doable. Somewhat ridiculous, but important all the same.

So here I am on that night, at the appointed hour, in the middle of a long line of passengers waiting to check in for the flight to Paris.

In front of me a couple of young people are arguing in low voices about the nature of their affair: Are they dating or are they in a relationship? If they are just dating, how serious is it? And isn't the fact that the boy didn't invite the girl to Thanksgiving dinner at his parents' house an obvious obstacle to its being a full-fledged relationship? It's certainly a mystery to me, since this most American notion of dating has no equivalent in French....This very un-French way of turning the date itself, and later the relationship as such, into a separate entity, living its own life alongside the two lovers... The oddity, too, of the mania these lovers have for verbalizing, evaluating, codifying, and, when it comes down to it, ritualizing anything that might happen within the framework of their relationship... For the sake of a series of social gestures, which suddenly become nothing but gestures, that sense of the unexpected, the romantic, is lost, which in France even the most trifling love affairs preserve.... I observe all of this with infinite curiosity.

Behind me, a woman who read my pieces in *The Atlantic* starts asking me questions—gently, though, with that extreme politeness that always makes me wonder whether this tone is feigned or sincere, and which in any case is the exact opposite of the outright screaming match I'd have been treated to under similar circumstances in Paris. A reader, smiling, benevolent, who reproaches me for the attitude I adopted in my analysis of the megachurch phenomenon, especially in Willow Creek: Why do I mock these new churches? Why not pay attention to the good they might bestow on the men and women of today? What about the community ties they establish? The generosity they exhibit? The fact that Bono, for instance, appealed to them when he launched his campaign for awareness of AIDS in Africa?

So it's one of those interminable lines, typical everywhere since September 11, that form whenever there's a counter open somewhere. Once again, I find it hard to justify the usual clichés about the impatience, feverishness, agitation, even brutality, of American crowds. Quite the contrary—there's calm, discipline, a mixture of docility and courtesy, gregarious submission and civilisation. The opposite of the French type of whining, line-cutting crowd; the opposite of the vicious, stamping herd in which individuals are intent to tear one another to pieces. Here, when your gaze meets someone else's, when people bump into each other, there's a flurry of 'It's okay,' 'You're welcome,' 'Enjoy your trip'—friendly commonplaces, outward signs of warmth, especially smiles, yes, those smiles that mean nothing, those affectless, emotionless smiles, smiles that seem to be there only to signify the pure will to smile and, by so doing, defuse any conflict that threatens. All that, once again, so quintessentially American…

And then, when my turn finally comes, the most comical of scenarios, because it's the only one I would never have thought of. Having discovered that this passenger Lévy is travelling to Paris to spend a total of two hours there and that the flight approval requested includes another flight on the same day going in the opposite direction, the company computer panics, blocks the request, and refuses to issue my ticket.

Red alert.

Sudden commotion.

Distress of functionaries, first from the airline company, then from airport security, faced with this curious situation.

What's all this about wanting to spend the day on a plane? What can you be up to, as you are planning to spend seven hours flying one way and then seven hours flying back, with just a few minutes on French soil in between?

Grandfather? Prove it…

Writer? No proof…

Tocqueville? No connection…

I recall—since it makes me hope for a quick resolution—the story of my good Tocquevillean cop back at the start of my journey, on the highway.

I recall—somewhat more alarming—the story about Cat

Stevens being sent back to England and, especially, the one about Ted Kennedy, who was prevented five times from getting into an airplane because they had confused his with another name on the 'no-fly' list.

I do understand American paranoia.

I can understand how a nation at war with enemies skilled at making themselves undetectable must equip itself with sophisticated warning and identification systems.

But at the risk of absurd queries?

Does every passenger need to become a suspect?

Every trip an irksome undertaking?

Why such theatrics when, every day, illegal immigrants cross the Mexican and Canadian borders?

Isn't there a way to avoid these scenarios?

Needless to say, I was finally able to spend my two hours in Paris.

But one thing is clear. These new surveillance systems pose nearly as many problems as they solve. And the brand-new Department of Homeland Security is still a long way from the 'smart borders' that have been promised to America and the world.

The Journey to America

IN BALTIMORE, IN the poorest neighbourhood of the city, in its landscape of empty lots and half-razed buildings, I wanted to see the redbrick house that's one of the few to have been restored, where a plaque tells us—what an irony—that here Edgar Allan Poe lived and died.

I wanted to visit Johns Hopkins University (Hopkins: the maiden name of Elizabeth, Poe's mother—is that merely chance?), where my teacher Jacques Derrida lectured and where Sartre scholars have gathered for a conference, the calibre of which is almost unimaginable in a European university.

But I also wanted to see the waterfront, where, in 1791, at the height of the French Revolution, a great writer dropped anchor: Francois René de Chateaubriand, who had set sail from Saint-Malô and who, having passed by the Azores and then by Saint-Pierre, invented the literary voyage to America forty years before Tocqueville (to whom he was, incidentally, distantly related).

It's quite strange, this business of a voyage to America. Strange, when you think about it, this passion writers have had, not just French ones but other European ones, too, for this particular journey.

Writers have always travelled, of course. Notwithstanding the famous—too famous, perhaps—saying of Levi-Strauss at the start of his *Tristes Tropiques* ('I hate travelling'), Europeans have never ceased to love travels and travellers. But I'm not sure there's any destination in the world that—from the author of *Genie du Christianisme* to that of *Oliver Twist*, from Céline to Georges Duhamel, from Franz Kafka to Mario Soldati, Simone de Beauvoir, Jean-Paul Sartre, and so many others, for better or worse, whether eliciting hatred or reluctant adoration—more continually, intensely, irresistibly, summoned them than America has. And although I can see what they were after when they journeyed to the East (the *exote* so dear to Segalen, but also to Claudel and Malraux), to Rome or Florence (the beauty of lines, the metamorphoses of art and its forms), to Jerusalem, Persepolis, Lhasa (mirage of origins and sources, cradle of civilisations), it's harder for me to grasp what it is that continues to beat in the heart of this desire to see America and that can't be reduced to any of those great canonic motives.

A search for sources? Nonsense, since here we have a new world whose sources are in Europe.

Beauty? Harmony? With a few notable exceptions—a handful of free spirits who were able to discern the beauty of skyscrapers and of the new urban landscapes of these great, mad, artificial cities—most of these observers deplored the poverty, the ignorance, the unsightliness of Americans.

The exotic? The cool gaze of the ethnologist, alert to the customs of a foreign civilisation? Those aren't viable reasons either. They bear no relevance to the European underpinnings of America, and also contradict this delight in the modern that, after three centuries, continues to haunt, shape, and draw along the nation of Jefferson and Kennedy and that is still the best antidote to whatever love of folklore or the picturesque the typical fascination with the exotic may be laden with.

No. The journey to America doesn't come into any of these categories. It obeys none of these traditional motives. And I even wonder if, point by point, methodically, it doesn't take just the opposite course.

First contradiction: not the exotic but the nearby; not the other but the same. Of course, in a sense, it is the other. America is other—but so much less other than the Asian, African, or Amerindian other! An other that talks to us about ourselves; an other that teaches us about our most ordinary, common, and, ultimately, shared reality; an other that always, or almost always, has the puzzling familiarity (or, which comes down to the same thing, the unsettling strangeness) of a caricature or a mirror, a way of changing places whereby you travel a very long route to meet not the other but yourself, once again and afresh. Observe how among the moderns the journey to America always has the structure of a phenomenological odyssey.

Second contradiction: the future. Usually this kind of mirror reflects the past; it says to us, 'This is what you used to be, where you came from, who made you.' Here it's just the opposite. A mirror that, to use a well-known title, lends us the image not of our past history but of scenes of future life as American anticipation allows us to imagine them. 'This is what you will be,' it tells us; 'this is where you're going and what kind of world you'll give birth to.' If the journey to America is, like all journeys, a journey in time as much as in space, the time is not that of our dreamed, nostalgic, or reinvented memory but of a future that, according to your taste, according to each person's temperament, threatens us or is promised to us—a machine not to mount but to descend the chutes of time.

And then, one last contradiction—a third trail that complicates the preceding one, and makes it more specific. America is skyscrapers, but it is also wide-open spaces and deserts; it is scenes of future life but also (I've seen so many of them!) landscapes of the dawn of the world that are certainly not (see the preceding point) 'our' European dawn but that, from Audubon to Baudrillard (along with all those movie westerns), are a kind of reminiscence of it, or a reminder. So there it is; perhaps this journey has the peculiarity, finally, of giving us a taste of both. Perhaps it's one of those very rare experiences capable of offering, in one single bundle of sensations, a whiff of the ultramodern and another of the extremely archaic. And perhaps the love we feel for the journey stems from the obscure conviction that here, and here alone, the possibility is offered to a human being to see concentrated the materialisation of these two dreams, pre- and posthistorical, both equally powerful, but which usually we can think of only as separated by thousands of kilometres and, even more, by millennia. The American journey, in one single space (a country), in one short period of time (scarcely three centuries, maybe four), in the scarcely one hundred years, for instance, that sufficed for the first American pioneers who entered the territory of Death Valley and the Grand Canyon to invent the hideous Las Vegas (and by doing so, to leap from the prebiblical to the postmodern): the American journey, then, or the endless passage from Eden to Gehenna, the permanent short circuit of the Bible and science fiction, the journey across humanity's golden age and age of lead…

Blindness on Tocqueville's Part?

PHILADELPHIA. EASTERN STATE Penitentiary. Probably my last prison, but one of the first, along with the one in Auburn, New York, that Tocqueville and his companion, Beaumont, studied. Everything is the same as it was, Sean Kelly tells me. He is chief of the office that, since the establishment closed thirty years ago, has been in charge of maintaining it, arranging tours, and, every year for Halloween, renting the site to groups of children short on ghosts and vivid emotions.

Everything is exactly as our two missionaries found it on that day in October 1831, when they were welcomed by James J. Barclay, George Washington Smith, and Robert Vaux, leaders of the Philadelphia Society for Alleviating the Miseries of the Public Prisons, an association of Quakers, human-rights advocates, defenders of the Cherokee Indians, and early opponents of slavery, who conceived, created, and, from 1829, managed this new kind of penitentiary, which was not meant to punish the criminal or repair the damage caused to society by crime or even, like Alcatraz, Angola, and, later on, Rikers Island, put the criminal in quarantine, get rid of him like trash, and banish him. Instead it was to help him, through silence and solitude, redeem himself, repent, and, in the pure Quaker tradition, elevate his soul, which had been led astray by the Devil. The same high walls. The same crenellated towers flanked by fake machicolations. The same moats, drawbridges, dungeons, arrow slits. The same Piranesi architecture, which the prisoner, arriving blindfolded, couldn't possibly see, but the mere idea of which—whatever was told to him—was enough, Tocqueville said, to inspire in him the beginning of a religious terror and a horror for his crime. And finally, inside this desolate setting, flooded by rain at night, resembling a haunted castle more than anything, the same prison complex, made up of a central tower from which seven galleries of individual cells radiate in perfect geometry, each one with a tiny garden, all of which lie open to the view of the guards.

Had Tocqueville read Jeremy Bentham's opus, published forty years earlier, at the height of the prison debates initiated by Beccaria and the French revolutionaries? Did he realise, when he marvelled at this system, in which, as he wrote, they 'translated the intelligence of discipline into stone,' that he was in the first detention centre in the world that applied the panopticon schema that the nineteenth century would use not just for prisons but as the principle of organisation for its schools, hospitals, barracks, and factories? As far as I know, Tocqueville never cited either the book or its author. But it is certain that he perceived this system's stroke of genius. He understood that because it gives guards the possibility to see without being seen; because it establishes a surveillance that is at once uninterrupted, invisible, and virtual; because no prisoner ever knows, in other words, whether the eye of power is at any given instant actually directed at him, it has the ability to throw souls into 'a deeper terror than chains and blows.' And above all, he appreciated this other peculiarity of the system, which is directly linked to the ideology of its Quaker promoters. In order to be absolutely certain of making the prisoners face their villainy; urging them to genuine repentance, which was the goal of their imprisonment; and hastening the intellectual and moral reform for which prison, according to the Quakers, should be the opportunity and the setting, they organised everything so as to isolate prisoners both day and night and cut off any kind of contact—not just with their fellow prisoners but with the outer world and even the guards. Visits were forbidden; the slightest attempt at speech was punished; any reading other than the holy scriptures was prohibited. Thus were they put in the situation of caring only about God....

Ten years later, Dickens would proclaim his horror at an organisation that was meant to convert delinquents to good but that, as far as he could see, managed only to push them over the line into madness. Learning that everything, from meals to religious services and bimonthly showers, was arranged so that no one ever met anyone else, he would denounce 'this slow and daily tampering with the mysteries of the brain,' which is 'immeasurably worse than any torture of the body.' Others, many other visitors throughout the entire nineteenth century, would denounce the insanity of a world in which the phobia of noise was so severe that the axles of the carts that stopped at the cell doors at mealtimes were wrapped in cloth; in which the last trick left to prisoners to hold on to the sound of human presence was to tap gently on iron sewage pipes to send one another secret messages; and in which, when a rebel couldn't cure himself of talking, they put into his mouth a piece of cast iron attached to a mechanism that buried it a little deeper in his throat whenever he moved his tongue or glottis and merely suffocated him if he did not cease to speak.

But not Tocqueville. He had no fundamental objection to this Quaker vision of redemption by meditation, prayer, and labour. He visited these little rooms whose only opening was a bull's-eye window carved out of the ceiling, looking onto the sky. He visited the prisoners and, despite the rules of silence, obtained permission to question them and extract vague confidences about their detention. And he found almost no faults with the system. He seemed scarcely moved by the notion that speech was the supposed vector of all contagions and, necessarily, of the vilest of evil spells. Beaumont even talked of these cells as a 'palace' that must have cost an 'astronomical amount' and that, at a time when the president of the United States had to content himself with a coal burner and pitchers of water, were all equipped with central heating and running water. In short, arriving from Auburn, where prisoners were isolated only at night and devoted themselves during the day to forced collective labour, and finding that here hygiene, food, and the material conditions of life were objectively better, observing that the jails smelled good and were clean, and also noting that corporal punishment had for the moment disappeared, the two friends found enough merit in this model to commend it to their own government.

Was that a shortcoming of Tocqueville's, or of his context? Was it the blindness of the time, or—perhaps—a faint shadow on the portrayal, so consistently flattering, that a parallel reading of his masterpiece and the great open book of the living America of today invites us to admire?

Woody Allen: Portrait of the Filmmaker as a Musician

DON'T TELL WOODY Allen he's a filmmaker. He thinks of himself as a musician. That must be what went through the minds of the hundred or so fans who saw him perform tonight in the café at the Hotel Carlyle, on the corner of Madison and Seventy-sixth, where he came, as he does every Monday, accompanied by his New Orleans Funeral and Ragtime Orchestra, to play the clarinet. Here was one of the greatest living American filmmakers. Here was the superb auteur of *Annie Hall* and *The Purple Rose of Cairo*. And here he was within arm's reach, sitting on a stool, without any special set, among diners who didn't think it necessary to stop their drinking and eating to listen to him. Here he was, dressed in corduroy trousers and a light blue shirt; concentrating, eyes half closed or fully shut; defined gestures; confident breath; fingers flat on the open holes of his clarinet; the muscles of his mouth tight, yet not puffing out his cheeks around the mouthpiece; his upper lip surprisingly mobile, at times seeming to inhale and swallow the top of the reed and at times curling back as if to convey its decision to keep its distance, disavow that nasty instrument and, all of a sudden, with sovereign authority, literally cut off its breath....

From Washington, D.C., back to Cape Cod

In the beginning you say to yourself, That can't be him. You tell yourself that the real Woody Allen wouldn't expose himself this way, in this bar; that this famous little man, the schlemiel with the physique of the eternal loser, heir to Keaton, Chaplin, and Harold Lloyd, epitome of the awkward oaf who has never been seen to take a step, come through the door, pick up any utensil, let alone a musical instrument, without tripping and getting his feet caught in the rug—he can't be this virtuoso, his technique so flawless, with such an impeccable presence and, when he stops playing and starts singing, such a perfect, well-calibrated voice. And then, after a while, you get used to it. Little by little you recognise him; when he gives the floor to Cynthia Sayer, his pianist, or Rob Garcia, his drummer, or Eddy Davis, the fat man with the plaid shirt opening onto a buffalo neck, who accompanies him on the banjo; when he starts nodding his head to the rhythm of the trombone or staring at the tips of his shoes with the look of a punished child, waiting for someone to finish a solo—you rediscover the sad gargoyle face, the furrowed mask, the long nose, and the dazed, 'nutty professor' side of the actor in *Take the Money and Run*.

And then, once more, the virtuoso gains the upper hand. And the musician launches into a wild rendition of a Glenn Miller or Benny Goodman tune. Now he's stopped being the director of *Manhattan Murder Mystery* and becomes the disciple of Gene 'Honey Bear' Sedric—the one you had to look for, that night twenty years ago when *Annie Hall* won four Oscars, at Michael's Pub, where he was performing in front of an audience pretty much like tonight's. Here he is no longer the world superstar who starts a riot in Paris just by stepping out of his hotel, but only little Allen Stewart Konigsberg, who chose his pseudonym in homage to Woody Herman, who called his last daughter Bechet in homage to the great Sidney, and who has said a hundred times over that the two most desirable destinies in this world have always seemed, in his eyes, to be those of a basketball player (which he had to give up rather quickly) and a clarinetist (to which he continues, here at the Carlyle, to sacrifice some of his desire, his time, and his fame). Oh, the intense joy on his face, this countenance of an old, consumptive adolescent metamorphosed into a semi-athlete, his air of absolute triumph, when he reaches the end of one of those solos and you don't know if that amazing breath comes from his mouth, his body movements, the force of his soul, or all three at once.

The history of art is full of these misunderstandings in which you see an artist living or acting as though he were convinced he had chosen the wrong genre. We know the case of Stendhal, thinking he would owe his immortality to his plays. And that of Chateaubriand, persuaded that his masterpiece was not *Les Mémoires d'Outre Tombe* but *Les Natchez*. I myself have seen Paul Bowles explaining, with his last breath, that his masterpieces, the ones that would stand the test of time and that had to be taken care of after his death, were not *The Sheltering Sky* and *Let It Come Down* but the delightful musical pieces he composed every spring for the end-of-the-year celebration at the American School of Tangiers and its director, Joe McPhilips. But this case, the case of this great filmmaker coming every Monday to perform, this case of the formal innovator you feel would give up the most beautiful shot in *Purple Rose* for a well-played bar of music, able to switch successfully from the sound of a bugle to that of a reed flute—this case surpasses anything I know.

I will get to see the other Allen. The next day, in his office on Park Avenue, I'll get to see the filmmaker and the intellectual, a New Yorker through and through, who will have many things to say, not just about his films but about the mediocrity of Kerry, the nullity of Bush, the state of political collapse of the country, the neopuritanism that's winning over the middle classes. Of which, I ask him all of a sudden, wasn't his affair with his daughter ('She's not my daughter,' he interrupts), just as much as the Lewinsky affair, the harbinger? And about his conviction (the height of pride, when I think about it) that a guy like him, Allen, doesn't have the right—do you understand? *the right*—to get involved in politics, since he's so unpopular, since he so perfectly embodies all that this puritan, suicidal America execrates, and since he is at the same time so incredibly famous that each word that might come out of his mouth would be held not *for* but *against* his champion and would thus only weaken him and contribute to his defeat... But the great moment, the real Woody, the hour of emotion and truth, the one that in any case most impresses me, since I feel that here we are in contact with his most intimate identity, is his euphoric, squandered jazz performance.

Three Tycoons

IT'S HIS HARDNESS that strikes you first. His air of icy, cautious ferocity. His wolf eyes, unusually far apart, very green, piercing, but which don't really go to the trouble of studying you. His way of making no excuses for himself, never explaining himself. His insistence on declaring, in effect, 'I am Henry Kravis, master of the world; I am head of Kohlberg, Kravis, Roberts and Co., the best private-equities business there is; I am the son of Ray Kravis, a small-time oilman from Oklahoma, and I have built this enormous business, this empire, where the very practice of forced takeovers has become an industry in itself. People are mad at me? I know. They see me as a predator, a lackey for Bush, an asshole? I couldn't care less. I won't bother to tell you the history of the New York City Investment Fund that we founded with a few friends seven years ago. I won't lower myself to telling you about the tens of thousands of jobs we create with our money in the neighbourhoods the state has abandoned; or about the state's moral code and our own; or about its principles and mine, which are those of big business—and I never for an instant doubted how good they are, not just for me but for America and the world....'

After a while, though, something else transpires. A crack in the mask. A fissure. Maybe an old clumsiness. Maybe fear, too. Yes, I'd swear it, Henry Kravis is afraid. Of what? Of whom? Of other people, his fellow men, and of the war of everyone against everyone else that reigns in the jungle of big American capital? Of his own violence, which he knows only too well? Does he, like Gatsby, live in the obsessive fear of seeing his original sins emerge and inscribe themselves on this face of his, which he has gone to such pains, over so many years, to make as smooth as the varnished mahogany panelling in the library where he receives me? All of that, undoubtedly. And then this picture, over our heads, which I hadn't really noticed at first, this hyperrealist painting, probably sketched from a photograph, which represents a charming adolescent in a blazer and a white shirt open over a hairless chest—college boy, little prince—his son, who died at the age of twenty, and about whom he is heart-broken.

Henry Kravis can talk for two hours without saying a word about his New York philanthropies. Barry Diller, though, does better. He asked Frank Gehry, the architect of the Guggenheim museums, to plan the future headquarters of his empire in Chelsea. For this, Gehry conceived of the first building ever constructed entirely of glass, without a trace of steel or concrete framework: a great ship of crystal, a transparent mirage, that will float over the Hudson. In other words, Diller is putting his mark on the city. He is imprinting his signature on it. He is legitimately joining the illustrious lineage of Stuyvesants, Rockefellers, Reynoldses, Singers, Woolworths. But Diller spends a large part of our meeting trying to convince me that, considering the absurd rent he pays here, in these old offices; considering the prices of downtown real estate and its potential for appreciation; considering the impact the building will have, the publicity it will generate, and the energy its sheer possibility is already radiating to his staff, this pharaonic project, this pure gift, this masterpiece, will not only cost his company nothing, it will in fact bring in a substantial profit. Arrogance again, or a supreme form of humility? Is this the honesty of a man who refuses to play the conventional (and excruciatingly European!) game of the ashamed billionaire who expiates his success and strives to appear acceptable—or is it the height of self-punishment and modesty?

I observe Barry Diller, with his powerful, vulnerable skull that conveys the air of a Picasso, with his smile that's usually so melancholic but which, now that I've stopped pestering him about his memories of Paramount, his tussles with Murdoch, his conversion to teleshopping, has become curiously disarming. I listen to him talk passionately about the architectural model, placed between our chairs, of what may be the great work of his life but for which he begs me to give him no credit, none at all. There is a kind of madness, too, in this man. A mixture of gratuitous talent, potlatch, glorious eccentricity, and, when he explains to me that he couldn't care less about posterity and only his own people count—that is to say, his close friends; his wife, Diane von Fürstenberg; his younger, heroin-addict brother, who died alone at the age of thirty-six, shot to death in a fleabag motel—there is suddenly a brash insolence, a mutely enraged violence, an amorality that's too flaunted to be completely sincere and not betray some kind of hidden wound.

And then Soros. The implacable George Soros, the impenitent speculator, the virtuoso of hedge funds who, when he was playing the stock market twenty years ago, almost brought down the pound sterling and, beyond that, the international monetary system. He doesn't regret anything either. He doesn't criticise the operating procedure of the American tycoon, or the notion according to which money is born noble and, everywhere, finds itself in chains. With one exception, though—which makes his case an interesting variation. His style. His looks. His tousled aspect, which reminds you of Elias Canetti. The slight sloppiness of his clothing, which lends him a professorial guise. His accent—this Hungarian accent that, in him, seems like the sign of a resistance to Americanness.

And then this way he has, during the lunch we're having in a rather modest dining room adjacent to his office, of talking only about prisons, about the new fascism that is looming, about public-spirited investments, democracy, open society, Karl Popper—this way of quoting his own Popper-like books as though everyone has read them, and his childish disappointment when he understands that I'm here not so much for Sunday philosophy as for the flamboyant, paradoxical billionaire himself. On the one hand, this supertycoon who, when I ask him whether he is sometimes burdened with a guilty conscience because of these fortunes that are so curiously won, isn't far from replying that attacking a whole currency, throwing banks into a panic, forcing them to react and invent, is not a crime but a service, a revolutionary gesture, a duty. On the other hand, his nostalgia for European values and concerns, which in his mind doesn't seem the least bit contradictory—a nostalgia that leads him to take back to Europe (especially eastern Europe) the money earned in America while importing to America (especially Democratic America) whatever European memories remain enclosed within himself. For his problem is Europe. He is in mourning not for a son or a brother but for Europe. And if there is but one thing about which he is inconsolable, it's being merely George Soros and not one of those Czech or Viennese philosophers he's admired since his youth. A part of him dreams of being their secret successor. Human, too human. Another embodiment of a system that is regarded by half the planet as inhuman, and this touching, pathetic share of humanity. Is he the most peculiar of the three? The most romantic? Or the most hubristic?

Three Days in Guantánamo

ACTUALLY, THAT PENITENTIARY in Philadelphia turned out not to be my last prison. There was one still to come. The last one. The definitive last one. And for a traveller looking for symptoms of the current American vertigo, surely not the least eloquent.

To tell the truth, I had resigned myself to not going there. Knowing that it was the most closed off of all prisons, I had sent in my request at the start of the journey; but seeing that nothing had come of it, I had got used to the idea of completing my travels without being able to gain access to what, throughout the world, has become the defining American prison, the symbol and synonym for the system—a kind of third example, beside Auburn and Philadelphia, about which I could only imagine what Tocqueville might have said....

What a surprise, then, when the response finally comes. What a surprise, as I'm in the process of going over my conclusions about this magnificent, mad country, laboratory of the best and the worst, greedy and modest, at home in the world and self-obsessed, puritan and outrageous, facing toward the future and yet obsessed with its memories—what an unexpected twist in this long adventure when an e-mail arrives from the press attaché John Adams saying they'll be waiting for me on April 25, 26, and 27 at the American base of Guantánamo.

Plane to Fort Lauderdale, Florida. A small plane, officially civilian, to Inagua, and from there to Guantánamo. Once in Guantánamo, scorching heat. Tropics, basically. Something in the air, the deep blue of the sky and sea, the faces of the base personnel, the passengers on the ferry that crosses the bay, the façades of restaurants glimpsed through the SUV window that remind you that you are in Cuba, quite literally, in Cuba. An astonishing situation that one has to see in order to believe and that I'll get a closer look at the next day, at the border, at the comic-opera frontier post where every year, on the same date, in a ritual that's been played out for years, the American commander of the base brings a check for four thousand dollars (corresponding to the annual rent settled on in 1903 and never revised) to his Cuban counterpart, who, after an on-site telephone consultation with El Líder Máximo himself, just as ritually refuses it. The extraordinary situation, half Dino Buzzati's *Tartar Steppe*, half Julien Gracq's *The Narrow Waters*, of this far-flung outpost of the empire stuck in the heart of the last colony of another defunct empire…

The naval base, then. The classic—but here surrealist—structure of all American bases, with homes for the officers, schools for their children, a Starbucks between two checkpoints, a McDonald's, diving and fitness clubs, nightclubs, malls, a golf course alongside the barbed wire. And then, finally, the prison camps themselves, clustered in the southern part of the island, near the shore, where at the time of my visit a little over five hundred 'enemy combatants,' most of them former Talibans, are basically being held without trial, without any legal protection or status. Camp X-Ray, historically the first, a veritable human chicken coop, whose metal cages, brought to white heat by the sun, are now abandoned to the weeds and the rats. Camp Iguana, on top of a cliff, where they used to keep 'terrorists' under the age of eighteen, but, since all juveniles have been released from Guantánamo, where they now keep other prisoners. Camp Delta, more modern, with wooden watchtowers, six metal fences covered with wire mesh and topped with electric barbed wire and, painted in white letters, a colossal HONOUR-BOUND TO DEFEND FREEDOM that echoes so eerily. A chance to attend one of the ARBs (administrative review boards) that in principle take place behind closed doors and where today an 'enemy combatant' with one leg, but still handcuffed, his one foot chained to a ring in the floor, is appearing, without a lawyer but accompanied by two soldiers, before the troika of officers supposed to decide if he still represents a 'danger' to the United States. Camp 4, still in Delta, reserved for 'cooperative' detainees, who have the right to play volleyball and read detective novels. John Edmondson, the chief physician, who discloses that one detainee out of six is treated for a psychological disorder. The woman cop who follows my every step and, the night of my departure, erases from my camera the images of detainees I managed to film. All these faces, at once pathetic and terrible, that will remain engraved only in my memory. All these men that Bush and Rumsfeld claim are either terrorists (why, in that case, are they not tried?) or prisoners of war (but then why not apply the Geneva Conventions?).

I'll go back over all of this, of course. Later on, I'll go back over the fundamental issues here and reflect in particular on what the existence of such a zone of 'exception' signifies in a democracy. For now, one observation. One modest, minute observation.

There are, in this prison, characteristics that are bound to seem familiar to anyone who, like me, has had the occasion to visit other American prisons. Its undertow of violence, which reminds me immediately of Rikers Island. Its policy of isolation and banishment, like that of Alcatraz. An indifference to human rights and to the rule of law, which perhaps is not unexpected from a country that, in Nevada, Texas, and elsewhere, invented the legal and moral monstrosity that the idea of a private-enterprise prison represents. The absence of perspective and of horizon, the methodical state of uncertainty as to their fate in which the detainees are kept—this literally unlimited detention, which makes me think of the programmed despair of the prisoners at Angola. And finally, in the way I am urged not to wear a short-sleeved shirt so as not to offend the detainees' modesty; in the insistence of one sergeant as he explains to me that each new arrival is offered a Koran that will be placed in a surgical mask hanging on the bars of his cell; in the conversation of another sergeant, not the least bit uncomfortable when he confesses that you sometimes have to resolve to be ferocious with a detainee who spits on you or smears his wall with excrement, who explains that on the other hand there are procedures that forbid handling the Book without wrapping it in a cloth specially meant for this purpose—in this multicultural comedy, in this affectation of caring for the 'spiritual needs' of the other even as he's being treated like a wild beast, there is something that must remind you of the hypocrisy of the Quaker soul uplifters of the Philadelphia penitentiary.

You can begin to wonder whether or not these good Christians have broken the rules and profaned the sacred Book (instinctively, I tend to believe that reports about this have been exaggerated). You can debate the pertinence of the word *gulag* to describe this offshore hell (this, too, I think is inappropriate). You can argue about whether or not Guantánamo should be closed—as Jimmy Carter, among others, urges (here I think the answer is yes, without hesitation, since the honour and, in any case, the health of American democracy is at stake). What you cannot possibly say is that Guantánamo is a UFO, fallen from some unknown, obscure disaster. What you have to admit is that it is a miniature, a condensation, of the entire American prison system.

Back to Square One (or Nearly)

BOSTON. ONE YEAR later—or almost. And in this loop that's closing, in this mixed impression of endgame and beginning, the curious feeling of finding myself in a city I scarcely know but where I already have memories.

I return to the Union Oyster House, where *The Atlantic* magazine hosted its breakfasts during the Democratic convention. I walk back to Copley Square, where on election night the population of Democrats waited so many hours, in vain, for their conquered champion to appear. I wander through the now empty hallways of the Fairmont, where the announcers offici- ated. I linger in the reading rooms of the Boston Public Library, which I visited briefly one morning between meetings with aides to Obama and Kerry. I didn't realise at that time how beautiful the city is. In the whirlwind of the instant, I didn't take enough note of its affluent, literate charm, aristocratic and European, which so impressed Tocqueville that he stayed here for three weeks, the longest stopover in his journey. Boston was the only American city to have so lastingly bewitched him....

Hence I take my time on this occasion. I look for the place on Washington Street where the Marlboro Hotel stood, where Tocqueville went as soon as he arrived. I have dinner at the Parker House, through which the ghosts of Emerson, Hawthorne, Thoreau, and Longfellow hover, as well as Tocqueville's own, of course. I even let myself be led on an informal tour organised by a friend, which, while not the official tour of the American Civil Liberties Union of Massachusetts, guides me through the city from one site of social activism to another: the house where Roger Williams was born, apostle of free thought and of the nascent separation of church and state; the first church in New England where the emancipation of slaves was preached; the marble bust of Robert Gould Shaw, colonel of the first regiment in the state made up exclusively of black soldiers; the street where, at the height of his combat for the equality of races and women's rights, a crowd almost lynched William Lloyd Garrison; the hotel where John F. Kennedy announced his candidacy; and even—a final avatar of this process of transforming everything into memory and museums that has continued to manifest itself until the very last day!—the house of the Kerrys, on Beacon Hill....

I like this city. There is something about its cheerful puri- tanism; its proud, provincial slowness; its hundred-year-old arborvitae trees; its houses that exude the rich perfume of polished wood, with period parquet floors, portraits of ancestors on the walls, fashionable, well-used furniture. There is, in its slow dawns and its nights slow to end, in the sight of its narrow streets and their too orderly cobblestones, in its reverberations of the past century—there is in all of this the source of a faint ennui but also an irresistible charm that places it, without contest, in that little cluster of cities (Seattle, New Orleans, Savannah) where I, too, could spend three weeks or more.

With, perhaps, two reservations.

For there were two bitter moments during these pleasant days.

The southern sections of the city—Dorchester, Mattapan— are also the poorest neighbourhoods, where you suddenly have the sense that you're on the threshold of another world. A world of brutality and narcotics. A world of abandoned buildings, squatted in by gangs, their walls covered with immense, multi-coloured, naïve murals. The world of that young, homeless Haitian woman who thought the hospital was for other people and who, ten minutes before I arrived, gave birth here, on the floor of a supermarket, with the help of a cop who was passing by, a feat for which he will be decorated by his unit.

The world, a little further on, of Adèle—a very old woman; spitting image of Priscilla Ford, the woman on death row in the north Las Vegas prison—who lives in the slums on Blue Hill Avenue and who is being taken to the emergency room by ambulance... But actually, no—she's not that old. When I talk with one of the neighbours huddled around the ambulance, I discover that she's only forty-five, and that she's just very poor, out of work for ten years, exhausted. 'Be careful,' the neighbour shouts to one of the stretcher bearers as she pats Adèle's sparse hair. 'Be careful, she's on cortisone and stress medication.' And Adèle, her lips white, sweat on her temples, eyes glazed, already gone: 'Is it the good Lord that's taking me away?'

And difficult, too, disappointing, although for reasons of an entirely different nature, my meeting with the ultra-Bostonian Samuel Huntington. I knew there was a problem with his last book. Like a number of his readers, I had been troubled by his thesis about Spanish-speaking immigrants whose uncontrolled influx would transform the white Protestant nation of the first pioneers into a bicultural polity. But here, in this elegant restaurant in Beacon Hill, where the food is too good and the wine too heady, now, to my great surprise, he throws all caution to the wind and in a few sentences expresses what his opponents have long suspected him of thinking without daring to admit it out loud. What startling violence wells up in his blue eyes when he says to me, 'The big thing, the big problem with Hispanics, is that they don't like education.' The sudden expression of hostility that disfigures the scholarly face of the professor when, anxious to tell me what, after all, annoys him so much in this rise to power of a hardworking, patriotic Mexican minority, he starts explaining that these people, because they'll have the advantage of bilingualism, will get 'preferences for jobs,' so they'll be able to 'take their jobs away' from the 'large majority' of other Americans, and that when these other Americans realise it all, when they understand that they, the whites—in principle the bearers of the old founding 'creed' of the nation— will henceforth be the object of 'discrimination,' they will react with a terrible concoction of 'resentment' and 'nativistic' racism.

And then Israel… His strange anger when, at the end of the interview, I put forward the idea that Israel, along with France and America, is one of the rare countries founded on what he calls a 'creed.' Oh, no, he says. That's not a creed! I forbid you to associate the fine word creed with a country based on 'ethnicity,' where Arabs and Jews have distinct rights! I answer back. I protest. I argue that talking about 'ethnicity' in relation to a people, Americans, whose very essence is to be made up of all peoples, doesn't make much sense. And when it's time to leave, when we're standing on the sidewalk, there's a shadow of doubt in his gaze, a sudden anxiety in his voice: 'Did I say some things I shouldn't have?'

Under the Eye of Eternity

CAPE COD. LAND'S end. Or—but it's ultimately the same—birth, beginning; the very place where, four centuries ago, the 102 Pilgrims landed, with their dogs, from the *Mayflower*. And today, in Provincetown, two hours away by car from Boston, these dollhouses, inexpensive art galleries, fishing shacks with painted clapboard façades gnawed by salt and snow—this typically middle-class seaside resort whose other peculiarity is to have become, over time, a gay town.

What on earth is Norman Mailer doing here? How could this boy from Brooklyn, this New Yorker in heart and mind, this supermale with six marriages, this man whom the feminist Kate Millet called the quintessence of the 'heterosexual, macho pig'—how could this man have chosen to live in a small town of four thousand souls, most of them homosexual, whose contribution to local culture consists (if I am to believe the waiter in the faux fisherman's restaurant where I wait till it's time for our meeting) of a festival of sexy bodies, a week for leather enthusiasts, and a colloquium on the problems posed by adoption by same-sex couples? of course I ask Mailer. It's even one of the first things I ask him when he appears in the sun-drenched living room of his house, short, thickset, all neck and torso, very round in his sweater vest, full mane of white hair, blue eyes that scrutinise me and that have lost none of their irony. But he doesn't answer. Or, rather, he does, but in a round-about way. He is with the comely Norris, his wife, and they both reply that that's just how it is. Chance. She for her paintings, he for his novels—they were both looking for a quiet setting where they could work at their own pace. So here they are. Cape Cod. And on Cape Cod, Provincetown. Don't look any further than that. There aren't any other specific reasons....

All right, then. I suppose it's possible, after all. Possible you should forget the *Mayflower* and the discovery of America. Possible not to convey too much meaning to that peculiar book *Tough Guys Don't Dance*, published in 1984 and set in Provincetown, the hero of which is gay. And possible, too, that Mailer is here simply because this beautiful, light-filled house in the dunes, facing the sea, was the ideal place to lay up a store of solitude and silence. What, he asks me in substance, is the main problem of writers in general, and of writers who know their time is short in particular? How to isolate themselves, seek exile in their own country. Sometimes, like Philip Roth, vanish in the confines of their own city. Leave the ranks not of murderers but of idiots, amnesiacs, noisemakers, culture haters, all those who seem to exist only to turn to ashes a writer's desire to write. And once you're finally set in this cocoon, in this sanctuary of rest, this chapel, then write books relentlessly, books the age wasn't expecting.... Norman Mailer is eighty-two years old. In a certain way he doesn't look it. No, despite the alcohol, the drugs, the excesses of his successive lives; despite his encroaching deafness; despite his legs that have trouble supporting him and lend him the deliberate gait of a little stone golem; despite his air of an old boxer who's just left the ring or an old sailor who's come ashore for good, he radiates an eerie, unsettling youthfulness. But the overwhelming impression he gives is of no longer being always or completely of this world. The only real visible mark of age on the face of this great living successor to Hemingway is the air of absence that appears when you try to talk to him not just about his books but about his exploits of long ago. The war in the Pacific? Vietnam? The Nixon and Kennedy years? His meeting with Castro? His candidacy for mayor of New York? The naked? The dead? The battles for civil rights, and the struggles against the culture wars? The old sailor responds, of course. But once again, halfheartedly. Without fervour. Without eloquence. As though his energy were elsewhere, reaching out toward the book he's writing now, gathered into the few years that are left to write it.

So he is economical, calculating, and has an altogether different intelligence of time, another quality of presence, a kind of colossal now that, unlike the classic diseases of memory, crushes whatever has been experienced and only trains its spotlight on what is actually happening. But he doesn't regret anything. He is not sad, or worried. He is even the type, like Ravelstein in his amiable enemy Bellow's book, who willingly tells his visitor that he 'loves existence' and 'is not in a hurry to die.'

And yet, he is counting. He keeps counting: The number of days that are left to him. The number of hours an interview steals away from him. The books he'll never read. His eyes, now so frail, need to be saved for writing his own books. The hours—maybe just the minutes—every day when he is truly master of his art. His hand, which needs to be in training for that very time. His breath, which he needs to hold in so as not to waste it, so that he can keep on creating. He does not, like another of his old foes, write to keep from dying; he keeps from dying so that he can finish writing. Not for posterity, that immortality of weak souls, but, like the character in Godard's masterpiece, *Breathless*, to be immortal, immortal right away, and then die.

So sometimes, at nightfall, the ghosts of Gilmore, Marilyn, Oswald, Muhammad Ali, return, those heroes of an America that seemed to exist only to end up in great books. Sometimes the door creaks open and the image rises up of an evening spent at the Kennedys', in Hyannis Port, where he had paid a neighbourly visit; of that cocktail party where he got into a fight with McGeorge Bundy, the ridiculous diplomatic adviser to his personal enemy Lyndon Johnson; or, more recent, of a dinner with the elder Mrs. Bush, who listened to him, with gaping mouth, describe the contracts her president of a son has with the Devil. But by and large all that has faded. His life, when I press him to recall it, is now nothing but a series of pale shadows, long spans of boredom, sterile provocations, misunderstandings. The most secular of American novelists, the inventor of New Journalism, the engaged writer par excellence, the man who covered the Republican and Democratic conventions and won a Pulitzer Prize for it, ends up like Proust or Kafka, his eyes fixed on eternity. This world is no longer my own. My last dream is not for you. I am facing up, albeit in a different way. My most daring novel. Wait and see. Cape Cod.

Postscript

A barometric depression hung low over the Gulf of Mexico.

The phrase is reminiscent of the opening of Robert Musil's great unfinished novel, *The Man Without Qualities*.

And it will be, if not the last sentence, at least the final note to this narrative, which I was just about to bring to an end at the very moment this hurricane with a Russian dancer's name struck the United States and plunged it into grief.

Not, of course, that America today is like the 'royal and imperial' Austria of 1913, experiencing its final hours.

Nor that a hurricane, even a Category Five hurricane on the Saffir-Simpson Scale, could actually be compared to that 'joyous apocalypse' that was about to sweep Musil's Kakania away.

Even less so since, as joys go, there is already something obscene (and something I wouldn't want to take part in, even remotely) in the ill-concealed joy of the enemies of America when presented with the first effects of this hurricane: the superpower brought to its knees by Mother Nature herself! The Empire, the formidable Empire, demoted to the level of some Third World country, receiving offers of aid from Sri Lanka, even Chavez and Castro—what a godsend for America's foes! For a friend of America, what a pity!

What is undeniable, however, is that an event of considerable importance really did occur.

That there was, in the spectacle of American corpses drowned in the streets of a city flooded like Nineveh, a whiff, if not of apocalypse, then at least of cataclysm and horror, is simply undebatable.

The destruction of New Orleans might not be, for the universal conscience of this dawn of the twenty-first century, the equivalent of what the Lisbon earthquake was for Voltaire's century—but what appears to stand out as I write these lines, and surely requires a few ultimate clarifications, is that there is a shock here, an authentic shock, and this shock is likely to modify, if not the way we contemplate America, then at least the way America contemplates its own image, its status, its destiny.

I am not thinking here—understand—of the purely political implications of the event.

I am not thinking—or rather, not thinking solely—of the unbearable off-handedness of those executive chiefs hesitating, during four days, to cut short their precious vacations in order to come to the aid of the disaster victims.

I don't even want to speak of the moment—more disturbing yet (but that's still not the main point)—when the same American president who had for years received extremely detailed reports that the New Orleans levees would inevitably break some day had the nerve to state that 'no one could have foreseen' what had just taken place.

Nor do I want to linger over the curious debate immediately launched by several of the president's opponents who, surprised at not seeing helicopters that could have rescued the thousands of men and women trapped on rooftops fly in right away, concluded that if the help wasn't there, it was surely because it was elsewhere; in other words, they took advantage of the situation to attach yet another piece of evidence to their interminable case against the Iraq War.

And if I don't linger over it, it's because there is something rather fetid, too, in the reasoning of these people—Michael Moore, for instance, in his 'Letter to George Bush'—who would like to force us to choose between building dams at home and giving birth to democracy abroad. There are enough reasons, as I've written, to oppose the Iraqi venture without adding—it always smacks of the populist right—some incompatibility of principles between New Orleans's way and Baghdad's way...

No.

I am thinking of the metapolitical lessons of the event.

I am thinking of those great lessons that America has traditionally drawn from its cataclysms and that it will draw—is drawing already from this one.

Nature, that social philosopher.

Nature, that political scientist.

Nature, that great book Americans have grown accustomed to learning from, as much as from their libraries.

The great Chicago fire and its contribution, so decisive, to the reshaping of the very idea of the American city...

The monster flood of the Mississippi, in 1927, and the role it played in the genesis, then the implementation, of Rooseveltism and the New Deal.

The myths and realities of the Big One—their function in the very definition of Californian space-time.

And now the Big Easy wrecked by Katrina—formidable analyst of American society, revealer of its unseen face.

The question of the poor, for instance.

I saw the poor of America all through my journey.

From the Boston slums to Spanish Harlem, from destitute neighbourhoods in Washington, D.C., to that street near Beverly Hills where I saw a mounted policeman whipping a homeless man, I didn't visit one city devoid of a nether side on this matter.

But I saw as well—I want to say, *especially* saw—the extraordinary denial of that sombre lining in this positivity-driven country, where the lights never go out.

I saw—I heard—the manner in which the American nation persists in viewing itself as an immense middle class devoted to the American Way of Life, despite the obvious refutation—the very real existence of the 37 million outcasts, the victims of social exclusion.

Well, here they are, these living refutations, crammed into the ruins of the city they couldn't leave because they lacked the means to follow the order to evacuate.

Here they are, these Poor, 'stuck inside New Orleans' with the Memphis blues of death buzzing in their heads—here they are, emerging out of nowhere and rising up in the face of an America that thought it had relegated them to the margins of its concerns, just as it was casting them out beyond its gated communities.

We believed they were safely penned in the deserted heart of cities, but here they are—on CNN.

People said to themselves: leave it to the aesthetes of old Europe to marvel at the spirit of a New Orleans that for us has been for a long time now nothing but a cesspool, a ghetto, a doomed city, at most, a regret—now the cesspool is invading the country's television screens; now this regret is the shame of America.

We thought they'd been reduced to statistics, but now the statistics have come to life.

We thought they were fossilised as sheer numbers, made abstract by dint of being so often repeated, but now the numbers have rebelled; at the very instant they are dying, the numbers are coming to life, incarnate in bodies and faces.

Katrina, or the paradoxical appearance of the invisible.

Katrina, or—with the help of the media—the sudden first surfacing of this Atlantis, since before the flood it had sunk beneath people's consciences: the continent of poverty.

The question of race

The question of these selfsame poor people who are also black people, about whom democratic America is discovering, again with shame, that their neglect is not unrelated to the colour of their skin.

I won't reconsider what I noted in my Alabama journal, about the path travelled over the past twenty years by the Old South.

I won't take back any of the genuine admiration I felt for a society that was able, in a very short time, to win the civil-rights battle begun by Martin Luther King.

And I will note, incidentally, that as revolting, as shameful, as *unpardonable* as those notorious four days remain (when men, women, and children were left to die—their only crime to have been born on the wrong side of the ethnic fence) those very days were followed by an outburst of energy—all in all a slightly better response, you'll agree, than that to the 1927 flood, when black neighbourhoods were completely inundated in order to reduce the pressure on white neighbourhoods....

Still.

Those faces of frightened poor people were black faces.

Those corpses floating in the current like dead dogs were black corpses.

Black, too, those survivors dying of hunger, thirst, and fatigue, on the road that should have led them to Baton Rouge, while they waited for buses that never came.

Death, on September 11, struck indiscriminately.

It didn't make exceptions for individuals, let alone races.

Here, it wrote up lists.

It selected its clients.

It revived the spirit and the letter of segregation, which we thought had been stifled along with the thing itself.

And that is why it is right to say both that the hurricane of August 28 is an 'anti-9/11' (Ross Douthat, in *The Atlantic Monthly*) and that this original sin of America that is the methodical humiliation of the black community is far from expiated (Jim Carrier, Morris Dees—let us praise these good men).

Katrina's other lesson

The violence. This violence, too, is not exclusive to contemporary America.

And we know, at least since Freud's *Civilisation and its Discontents*, that civil peace is never, in all societies of this world, anything but a thin layer, a froth, on the surface of savagery.

But what is (was?) perhaps unique to the United States is, here again, its rejection of the bluntly evident.

What struck me, in any case, on each stage of this journey, was the extraordinary use of language and rules, rhetorical courtesies and at times absurd formal constraints, designed to confine, domesticate, banish, and basically deny this inherent savagery and drive it away into limbo.

Well, here the shock is equally brutal.

Here, too, Katrina will have the twofold effect of both chipping off the veneer and opening America's eyes.

The violence of the Rich and the White fleeing the city, every-man-for-himself, just as you flee a rabid animal.

Violence of society's outcasts, poor and black, destroying what was left of their own city with the same kind of strangely desperate anger I witnessed in the ghost towns of the forgotten wars of Africa and Asia.

Violence of the policemen, deployed to assist people but whose first reflex was often to attack and even shoot—and violence of those National Guard members we watched in their Humvees, clutching their weapons, spontaneously rediscovering the gestures of war while dealing with fellow citizens they were meant to protect.

Violence, finally, of those images of corpses that were, we remember, the chief undisputed taboo in the wake of the 9/11 attacks—but here, too, the levees gave way; here, too, the barriers broke down; and here, too, it's the terribly brutal and possibly devastating return of one of the most stubborn 'represseds' in America's consciousness.

A moral and symbolic Ground Zero.

Worse: a kind of Ground Minus-One, where it's the social bond itself that is breaking.

Hobbes against Tocqueville.

Mad Max versus *Mr. Smith Goes to Washington.*

Hobbes's illustrious state of nature that is, in general, only a hypothesis, a fiction—and then in the space of a few hours you'd think it was actually there, a reality risen from the depths.

Except that it was not that state of nature, obviously.

It was the—alas, social—state of an America that I had sometimes suspected, in Fort Worth for instance, at that gun show the Texas comptroller sent me to, has a core of latent ferocity that has never been fully tamed. But there it is.

Just as 9/11 revealed the country's vulnerability to foreign attacks, so the anti-9/11 has unearthed yet another, inner, vulnerability, which American society didn't want to know anything about either: a vulnerability that is all the more treacherous since, this time, it put on the mask of violence.

The limits of compassion

The frailty, thus the limits, of the compassionate response the

United States has always tended to privilege when a natural and, logically, social catastrophe occurs.

This compassionate behaviour has its virtues, no doubt.

And we observed clearly, in New Orleans, that the main virtue of American compassion was the manner in which it set in motion mechanisms of solidarity that ought to have stunned the world as much as the disaster itself: a retired politician chartering two planes to provide the Superdome with supplies; actors wading through the water, or crouching in boats, to bring food and clothing to stranded old men; a television anchorwoman mobilizing money and friends to make up for government inadequacies; churches, starting with the powerful Second Baptist Church, taking over the national fund-raising effort headed by two ex-presidents; a chain of stores—the very symbol, theoretically, of 'antisocial' America—donating by itself alone as much as the entire country donated a year ago to the victims of the tsunami in Asia; the inhabitants of Houston, Texas, opening their arms to hundreds of thousands of refugees flowing into their schools, their hospitals, their houses—this generous impulse, this multiplication of gestures the likes of which I've never seen in any other country—yes, they certainly are illustrations of the noblest and best the system can produce.

But is that enough?

Faced with a calamity of this magnitude, can relief be left to the goodwill of people alone?

Isn't there a threshold of distress beyond which you'd like to see the authorities recall that it is also their duty to protect their citizens?

And especially—especially—if charity manifestly works wonders *afterward*, isn't it terribly impotent *beforehand*? If no one could do any better than the most popular of former presidents in raising money for the victims once the catastrophe had already occurred, wasn't it the role of the president in charge to watch over the levees, the locks, the evacuation and pumping systems that alone could have prevented this kind of catastrophe?

In short, in the eternal dilemma of charity versus justice or, if you prefer, of the law of the heart versus the law of concerted political action, hasn't the United States gone too far, way too far, in the direction of the former? And, faced with a neo-Darwinism that threatens and selects, this time not species but human beings, isn't it time—high time—to take a step in the other direction: the one that indicates that the government's most urgent task is to care for the well-being of its citizens?

Those are the other—altogether straightforward—questions posed by Katrina.

Those are the issues that—just like the reflection on terrorism—should dominate discourse in the coming years in America.

And then, of course, the state.

This insistent questioning of the role of government that I continually discerned as I spoke to doctors in Rochester, or to the wife and sister of miners in Grand Junction; faced with the ruined cities of the North and the preposterous masses of homeless and destitutes in Las Vegas and Los Angeles—this question, or rather, this *answer*, is the methodical weakening of government that the neoconservatives have sought for twenty years, and which has now, perhaps, after Katrina, run into its first check.

Not long before my stay in the Cajun city, in order to better understand how societies dependent on great rivers actually function, I reread that classic from my youth *Oriental Despotism*, by Karl August Wittfogel, which established the correlation between the mastery of rivers and the birth of empires.

So I flew over the Mississippi in the light of day; I watched that immense and menacing delta; I surveyed those neighbourhoods that were already wrecked, and I plainly saw, as all honest observers do, and as the journalists, principally of *The Times-*

Picayune, have been writing about for years, that one final flood would, of necessity, wind up submerging them.

And then I meditated on the luminous 'hydraulic hypothesis' of the brilliant geographer who, in that same book, and later in the polemics that pitted him against Arnold Toynbee in the 1950s, turned the regulation of rivers, the control of their unstable and turbulent waters, the damming, in a word, of that other 'boundlessness,' that other form of 'hubris,' that is the ever possible explosion of nature in its aquatic form, into the basis not just for despotism but for the birth of great governments and, more generally, of politics.

Does this mean that the United States had no other option but despotism in confronting, yesterday in Louisiana and tomorrow in Florida, a particularly wild and hostile nature?

Obviously not.

And incidentally, I am careful not to forget that, faced with this very ancient dilemma of anarchy versus despotic control, the United States devised a third response, fashioned out of liberty and courage, that is called, quite simply, the pioneering spirit.

But this surely signifies, when all is said and done, that the United States now has the obligation—if it wants to grant itself an additional chance of limiting the limitlessness of catastrophes—to reinforce its systems of early warning and prevention.

It signifies that, since the least deficient levees were often the ones built and certified by the federal government, America is summoned, here and elsewhere, to reinforce its institutions and hence, whether it likes it or not, its apparatus of government.

Last, since government in America exists on many different levels, all of which entered into a head-on and suicidal collision in New Orleans, this signifies that it's the entire balance of power, as the American ideology of the last twenty years has measured it out, that crumbled along with the levees of Lake

Pontchartrain—a balance that must be re-arbitrated, urgently, in favour of federal authority.

This debate is as old as the United States.

It dates back to the old division between the federalists and the anti-federalists, at the time of the first New England colonies.

It traces back to the conflict between the Hamiltonians and the Jeffersonians (to revert one last time to the Roman paradigm: Brutus and Caesar, Cato and Cicero…), as the Philadelphia Assembly had provisionally outlined it.

This means that there is, in the philosophical and political heritage of America, all the vibrant material—concepts, traditions, practices—essential to taking up the challenge; this means that the America of Washington, Roosevelt, and Kennedy is indeed finely equipped to deal with the great intellectual and moral reform that will allow it, without renouncing any fraction of its identity, to revive its reasons for believing in itself.

En Route!

FOR A LONG time, Alexis de Tocqueville was perceived, in my country, as a second-rate author.

For a long time, a very long time, this apostle of freethinking was hardly taught in French universities. Had we realised his importance earlier on, this prophet of the anti-totalitarian trends of the end of the twentieth century, precursor of Hannah Arendt, herald of freedom, might have saved us precious days and kept us from a fair number of pointless debates.

And the fact is that I spent the first half of my life regarding this theorist—who also happened to be a fine writer—as most of my contemporaries did: as an old-fashioned, hiccupping aristocrat, an adept of lukewarm thinking and happy half-ways, a quibbling, over-scrupulous dilettante, a moaning 'sensitive', a sad Narcissus, a boring, reactionary public intellectual, a sententious activist, an intellectual who amused himself by posing as a writer, a failed politician, a pale imitator of Montesquieu, a lightweight version of his uncle Chateaubriand (who seemed to have pre-empted the entire gamut of attractive roles), the author of a *Recollections* that could only be read as proof of a forgettable era and, prior to that, of the long account of a journey that had almost immediately fallen into the void destined for topical writing.

Times, of course, would change. With the collapse of grand political theories, the decline of the materialist visions of the world and their rigid, simple mechanisms, the need, above all, to reflect on the failure of socialism, on the desirability of the idea of revolution itself, and on the possibilities of democratic renewal, French intellectual attitudes would change and grow closer to a form of thinking that was to break our sterile deadlock with the inheritors of the ideas of Auguste Comte and Karl Marx.

But for a long time indeed, this was the case.

For my generation at least, for someone who came to philosophy near the end of the 1960s, at a moment of ideology strongly dominated by radicalism and Marxism—for someone who, like me, was twenty years old in a France where the last word in fashionable thought was Mao Tse-tung and where the new spirit, expressed with boldness, intellectual and political weight, obstinacy, combined revolt with structuralism, freedom of thought with abstract anti-humanism, for the witnesses of this pivotal moment, at once ferocious and unyielding (the prevailing mood of our youth), for people like us—ignorance of Tocqueville, this moderate spirit straddling the Old World and the New, the Orléans and the Bourbons factions, resignation to democracy and fear of revolution, was, I'm afraid, the norm.

I knew much less about him than did Americans of average education and background who had, for a century, recognised in *Democracy in America* not just a monument, not just a manual or handbook, but a kind of mirror where, as in westerns, as in Griffith's film *Birth of a Nation*, as at Mount Rushmore, they judge their virtues, their vices, the noble or ominous temptations that beckon, their auspicious birth, their future.

And this is also to serve as a warning that even if I plunged into his texts right away, even if I took the time, before setting out, to go over my predecessor's itinerary, even if my new-found interest, my wish to make up for lost time, as well as my desire to see this excellent mind at work, all led me to take up not just his book but his notes, his correspondence, his accounts of travels to Algeria, to England, to Switzerland, as well as the writings of his companion on this venture, Gustave de Beaumont—even so, you must not, alas, expect this book to honour Tocqueville to the letter. Times have changed too much. The country has become too different from what it was when America ended at the shores of the Mississippi. And I myself, once again, am too fresh an admirer of Tocqueville for my account, my travelogue, my daily journal, to be read as the reply, the extension, even the continuation or addition, of his famous example.

At the very most, whenever it was possible, I repeated some of the stages of his journey—for instance, the investigation into prisons that was the official pretext for Tocqueville and Beaumont's journey and which I set about updating. There are several prisons in this text. Five, to be exact. And a sixth one, Guantánamo, which, as we'll see, is not unconnected to the other five. And whose most revolting and unacceptable characteristics can quite quickly be explained by the general prison regime that I was able to observe elsewhere and that says much, unfortunately, about contemporary America.

I know that the idea of interrogating a penal system and expecting it to provide you with answers about the nature of the society that has bred it, the pattern of thought that seeks to expose the secret workings of a society by examining not just what it hides but the way in which it hides it and, once it has hidden it, excludes it—I know that all of this has to do with a typically modern view of things, one that is based on Foucault, and Nietzsche, and one that doesn't need Tocqueville for its formulation or execution. But in the end I still believe the two are intrinsically related.

I don't think I would have lingered for so long in New York's high-security prisons, in the ruins of Alcatraz, or in the corridors of death row in Nevada and Louisiana if I hadn't had in mind the Tocquevillean precedent. I don't think I would have spent so much time, from the Quaker-inspired penitentiary in Pennsylvania to the camps at Guantánamo Bay, exploring the other side of the American scene, without this discipline—a rather formulaic one, of course, but one that, like all formal constraints, may have served as an effective instrument for seeking truth and meaning.

I also armed myself, whenever appropriate, with some of Tocqueville's insights—so extraordinarily far-sighted—which I tested, book in hand, to see swiftly confirmed by American reality. The triumph—which in his time hadn't yet fully played out—of equality over liberty. The tyranny of the majority, which he was the first to point out and which isn't any less fierce than other forms of dictatorship. The 'pressure,' to phrase it differently (and especially to put it in words that, as I now see, could be those of the 'identitarian' America of today), 'of the minds of all on the intelligence of each,' of the group or ethnic mentality over citizens' 'freedom of action.' And, on the other hand, the new layer of 'individualism' that (as it reaches its culmination, letting people become intoxicated by their independence rather than their powers, as it spurs them to sever the ties that bind them to one another and to the body politic, as it reduces them to the 'innumerable crowd of men, all alike and equal, turned in upon themselves in a restless search for those petty, vulgar pleasures with which they fill their souls' that the end of *Democracy in America* glimpsed and that I found again in malls, megachurches, and leagues of virtue) risks turning into a dictatorship whose 'immense, protective power,' as 'absolute' as it is 'meticulous,' as 'ordered' as it is 'provident and kindly disposed,' 'seeks only to keep them in perpetual childhood,' and eventually removes from them even the 'bother of thinking' and the 'troubles of life.'

It would be absurd for me not to admit how endlessly vivid and present these theories were in my mind. Theories whose almost palpable presence in contemporary America is at times so blinding that you might accept the inferences from which, they say, reality draws its inspiration, not vice versa. All these theories—you might even say these fables or these myths— which you sense didn't so much foretell America as actually shape it.

And then, of course, there is a certain kind of style. A way— Tocquevillean once again—of trying to mingle what is seen with what is thought, the visible flesh of facts with their secret code, the text we can glean from institutions with the more arcane principle that forms their structure, as in Aristotle or Montesquieu. A way to relinquish oneself methodically without, however, rejecting one's own view of the world. Above all, a way to go from one subject to the next, not to dismiss, *a priori*, any incident or observation, and to find in a fact of daily life, or in a debate of ideas, in the dreary poetry of a motel or a highway just as in a meeting with a writer or a high-ranking member of the administration or the entertainment industry, the equally fertile substance of reflection. The determination, if you like, to write a flowing, variegated, and, at the same time, obsessive book whose style I do owe to the man who, in a letter to his cousin Comte Molé, described his America as 'a forest with a thousand roads' all converging on 'one single point' and who, at the very instant he seemed to be wandering, dawdling, or giving way to the rewarding demon of curiosity and chance, didn't stop bending what he saw to the rigorous logic of relevance and meaning.

Isn't the author of the two volumes of *Democracy in America* the inventor, after all, of this modern form of reportage where attention to detail, the taste for personal encounters and circumstances, did not preclude—quite the contrary, made possible—faithfulness to a fixed idea? Isn't Tocqueville the prototype of those 'philosopher-travellers,' as Jean-Jacques Rousseau calls them in a famous note in *Discourse on the Origin of Inequality*, whose entire art consists of drawing valid links between the slightest vicissitudes of a journey in an unknown country and the eternal (or new) principles of what was then not yet called sociology? Was there a better guide to lead me in America?

Nonetheless, the questions, for the main part, are my own. I went to answer questions that are about us all just as Tocqueville took to the road in the United States to try to answer questions raised by the situation of France in his time; just as he travelled there to discover and explain the 'inexplicable vertigo' that was, for his contemporary Benjamin Constant, unique to the Reign of Terror; just as his concern was to go and look in the colonies of New England for the chemically pure form of this 'democratic revolution' whose irresistible triumph he felt he was experiencing, in Great Britain but especially in France; and just as, finally, his great concern, once this form was identified, was to distinguish between the two paths liable to lead a people 'to slavery or freedom, to enlightenment or barbarism, to prosperity or wretchedness.'

First and foremost, the unsavoury and ancient French and largely European passion that is known as anti-Americanism and that was—when I undertook this journey—sweeping through European public opinion as never before. It's one thing to acknowledge this, to denounce the absurdity of a way of thinking that turns the United States into a symbol, a cliché, as well as a scapegoat for the mistakes, insufficiencies, and inconsistencies of other countries.

It's one thing to laugh (for you do have to laugh about it) at the monomaniacs who, when war is ravaging Darfur, when hundreds of thousands of men, women, and children are dying of hunger in Sri Lanka or Niger, when the neo-Talibans are humiliating the women of their Afghan villages, when the Pakistani Islamic fundamentalists prefer to burn women alive and call it a crime of honour, when the incompetent and corrupt leaders of the poorest countries bleed their own people dry and sacrifice them for their mediocre interests—when confronted with all this, can do nothing but repeat, like mindless machines: 'Blame the United States!'

One and the same thing to study the origins of a virus that, before entering the bloodstream (that is to say, the language) of a people, began with a long—very long—process of osmosis, passing through the laboratory of scholars (Buffon linking corruption of souls and bodies in the New World to the excessive humidity of its climate), the writers' cabinet (Drieu la Rochelle, Céline, Bernanos, so many others, denigrators of an 'internal America' thriving 'inside people's heads,' which, from the 1930s to the present, was one of the most frequent commonplaces of the literary right and the extreme right), and the library of philosophers (the great Heidegger denouncing, while cleaving to Nazism, that 'emergence' of 'monstrosity' in 'modern times' which, according to him, was the birth of the United States).

In other words, it's one thing to show that anti-Americanism has in Europe always gone hand in glove with our baser instincts and that it is now, at the beginning of the twenty-first century, becoming the most powerful 'magnet of the worst' for all the abandoned theories, all those little dark stars fallen from doctrinaire galaxies, all that scattered debris, the directionless iron filings in search of a new pole.

One thing to show that anti-Americanism *has* become the magnet that was missing since the collapse of the totalitarian megatheories; and now, in Europe, in the Arab world, in an entire region of Asia, in Latin America, is unleashing chauvinism, hegemonism, the thirst for purity, ethnocentrism, racism, anti-Semitism, and of course fundamentalism.

But it's altogether *another* thing to go out into the field, to judge on actual evidence; it's another thing to contrast that chimera with the concrete body and face of America today. At times, this face will be rather flattering. At times, it will prove more unfavourable and, for friends of America, disappointing and despairing. But at least it will have the merit of no longer being imaginary. At least it will break, or try to break, with Manichaeanism, essentialism, and the reign of clichés. That, from my point of view, is the main, most honest, and, especially, most effective response to the anti-American phantasmagoria.

Then there is the question of Europe. Not the question of the image of America in Europe, or even of Europe in America, but the question of the role reserved for Europe, for its culture and its values, in contemporary America.

We know how determined the Founding Fathers were to detach themselves from Europe. We know—Tocqueville, in the introduction to his book, insists on it—that the whole idea of these pioneers who had failed, in England, then in Holland, to create the city of their dreams was to separate 'the democratic from all those other principles it had to contend with in the old communities of Europe,' to 'transplant' it to the supposedly virgin territories of the 'New World' and there, in that laboratory, greenhouse, new land untouched by the corruptions of history, to allow it to 'grow freely.'

But we also know that since then, America has never stopped wavering between two poles, two aims, and, at core, two identities. At times: 'We are the inventors of a civilisation that owes nothing to anyone else and which will be an anti-Europe.' At times: 'Just as Polybius said that Rome would remain a Hellenic power, we were Europeans, and we know we have no other choice but to remain so.' At times even, just after the Second World War, when the Soviet empire's offensives had to be thwarted: 'Europe is what is at stake for America; Europe is an American idea; we Americans of the Marshall Plan era are the true founding fathers of a Europe that has been saved from disaster and abjection.'

So where do we stand now, today, in this debate that is as old as the United States? What does the country think about its European component now that its immigration has become mostly Hispanic and Asian? Does the idea of the West still have any meaning now that the Cold War is over and now that, faced with new threats, faced with the new war heralded by terrorism, the two allies seem to be standing on separate ground and holding to distinct, sometimes divergent strategies? And what should we think of the denunciations aimed at 'old Europe' (a phrase of Hegel's, from a passage of *Reason in History* where he mentions Napoleon's famous quip 'this old Europe bores me,' as well as 'those wearied by the historical bric-a-brac of old Europe') by those 'neoconservative' American intellectuals who have taken up so much space in the public debate and in the workings of government—and taken so many places in the French and European political bestiary? [When they call, with such senseless rage, for dissociating themselves from a spineless, feminine Europe, immoral and corrupt, daughter of Venus and sister of the most abominable dictatorships, when they call attention to its allegedly dishonest compromises, first with the wardens of Soviet prison camps, then with Saddam Hussein's Baathists, and now with the proconsuls of the Axis of Evil, is it just a matter of ill humour, a convenient quarrel—or is it the manifestation of a more profound rift? For whoever believes in the universality of the European message; for whoever considers Europe as the theatre of the most horrific massacres in history as well as the paradoxical wellspring of discourses that have allowed these massacres to be reflected upon and that might, tomorrow, make it possible to avert their repetition; for the upholders of a Europe understood as a faith born, as Husserl wrote, from the idea of reason and the spirit of philosophy, this question is an essential one. It is essential for an America that, had it to turn its back finally or even for a long time on its European source, would lose a portion of its memory, a part of its soul. But it is also essential for Europe, which, if it lost its American resource, if this chance, celebrated by Goethe, of seeing its own history begin again in American liberty were to fade, if it lost sight of this American model that is, in its moments of doubt, the only tangible proof that its own supranational dream is neither a piece of nonsense nor an unattainable ideal, would lose a little of its reasons for belief and, hence, a little of its motivating force: its famous constitutional patriotism, its aim of adding to everyone's national feeling the liberating allegiance to an Idea—what warrant do these notions have, in reality, other than the living evidence of America?]

Then there is one final question. Perhaps, considering the time chosen for my journey, it is really the main one. What shape is this democracy in, the one Americans (with good cause) are so proud of and which they have always wanted to hold up as an example for the rest of the world? Some voices are being raised in the country to denounce the attacks on constitutional rights brought about by the struggle against terrorism, infringements to which public opinion—drugged on patriotism, stunned by the 9/11 attacks—is increasingly reconciling itself. Other voices—or perhaps the same ones—worry about the series of micro-shifts that, even before 9/11, began to affect the fragile equilibrium of the executive, legislative, and judicial powers (here, an abuse of power... there, the excessive zeal of an intelligence organisation... or else the problematic and suspicious crusade of an independent prosecutor hot on the trail of a libertine president...). Still others say they are witnessing the implementation—insidious but relentless—of both immense and minute mechanisms of surveillance, whose triumph, should it come about, would prove Tocqueville right,

not to mention Foucault and Nietzsche, who saw in the prolif-
eration of laws transforming any attempted divergence from the
collective norm into a criminal offence the sign of either a
world without desire or of a deliquescent sovereignty or both.
All of this would be nothing, the worst pessimists add, if those
people whose profession it is to monitor these tendencies and
think critically about them weren't themselves the object of unprecedented disciplinary actions—all of this would be less
important if the American press, that model, that beacon, wasn't
undergoing a crisis in which it isn't clear which weighs more
heavily: acquiescence to the big lobbies, especially the lobby of
money; the temptation of self-censorship in the face of government propaganda; the personal risk journalists take when, protecting their sources, they remain faithful to the rules of their
profession; or (when the press too easily becomes the echo of a
politics reduced to scandal), assenting to the vilest tendencies of
our times. And I am not speaking here about that cancer of
poverty that is ravaging so many American cities, which the
federal government seems to lack both the means and, especially, the will to cure. And I am not speaking either of that
onslaught of moral values, that neopuritan wave, that obsession
with belonging and transparency, that could, according to some,
be well in the process of becoming a new mode of American
citizenship. I am not talking about those right-thinking activists,
those militiamen of Virtue and Order, those witch-hunters of a
new Salem, extended throughout America who are coming to
preach the end not of history but of the world and, in this end-
of-the-world perspective, general mobilisation, an aligning of
minds, and, in sum, an internal holy war. So what about this
democracy? What should we think about this debate? Has the
model broken down? Is democracy ill? Is America at a new
turning point of its history, as it was during the Civil War, the
Great Depression, and the New Deal? is it the tyranny of the
majority that threatens? Or of minorities? And aren't they both

one and the same thing? The same model, one a miniature? When the latter use the language of the former, when their style, their reproaches, their ways of imposing their canons and constraining the recalcitrant to toe the line, are inspired by the example of the majority and eager to duplicate it, isn't it at bottom the same danger? What of American exceptionalism, in this case? What has happened to the wild but inspiring dream of building a model republic in keeping with the manifest destiny of a people no less admirable? In short, have we returned to the dark days when Sartre, friend of John Huston and John Dos Passos, lover of Manhattan and its skyscrapers, admirer of the American way of life and its programmatic wrenching away from the evil demon of roots and origins, exclaimed, in the midst of McCarthyism: 'L'Amérique a la rage' ('America is sick with rabies')? Just as another great writer, Thomas Mann, a few years earlier, in a historical context obviously not comparable, notoriously warned 'Europe, beware,' should we, today, advise our American friends to watch out for this America that has inspired the world's esteem, fought fascism and communism, but might be starting to show, by its own admission, signs of weariness? Should we remember—and, if need be, remind our friends—that there is no example yet of a civilisation that has survived entering into what Walt Whitman called the 'Sahara of the soul'?

These are the questions.

They made up my implicit checklist of topics for a journey that lasted, by chance, almost exactly as long as Tocqueville and Beaumont's own (but with pauses and short journeys back to France).

To which, for the sake of accuracy, it might be useful to add a few other concerns, less American but no less Tocquevillean. The instant distaste, for example, that seemed to affect the idea of and even the word *liberalism* during the very same period in France, in the heated debates over the adoption or rejection of a European constitution. [It was a long time in forming, of course. This hatred of liberalism as such, this strange semantic reversal, the transformation into a mark of infamy of this fine word used by the Carbonari and French revolutionaries during Tocqueville's time, is an old, sombre story that dates back to the last years of the nineteenth century, at the time of the first wave of French anti-Semitism and fascism. But still… Noting the migration of this old, obsessive theme from the extreme right over to the other side, then hearing a good half of the French left take up the cliché, whose despicable undertones you didn't need to be keen of hearing to detect, then seeing this faction of the left shamelessly liquidating in this way the entire wealth of popular, and even revolutionary memory, from which liberalism—the word and the phenomenon—drew its true substance, thus witnessing once again, just as with anti-Americanism, just as with anti-Semitism, one of those crossovers France is so adept at, was terribly disturbing. And this disarray, seen from America—that is to say, from a country where both the word and the phenomenon have followed their semantic and conceptual career, have been improved, enriched, and, in the end, metamorphosed—was all the more distressing, and yet, in a way, more intelligible.]

The method would be as simple as the questions and concerns were complex: the road, essentially.

From east to west, from north to south, then from south to south, then north through Texas, Arkansas, the mythic cities of Tennessee, the two Carolinas, Virginia, the states of New England, this road—*hodos* in Greek, which has given us *method*, from *metahodos*, literally 'along the road'—which another writer, this time an American, Jack Kerouac, has shown is not the worst method for capturing the reality of the country: provided you travel it as he did; provided you put yourself in the same spiritual and perhaps physical mood as his; provided, for instance, you stay, as he recommends, well to the right of the driver and try to adhere bodily, almost sensually, to the ribbon of miles that unfurls beneath your wheels; provided you devour the miles as the biblical prophets prompted us to devour the Word of God. (Aren't road and language, after all, humanity's siblings? Isn't it when both roads and languages are invented that commerce, mediation, civilisation, begin?)

Of course I can't compare a modern journey like mine, monitored, from Washington, D.C., by vigilant assistants, to the presituationist driftings of the celestial tramps, semi-outcasts, and angels of desolation of the beat generation.

And truthfulness obliges me to say that I made some notable exceptions to the rule of the road: a flight over the Mexican border; another over the Nevada deserts; yet another over the Mississippi delta, then over an oil rig out in the gulf of Mexico; a sudden meeting that forced me to retrace my steps or skip a stop; three days in Guantánamo; attending the conventions of an electoral campaign that coincided with this plunge into the American heartland and that, even if the campaign wasn't in any way my main concern, sometimes imposed its own schedule on me.

But that is essentially how things happened.

These fifteen thousand miles of slow travel were made by road, through the fabric of a nation that, like so many Americans, I quickly realised I didn't know all that well. Roads great and small; mythic roads and forgotten roads; Route 101 from the Oregon border to the Mexican frontier; Route 1, Robert Kramer's road, but taken backward, toward Florida; Route 49, along the Sierra Nevada; Route 61, from north to south; Route 66, or at least what's left of it, west of the Grand Canyon, where the phantoms of *The Grapes of Wrath* still hover; numbered roads; official roads; roads that have been paved, planned, and standardised and roads that, whether they run alongside the Mississippi or the Pacific, whether they cross the hills of Nebraska, the pine forests and gorges of Colorado or the stone gardens, mounds of sculpted granite, and sudden dust storms of the South Dakota plains, all reinvent their landscapes, resketch their borders, and appear once again almost exotic; this endless intermeshing of roads that I sometimes feel, along with the railroad, made the United States, made them united and, at the same time, helped preserve the country's uncompromising and vigorous diversity....

I mention Kerouac. But I could also have mentioned film-makers. I could have mentioned Wim Wenders. Or the Hitchcock of *North by Northwest*. Or *Easy Rider*. Or *Vanishing Point*. Or even, but at greater length, Kramer's film *Route One/USA*. I could, in fact, have mentioned any one of those road movies that, much more than Tocqueville, much more than any European essayist, have shaped my imagination of America as well, I think, as that of an entire generation born after the Second World War. And I could also have quoted the H.D. Thoreau of the 'old, meandering, dry, uninhabited roads, which lead away from towns.' Or the Whitman who, 'afoot and light-hearted,' takes 'to the open road' on this 'rude, silent, incomprehensible' earth. Or even Nabokov, claiming that the car is 'the only place in America with no noise and no draft,' which is why he so liked to travel by automobile.

If I mention Kerouac, then, if I immediately thought of Kerouac when I arrived, for instance, in San Francisco, if *On the Road* was, from one end of my journey to the other, a service-able and secret guidebook, it's because proceeding thus, taking the time, like him, to cross this country on the ground, following these four-lane ribbons, these lifelines of the landscape, merging with the tongues of asphalt and sometimes, in the desert, the tongues of fire that are American roads, choosing, in other words, the paths that seem at first the longest, offered an entire range of advantages that, for a writer, soon turned out to be decisive.

It's the possibility of daydreaming.

It's an exercise in pace and patience.

It's a way of entering into that trancelike state, that alert and vigilant lethargy that lovers of high speeds know, that makes one all the more receptive to the sudden appearance of the unexpected.

While flying in an airplane abolishes time and distance, while it puts you in immediate touch with a point of arrival that is never really foreshadowed, while the train itself is, in Proust's words, a 'magical' vehicle that transports you as though by enchantment, with almost no effort or gradation, from Paris to Florence and elsewhere, this journey, this long, enduring journey by car, this ground-level journey that spares you nothing of the tectonics of space and hence of time, allows the traveller to experience a mode of the finite that alone can allow him to come to terms with the finitude of landscapes and faces.

Or rather: by yielding that sense of distance and gravity of places back to the traveller; by adding to that a sense of immensity, previously inconceivable; by pursuing a frontier that seems to keep hiding, growing ever more distant as he approaches it; by a continuous alternation of deserts, mountains, plains inhabited and deserted, huge cities and makeshift villages, more deserts, Indian reservations, parks; finally, by playing remorselessly on this yearning for freedom that, in most modern modes of travel, lingers only as an improbable memory, this kind of journey has the additional merit of offering a reminiscence, a kind of condensation, of the great founding myths of the American nation: land promised and refused, lines of escape, shimmering horizons, the wall of the Pacific, the American dream—the last chance, in this world, to have even a whiff of that rite-of-passage experience that for centuries was the discovery, by each individual, of America.

And then, finally, choosing asphalt rather than flight and the thoughts that go with flight, riding 'the white line in the holy road' (Kerouac again) 'to a nonexistent destination,' rolling along, not letting yourself be discouraged either by those supermarkets of sleep that the motels of the past have become or by those Potemkin villages that, from time to time, between two franchised feeding machines, are meant to reinject a little actual humanity into a space that tends to neutral impersonality, riding on, always riding—isn't that form of travel the only one suitable for a writer: wandering along, dallying, going somewhere and nowhere at the same time, hesitating, testing the wind, letting chance flirt with you, improvising?

There wasn't much actual logistical preparation for this journey.

Aside from a general itinerary glanced at before leaving, which I'm not even sure I kept to all that scrupulously, there wasn't much organisation; little premeditation; not too many preordained appointments, organised well in advance from afar; or, if there were, they were a beginning, not an end; a point of entrance, never of completion; a trick to tame the place and, afterward, lose yourself in it.

One day, the shock of an anonymous face.

Another, the 'devouring haste' of a suburbanised urban landscape.

Another, an incident; an accident at first stripped of meaning; a Tocquevillean policeman demonstrating that the American road has also, alas, become a place of choice for the insane injunction to 'keep moving'; the disturbing strangeness of a cliché; a scene of daily life, seemingly ordinary or, rather, infra-ordinary—a poor, laughable county fair in what Gustave Flaubert called 'the litter of the everyday.'

Still another, a meeting with an anti-Semitic Indian chief; a childlike archdemagogue who happens to be president; a would-be future president; a Hollywood star talking away like a politician; a writer mistaking himself for an Indian; a clarinet-playing filmmaker; a waitress at a bar singing, in a low voice, the black sun of her cursed existence; a tycoon; a poor white man in New Orleans; a Louisiana journalist predicting an imminent flood; an evangelical zealot of God; a severe, enlightened higher-up in the Mormon Church—all of them leading roles in the prodigious human comedy that is also America; the colour-studded, larger-than-life characters of the great permanent performance it has always offered—a show that seems less likely than ever to shut down.

And then yet another: nothing; a sensation; an impression; the vision, like a lamp floating in a pink sky, of the tip of Seattle's first skyscraper; the friendly spirits of Savannah; the dreamy sensuality of a young girl in San Diego; the new, endless light of the Los Angeles freeway; a conversation in a countryside brothel on the edge of Death Valley; the ghost of a gold prospector; the impalpable, almost unfindable, but all the more tragic traces of Fitzgerald and Hemingway; a jazz tune in New Orleans; a storm in Florida; the good, cheerful presence of a lifelong companion; a minister in Birmingham crying as he remembered the civil-rights struggles; the tumult of song rising to the rafters of another church, in Memphis; a sentence left unfinished; a sign not necessarily decoded; all these miraculous or malicious nothings, sometimes those moments of happiness that I have tried to capture in words and that form the other prize, in my eyes, of this journey.

Is it the route that creates the traffic or vice versa, asks Leopold Bloom in Joyce's *Ulysses*.

It's the road, in any case, that made this book. The road has made the method that in turn inspired this impossible portrait of America.

REFLECTIONS

What Does it Mean to be an American

THE FIRST QUESTION to emerge at the end of this journey is the question of American identity.

It was the question posed by Samuel Huntington in the book he and I discussed in Boston. Looking back, I see he has recycled the most hackneyed commonplaces of the beginning of the twentieth century about the 'amorphous, heterogeneous mob' of 'Latin-Slavs' and 'Jews from the East' who were flocking to corrupt 'the political and moral personality of the United States': Who are we? What remains of the old British Puritan credo that spawned our fine, noble nation? Are we a white or a mixed-race people? Mono- or multi-ethnic? And how will this nation resist the hordes of new Mexican immigrants that Huntington claims cannot be assimilated and that dream only of reclaiming the territories lost in the 1840s, by sheer force, in a new civil war?

This is the question posed by a whole series of other books, not as renowned or as skilful, but also not as dubious and certainly not bearing the mark of that historic nativism bred with both neo-Darwinism and racism that forms the accursed share of American ideology.

A whole series of books, in other words, that I saw, over many months, from city to city, spread out over all the local Barnes & Noble tables and that I sometimes have the impression—seeing them again in my mind's eye—contributed to the rhythm of this journey: America and its elections; America and its foundations; America and its Indians, its blacks, its associations; America at war; America and its myths; the red and the blue in America; the Hispanics and the Germans in American history; the myth of the frontier since the era of the frontier ceased to exist; Lewis and Clarke; Tocqueville; What Went Wrong in Ohio? What's the Matter with Kansas? Who are we, once again? What the hell is happening to us? What about our 'manifest destiny' in these times of turmoil in Iraq? What about our 'exceptionalism'? Or the message of the first Pilgrims? Or the mission of the Founding Fathers? What about our innocence? Our lost purity? So many books! Rarely has a country questioned itself so anxiously about its destiny; few are the nations prey to such a vertigo of identity.

And then there is an issue that leaps to the traveller's eyes, independently of this or that book, or even an avalanche of books. It's an issue that, at almost every step, at every stage of the journey through this mind-boggling, multifarious America, in the Old South that no longer knows what to make of its heritage and in the North stricken by post-industrial trauma, in the vast and small cities, in the well-off neighbourhoods and the dirt-poor ghettos, in the minds of the harpies of the neo-moral order as well as in the families of Wisconsin miners—wherever you go, in fact, the issue can be read between the lines, seen in men's and women's eyes, in the systems of social interaction, in the ways of working and loving of these myriad Americans who continue to be viewed as an elite people, sure of itself and domineering, whereas in reality no large modern nation today is as uncertain as this one, less sure of what it is becoming, less confident of the very values, that is to say, the myths, that founded it; it's a certain disorder; a disease; a wavering of points of reference and certainties; a *vertigo* once again that seizes the observer as well as the observed and in which, if I try to summarise it, I see at least three or four series of symptoms.

First symptom: the derangement of the mechanisms of memorialisation, which I noted so many examples of, from the Baseball Hall of Fame in Cooperstown to the Henry Ford and William Randolph Hearst museums, the Dinosaur Park in Rapid City, the museum of petrified stones in the Badlands, the Pliosaurus excavation site in Deadwood, and John Kerry's instantaneously museumified plate of cheese in Des Moines. I am reminded of the distinction Nietzsche draws in his *Untimely Meditations* between the three principal types of memory: monumental, critical, and antiquarian. The first serves to reassure a people by presenting it with the elaborated and, one hopes, inalterable image of its past grandeur. The second fortifies it by subjecting this image to the harsh but just tribunal of scientific history. The third, meanwhile, the memory Nietzsche calls 'antiquarian,' which is linked to what is 'small, limited, crumbling, and archaic,' the memory that stems from a 'blind mania for collecting' and from 'a restless compiling together of everything that ever existed,' is a useless memory that instead of reinforcing the individual 'cripples the active man' and, 'whether it is a person or a people or a culture,' inexorably winds up in 'annihilation.'

Well, it's into this third scenario that the United States, with its ubiquitous halls of fame, appears to fall. These museums that frenetically stock up, places that combine everything and no longer discern what is worth being memorialised from what isn't, villages and county seats where they seem to have forgotten the liberating benefits of oblivion, and where one sinks down beneath the relics of almost anything at all—all of this is like a giant caricature of that 'insomnia,' that 'rumination'; Nietzsche also says that 'resentment,' or that spirit of 'revenge'—

that are the markers of 'antiquarian history.' This form of absurd, pathological memory, a memory that is both anxious and lazy, febrile and idle, a memory that is, at bottom, 'un-American' since, by a singular reversal of roles, it is in the process of turning that great America of the Enlightenment, the America about which Goethe wrote that it had freed itself both from its European past and from the European obsession with the past, into a country even more enslaved to the past than the most past-obsessed European countries: this memory, then, is a memory that, if the world resembled what philosophers say of it, if we followed Nietzsche to the conclusion of his most sombre premonitions, would turn into not the stimulus but the grave digger of the present time, and would be, for the American nation of today, a harbinger of identity crises at least as formidable as those actually symmetrical crises that stem from absolute non-memory and from a settling into that 'vegetative present' that Nietzsche's *Untimely Meditations* also speaks of, and which hypnotise peoples just as powerfully. How can the same country be home to both one of the most remarkable Holocaust memorials in the world and, alongside a South Dakota highway, a permanent exhibition of fossils supposed to call evolutionary theory into question? How can remorse for the Indians, the rightful obligation to remember the genocide and segregation of Indian tribes, the brash intolerance, the social and cultural desire of extermination, which continued to persecute them until quite recently—how can these contradictions come to be embodied in the admirable Smithsonian National Museum of the American Indian in Washington, while at the same time, throughout the desert states, a parade of phoney memorial sites, each more garish than the next, border the road: here the fake grave of a fake Lakota chief; there a reconstructed Oglala village; there again, a small exhibit of vintage Cheyenne feathers; then a pharmaceutical museum, a conservatory of thirty-million-year-old fossil trees, and a retire-

ment home for authentic wild horses, whose upkeep is sub-
sidised by the states of Oklahoma and Idaho—all of which
antiquarian piety ultimately places on the same level?

Another sign: obesity. Not the obesity of bodies obviously.
Not that notorious obesity that European anti-Americanism
regales itself with and that, as I observed in California, is no
more spectacular or worrisome here than anywhere else. But
another brand of obesity. A stranger obesity for which the
reputed expansion of bodies is perhaps only a metaphor as well
as a veil of flesh and smoke. A social obesity. An economic,
financial, and political obesity. Obesity of cities. Obesity of
malls, as in Minneapolis. Obesity of churches, as in Willow
Creek. Obesity of parking lots that, in these malls and churches,
sometimes grow so enormous that they generate a full-fledged
miniature society, an entire way of life with its own rhythms,
spaces, distraction and rest areas, cafeterias, shuttles, even—and
this takes the cake—specially organised shuttles so that, once
your vehicle is parked, shoppers or worshippers can be loaded
into yet another vehicle, thus saving them the trouble of
walking. Obesity of SUVs. Obesity of airports, too massive for
the cities they're designed to serve. Obesity of election
campaign budgets, too hefty to be completely spent. Obesity of
Hollywood box-office sales, constantly breaking previous
records and, once those records have been topped, interpreting
the exploit as a sure sign of the new film's quality. Obesity of
large memorials, like the one for Crazy Horse in Rapid City,
that make monumentality the main criterion for statuary excellence (even though, of course, political support doesn't
always follow). Obesity of enterprises subject to the law of
forced growth, or—but it comes down to the same thing—
Gordon Gekko's famous dictum, in *Wall Street*, twenty years
ago: 'Greed is good; greed is right; greed works; greed clarifies;
greed will save the United States.' Obesity, finally, of public
deficits, whose exponential progression—their example

stemming from the above—is becoming a warning flag thrown at the whole society. The bigger it is, the better it is, says America today. Large is beautiful, it repeats over and over in a kind of hysterical reversal of the 1960s slogan. A global, total obesity that spares no realm of life, public or private. An entire society that, from the top down, from one end to the other, seems prey to this obscure derangement that slowly causes an organism to swell, overflow, explode.

A nation that, like a group of women 'from eighteen to sixty' I read about in a Rochester paper who meet in their parish church to practice the celebrated 'First Place Diet' (a miracle diet that compels the body's excesses to toe the line, provided you put the Lord in first place), a nation, then, that, like these women who had reportedly 'lost control of their eating situation,' has lost control of its own situation—not just alimentary, bur mental, cultural, metaphysical; a nation, one feels, that has strayed from, or broken, that secret formula, that code, that prompts a body to stay within its limits and survive. The Greeks had a concept for this. They had a word—two, even—to describe bodies that have lost, or not yet found, their medium, their limit. *Hubris*, of course. That immoderation, excessiveness, force of stress and unreason, which Sophocles said the gods punish by death and about which Hobbes, twenty centuries later, asserted that by reducing 'felicity' to 'a continual progress of the desire from one object to another,' by describing 'a general inclination of all mankind' as 'a perpetual and restless desire of power after power,' leads, inevitably, to 'death.' And then, particularly, *apeiron*, that representation of the boundless that was, for the pre-Socratics, the principle of all things, their unengendered origin, the primeval chaos that makes those it brings into existence guilty and potentially monstrous (that is to say, literally, insufficiently provided with form)—and that became, in Plato, the other word, either for the indeterminate, the receptacle, the unnameable, pure and motiveless materiality, or for the tyrannical insatiability of desire and, hence, once again, for death.

Has America reached that point? Is it on the brink of that darkness? Its position in the world, its geopolitical hubris, the increasingly consumption-crazed and debt-laden personal lives of middle-class men and women—are they avatars of these ancient laws? Another symptom. Another sign. Another bad omen, if you're in a sombre mood, for contemporary American identity.

Third sign, indirectly linked to the preceding, but this time with consequences for the country's essential institutions. The chopping up of American social and political space; its increasing differentiation, some say its disintegration, its Balkanisation, its tribalisation—the transformation of America into a plural nation, a mosaic of communities, a rhapsody of ethnic groups and collectivities that make increasingly problematic the realisation of the venerable project set forth by a great writer—not Greek, this time, but Roman—and inscribed as the motto of the country: *E pluribus unum*. The phenomenon, I am well aware, is not a recent one. It has been studied at length by such scholars as Denis Lacorne, Gordon Wood, and Elise Marienstras. From the origin—the arrival, in fact—of the innumerable rival sects condemned to live together who disembarked in the British colonies of New Jersey, New York, and Pennsylvania, the problem was posed, this difficult dialectics of *pluribus* and *unum*, of the many and the one, the democrat and the republican. One has only to contemplate the liveliness of the debates that preceded the ratification of the Constitution; one has only to recall the virulence of the anti-Federalist dispute, the harangues of Jefferson and all those who, like him, were afraid of seeing the tyranny of a central government merely replace the English yoke from which the War of Independence had just freed young America; one has only to remember the great ideological battle launched by the heralds of the first American populism against the 'Republican' appropriation of the theories of Montesquieu, simply to convey a sense of how perennial the problem is.

What's new, however, is that what had once been one trend among many has become, two centuries later, the consensus. What the Hamilton-Madison-Jay trio had described as the 'evil of factions,' which everyone believed would in time be conquered, ultimately ended up conquering time, and now looms as a dominant component in American discourse and institutional practices. The novelty, and the reality, is that a certain number of events (one, especially—massive, colossal, a veritable cultural revolution born in the 1960s whose full effects we are still trying to decipher) have occurred over a period of twenty or thirty years, and have bestowed dignity and legitimacy on what was for a long time just one temptation among many, unsure of itself, at times ashamed. This massive event is the rise of minority-rights movements. It is, to paraphrase Chateaubriand, the 'revenge' of those members of the American people who, because of too long a humiliation, have been imbued with a desire to overassert their identity. It's the demand for reparation for the Indians, or for the blacks. It's that other great awakening stirring up communities who, not without reason, think American land is haunted land, peopled with their own martyred phantoms, covered with blood, their blood, which cries out for justice to be done. It's the semi-religious awakening—more religious, at any rate, than many so-called religious awakenings—that strikes entire groups of men and women professing, in a strange gesture that appears suddenly in line with all the great American eschatologies, that this world will be inhabitable for the living only when it has, at last, become inhabitable for their dead. It's the whole movement of affirmative action. It's political correctness and its whiff of grand historical retribution. And it carries in its wake, by mimicry, thanks to the familiar mechanism of rivalry for victim status, the insurrection of other minorities who, putting forward the real or imagined wrongs that were done to them, too, also demand reparation.

So it is minorities who, like the Hispanics, have no metaphysical wrong to deplore, no transhistoric outrage that demands expiation, but who follow the movement and, in the name of their cultural heritage, in the name of their language, their religious practice, their faith, or, of course, their actual distress, covet a piece of the identity pie as well. In short, it's a vast movement that is only imperfectly categorised as the 'right to difference' since, in this case, *competition* is as much at stake as *difference*. It's a problematic whose model of mimetic rivalry doesn't reveal the whole truth, either, since it's *also* a question of differences that are not competitive and that result in countless demands for unlimited rights, thus gnawing at public law and running the risk of dissolving the social bond. In the end, after a process that comes to an unnatural but logical completion, it's these artificial cities, these reservations for the rich and the old, these private, fortified spaces, these gated communities, whose prototype I saw in Sun City, Arizona, that might be foreshadowing a possible future for this country; it's that temptation of apartheid that, if nothing comes along to oppose it, might bring together in distinct enclaves not just those obsessed with security or a good climate but also Jews, gays, lesbians, dwarfs, the blind, and so forth, and that would bring crashing down, once and for all, the entire institutional edifice built by the delegates of the Constitutional Convention of 1787....

And finally, this last sign, which I'll bring up briefly, since I was so often reminded of it throughout my travels. The expansion, everywhere, of the gray zone, this social and civic no-man's-land, which is the realm of extreme poverty. I know, of course, that the concept doesn't have the same meaning in the United States that it has in Europe. I am aware that in the United States you're poor if your annual income is less than

$19,300—which, in a country like France, would correspond instead to lower-middle-class earnings. And I have read the statistics stating that half, or even two-thirds, of the thirty-seven million American 'poor' will not long remain that way and for now, at least, own their car or their housing. Still, the others remain. The last third, or second half, remain—I'm not sure where they stand in the statistics, but I personally can testify that they live in a universe where the very idea of owning a home or one day finding work is the stuff of mirages. These battered human wrecks remain, these people that society has determinedly cast off, who live in the dumpsters of the 'ungentrified' sections of Harlem, Boston, or Washington—these human beings who are all but excluded from reality. I kept coming across them as soon as I left the marked perimeters of Las Vegas, Los Angeles, or San Francisco, people who seem to have once and for all cut loose the moorings that tied them to the American Way of Life and its customs.

And, above all, there remain, from Rikers Island to the women's penitentiary in Nevada, those terrible American prisons. I realise with hindsight that the dread they roused in me was perhaps due less to their systems of detention (which are not so much worse, really, than those that hold sway in most of the countries in Europe, or in my own country, at least) than to the kind of inhabitants they seem now to be recruiting (a great many petty delinquents; many prisoners who have been charged but still await trial; many young blacks or Hispanics, out of work for a long time, pathetic drug users or dealers, immigrants of varying degrees of legality, without any rights—I'm not sure, now that I think about it, whether they would be in prison at all in France). Does this mean, as the far left wing in America would have it, that America has opted for a repressive treatment of poverty? And should we, like a disciple of Pierre Bourdieu, Loic Wacquant, conclude that it has chosen to set up the penal state in opposition to the social state, the model of the penitentiary state against that of the providential state, proposing a net of control that involves first police, then prison, as against a minimum income and guaranteed medical care? Of course not. I will certainly not go so far as to say that.

But that America is, just after Russia, the world champion of imprisonment is a fact. That it does not, however, actually have such a large number of major criminals incapable of rehabilitation into society is another fact. And that its prisons are participating in this way in a global system of producing and concealing, manufacturing and then condemning to invisibility, a population of the absolute poor, excluded from the space of the polis, who are turning into zombies, troglodytes—a physician would say 'foreign bodies'—in a society that finds here the insurmountable defect in its armour and its image—that is a third fact, and one that is not the smallest result of my investigation.

So?

I still don't think there's reason to despair of this country.

No matter how many derangements, dysfunctions, driftings there may be, still, the danger of secession, of an internal war of civilisations, seems, as far as I'm concerned, much less of an issue today than some would make it.

No matter how fragmented the political and social space may be; despite this nihilist hypertrophy of petty antiquarian memory; despite this hyperobesity—increasingly less metaphorical—of the great social bodies that form the invisible edifice of the country; despite the utter misery of the ghettos; despite these ill omens that, anywhere in the world, would be the forerunners of a flagging, a crumbling, and, in the end, an implosion of national identity and the sum total of political forms that embody it, I can't manage to convince myself of the collapse, heralded in Europe, of the American model.

And that, once again, is due to a series of reasons that have as much to do with history as with a multitude of impressions gleaned throughout my journey.

The first thing that strikes you when you begin to meditate—as Lacorne and others have—on this question of American 'national identity' is that there has never really been a nation-state in America, not in the sense that we know it in the nations of Europe, especially France. Those nostalgic for pure Federalism; those who longingly bemoan a whole, indivisible republic, which, they profess, has been damaged by tribalism; those partisans of a traditional 'melting pot' capable of producing what a century ago was called 'hundred-percent Americans,' are mourning a model that never actually existed, and one that is quite simply inconceivable in a country that remains gripped by an almost obsessive fear of monarchism, tyranny, and abuse of power.

The United States, as Hegel pointed out, has never been, and never sought to be, one of those 'united states' whose paradigm lies in the very ability to deconstruct the idea of unity by separating the concepts of 'state' (always territorial) from 'government' (what, in Europe, we simply call 'the State'). The notion one should bear in mind is that the very identity of the country, its foundation, its name, 'America'—or, rather, its decision to adopt a name that barely meant anything at the outset (Amerigo Vespucci, the name of a Florentine explorer immortalised by a German cartographer!), then, as time passed, delineated a continent that went, in principle, from Tierra del Fuego to the Bering Strait (can you imagine the French or the Germans baptizing themselves 'Europeans' with the same casualness the New England settlers called themselves 'Americans'?)—this very gesture, this significant original off-handedness, this odd but obvious indifference to an act of naming that, for every country in the world, has always had an extreme importance, this shabby baptism, affects the very reality it designates with an inevitable but native and, so to speak, consubstantial fragility.

And that's not even counting the other error of perspective, also historical, that doesn't take into consideration the long—very long—period of its history when Americanness was even more problematic, unstable, uncertain, and vulnerable than it is today. (In 'What Is a Nation?,' his renowned 1882 Sorbonne lecture that outlined what is still the most accurate definition of what a nation is, didn't Ernest Renan posit that, unlike Switzerland, where they speak 'four languages' but form 'one nation,' the United States speaks 'the same language' and yet, just like 'Spanish America,' does not form 'one single nation'?)

It doesn't reckon with the interminable time during which what we now call 'minorities' could not endanger the democratic contract for the simple reason that they weren't really a part of it (those centuries—then, after the Civil War, those decades—when the blacks were Americans but could not vote; those dark times when the Jews, fleeing the ghettos of central Europe, found, when they arrived in America, another form of anti-Semitism, which, although it wasn't in the least comparable to the soon-to-be exterminating violence endemic in their native countries, was virulent enough for someone like Henry Ford, in Dearborn, to popularise *The Protocols of the Learned Elders of Zion* in his newspaper; or that time, during and after World War I, when speaking German became a crime and when the bilingualism practiced by the 'Teutonic' minorities of Colorado, Iowa, Kansas, Indiana, and Illinois was popularly and officially perceived as an attack on national security—true, these debates go back to another time and are all but forgotten, but their resonant violence causes the present debates on the bilingualism introduced into the southern and western states by Hispanic communities to appear less significant in comparison…).

I should add to these general considerations the fact that throughout this entire journey I was also struck by the vigour and fervour of patriotic sentiment.

I should add that, from New York State to California, from

the Cuban immigrant communities of Miami to the Baptist churches of the southern states, I heard more 'God Bless America's, more 'United We Stand's, more references to the country's 'manifest destiny,' more pledges of allegiance and rallies around the flag, more 'ecumenical masses,' more vigils of support for 'our troops,' and, since we were in the midst of an election campaign, more incitements to 'register to vote'—in short, more testimonials pertaining to the 'American creed'— than I heard confessions of disenchantment or dissatisfaction with America.

I should add the example of those Indians in South Dakota, all of whom, at one moment or another in our conversation, found a way to remind me that it was their community that provided the strongest contingent, proportionately, of brave men for the recent American wars. Or the black people in Memphis and their 'double pride,' black and American, American and black, one inseparable from the other—how remote the time of my first travels to America now seems, when anti-Vietnam War peaceniks held the political limelight and when the same 'sons of slaves' were ideologically dominated by the ultraseparatist theories of Malcolm X and the Black Panthers! I should also add the example of the Iranians in Los Angeles, the Koreans in New York, and, yet again, those well-known Hispanics, about whom the most serious surveys reveal that they speak impeccable English in the second generation and forget Spanish in the third. I should add that, with all these disparate populations, with all these dissimilar peoples who are not in the least disposed to renounce their difference, one may perceive the same paradox of a desire for Americanness, or even, as Richard Rorty would put it, a wish to 'do something' with their country, which, far from appearing, in their own eyes, incompatible with the exercise of their 'ethical option,' seems increased tenfold by the sense of adding on to it a heritage and a set of qualities that, in the end, work to the greater glory of America.

And then this. Much has been made, in Europe, of the 'political correctness' that, taken literally, can seem in fact like the culmination of the crisis, the height of differentialist absurdity, and the sign, above all, of a complete disintegration not exactly of America, but of its representations, its intellectual schemes, and its language.

What actually is it? Isn't there something admirable, first of all, in this way (which has been so derided by the Europeans) of training the spotlight on minorities and victims? Isn't there a form of generosity, even nobility, in the design to let none of the automatic reflexes of language, in which the history of the humiliated is fossilised, pass by unnoticed? Isn't there a profound form of truth in the idea that the misfortunes of peoples inescapably end up being inscribed in the history of their words, and that you need to go there, right to the hollow centre of language, to its most arcane or well-hidden etymologies, to track down the sediments of infamy?

Can one, as we rightly do in Europe, ask for generalised penitence and then suddenly ridicule an examination of conscience that, as far as Americans are concerned, sets out to search in the subbasements of discourse, hence of being, for the imprint, almost the testimonial, of the original crimes that constitute them? Or rather—and here I am thinking, among other things, of the interminable martyrdom of the Indians—when it is a matter of dead men stripped of faces, of names, and even of head counts, when it is a matter of hidden ossuaries and, in the true sense of the term, 'perfect crimes,' isn't it not only just but urgent to look for whatever traces they've left, which are now lodged in language?

Finally, as to the rest, as to the obvious excesses this undertaking has given rise to, as to the most outrageous aspects of this generalised victimocracy and this masquerade of Untouchables that the PC trend, in its most extreme manifestations, at times resembles, was it necessary to give it such importance? Was it necessary to blow out of all proportion the provocations of some small group plotting to rewrite the Grimms' *Snow White* so as to erase any traces of offence against the seven dwarfs? Because a tiny band of lesbian archivists had decided to say not *history* but *her story* and because some professor—sorry, professess—had, according to a rumour that was, incidentally, never verified, demanded that a reproduction of a nude Goya that she accused of sexual harassment be taken down, did we need to conclude that universities were turning into 'concentration campuses' or were being invaded by 'new Red Guards'? When a publishing house printed an edition of the Bible in which 'God the Father' had been replaced by 'God the Father-Mother' and in which, so as to avoid insulting left-handed people, they translated 'the right hand' as 'the powerful hand' of the Lord, when a Californian professor was booed in a lecture hall for having bluntly called one of his students 'handicapped' instead of 'alternatively endowed,' should we fall into the trap by announcing the triumph of linguistic fundamentalism and the destruction of Western culture? In brief, shouldn't we have treated the whole affair with that share of humour and detachment, that talent for seeing beneath things, that so often spurred on those very activists of the movement?

After this year spent in the United States, I am convinced that the answer is yes. I am convinced that the European and American disciples of Allan Bloom have overinterpreted these phenomena, words and deeds that perhaps had no more meaning or impact than those declarations of French intellectuals explaining, in the name of the same linguistic radicalism, that language itself was fascist and that a revolution worthy of that name had to begin, as Pol Pot and the Cambodians had proven, by throwing all the dictionaries into the fire. More precisely, I also have the feeling that there was, in this entire business, not only an undeniable and venerable desire for reparation and justice but also, no less important, a measure of provocation, of outrage, and almost of farce, which in any case would have fizzled out, and against which it was perhaps not that useful to pull out the rhetorical arsenal of an anti-McCarthyism that had merely changed its colours. The result, nevertheless, is there. Besides the fact that, in the linguistic habits of the black communities, for instance, I clearly sensed a return to the good old term *black*, as opposed to the politically correct and enforced terms introduced in the 1970s and '80s, I am ashamed to admit that I didn't meet anyone who, today, says 'optically challenged' instead of blind, 'hair disadvantaged' instead of bald, or 'endowed with part-time sobriety' instead of alcoholic.

Perhaps it's a question of historical conjuncture and circumstance.

Perhaps it's linked to the fact that I arrived after 9/11, and after the extraordinary movement of national solidarity to which it gave rise.

Perhaps I was also too impressed by the unfurling of American flags that was, just a year ago, my very first impression of America, in Newport.

But my conclusion remains the same. If I had to offer a prognosis, it would be a crisis, not an extinction, of the model. If I had to risk a hypothesis, it would be that of a new dialectics between the *pluribus* and the *unum*, alterity and identity, between the two ideals, ethnic and civic, democratic and republican, that continue to form—in a different way, of course, according to a differently negotiated compromise—that daily plebiscite that is still called America. If, despite everything and despite, especially, the accumulated evidence of American vertigo, I had to make a bet on the future, it would be that of a newly defined reconstitution—around parameters that are ancient but arranged in a new order—of that old national model, which is really unlike any other in the world, where a subtle equilibrium of talents and countertalents, devotions and predations or, to phrase it in religious terms, fidelities and heresies, have allowed the affirmation of a given identity to think of itself as enriching the nation with precisely what it had chipped away from it. If I had to make a bet, it would be that this double affirmation, this symbolic deathless exchange, will continue—and that America's identity machinery has not said its last word.

Of course, this is not, and will never be, a model of the kind we know in Europe.

America never was, and never will be, founded either on the continuity of a 'race' (that goes without saying) or on the solidity of a soil, on an intrinsic autochthony (no people is more mobile than the American people, none less indigenous) or even on a thoroughly shared history, a once and for all common memory (at the end of the day, this last attribute of nations, which is memory, this remainder when nothing remains, this 'legacy of memory,' this 'long past of efforts, sacrifices, and devotions' that Renan said is the final rampart of national existence when the roles of race, language, religious affinities, geographic proximity, and collective interests have been successively called into question—isn't this precisely what the renaissance of minorities targets and complicates when, for each group, it goes in search of another hidden memory, other roots, other myths, other heroes, in short, another romance of origins constituting a kind of microstory coming not, of course, to replace but to enrich and, whether you like it or not, to scramble the great national epic?).

It will surely be abstract.

It has always been abstract. It has always been this artefact, forged by people of diverse origins who had nothing in common but this sharing not of a memory but of a desire and an Idea. And so it will be ever more abstract. More than ever, this nation without foundation or substrate, literally without 'hypo-thesis,' will be held together by the sheer force of the Idea, that is to say, of a fundamental Law. It will be—it is already—that enigmatic nation, eluding all classical national theorems, whose very origins are unclear. A social contract? There is nothing in common between that complex federation of entities foreign to one another, that juxtaposition of idioms and communities recognizing one another in an endlessly reworked Americanness, and that relationship, according to Rousseau, of fragmented subjects that constitute a people only in the instant of grace of the contractual decision. The paradigm of national will? No, there is nothing, in the relationships between communities and the federal government, nothing in the discontinuous but incessant series of compromises thus formed according to material and symbolic relationships of force, that can be resolved through the abdication of will that the scheme of a national spirit implies. No, none of these theorems holds true, and yet the fact seems undeniable: this nation continues to obey the principle of 'perpetual endurance' dear to Thomas Paine; it embodies the genuine prodigy of a patriotism that isn't just constitutional but concretely, almost carnally, lived out: it allows for the miracle of an allegiance, a bond, which, in San Diego, along the Mexican border, gave free rein to Sergeant Santa Ana to hunt down, without many qualms or much guilt, illegal immigrants who could have been mistaken for his parents and grandparents.

A strong bond holds America together, but a minimal one. An attachment of great force, but not fiercely resolute.

A place of high—extremely high—symbolic tension, but a neutral one, a nearly empty one.

An empty nation, yes, in the sense that Kant wrote of the Idea; a concept void of intuition and object, unlike Rousseau's conception of it. A Kantian nation, in that sense.

Not the Kant, of course, who in *What Is Enlightenment?* described the nation as an aggregation of autonomous individuals, torn from their determinations and situations.

But the other Kant, that of the *Critique of Pure Reason*,

who held that the Idea is the enlarged concept, the ideal of practical reason and action, the projection into the Absolute and Unconditional, to which, however, no object or intuition corresponds.

A nation without substance.

A nation without essence or fixed being.

A nation 'in perpetual construction' about which Habermas says, in a text on Rorty, that it has never been that 'gift of nature' the hurried readers of the founding texts of American exceptionalism believed it to be.

An agnostic nation, in a word.

A nation that, inverting the Kantian move, undertakes to limit faith and leave room for reason.

A nation that, if words have any meaning and if one wants to take literally the deflation that all of the master signifiers of natural, idolatrous, traditional nationalism have undergone, is infinitely more unbelieving than is generally thought.

A country that, still in this sense (and as surprising as it may be to the simpletons who, with the notion that this people is a religious people, even pious and devout, with the notion that it believes—I'm coming to it—in its manifest destiny and its civilizing mission, repeat everywhere that the nation is threatened by the evil spirit of fanaticism, and that its patriotism quite resembles that of its fundamentalist enemies)—a country, then, that invented and, in the strict sense, continues to invent one of the most authentic atheist nations in modern times.

An America, in short, that is a strange, almost indefinable autonomous entity whose bond seems to consist in the infinite but sonorous repetition of its quasi-common name or, rather, in the dry, almost vain, but self-realised prophecy that President Bill Clinton had in mind when he declared, during his inaugural speech on January 20, 1993, that it is up to 'every generation of Americans' to 'say what America is': an America about which I myself want to say that it is nothing else, when all is said and done, but a prodigious yet mundane machine whose purpose is to produce more Americans—a magnificent illusion, an Idea again, or, to return one last time to the Nietzsche of *Untimely Meditations*, one of those 'useful errors,' one of those 'tall tales,' that allow a human being, whoever he may be, to represent what he is and what he has to become in order to survive.

Is that too little?

True, it's not a lot.

But still, what a relief...

What serenity there is, when you think of the drums, cymbals, big thundering orchestras of our French national, Jacobin religion.

What a chance America is, what an achievement, when you think of the struggle to the death that in France those two homonymous principles have been and are still engaged in, those two nationalisms of heaven and earth, Idea and Ground, Gaullists in the Resistance and Vichyists who never for a moment imagined separating from their sacred occupied land and, for that very reason, took the side of the worst. What a chance, yes, to spontaneously have at your disposal a national and, dare I say it, a naturally republican identity whose foundation is in the clouds, in people's heads, in texts, in law.

In short, what a miracle, when you compare the inorganic neutrality of this wish to be American and the representations that ensue from it with the coarse European animal, the ugly hairless beast, gorged on sense, blood, and arrogance, which the Sartre of *The Condemned of Altona* turned into the very symbol of the evil nation.

Not, of course, that there isn't any arrogance in America. But here, too, we should be in agreement.

We need to agree on words and know what they mean.

This American arrogance is an identitarian one. Tribal. Separatist. Possibly individual. But not really national.

There is a kind of self-importance of minorities in America. A haughtiness. A pride. But I am not convinced, upon reflection, that you can talk about 'double pride' or that this pride is of the same nature as that other pride—poorer, more tenuous, and, all of a sudden, lighter—linked with being American.

Or rather: no doubt there is, bound up in identitarian allegiances that have always made up—now more than ever—the national pastoral, a form of pressure exercised on subjects; perhaps this pressure, or, in some cases, this intimidation, forms a prison for individuals compelled to define themselves in relation to their sexual identity, their race, their ethnic background; yet Americanness as such is not, or is no longer, or is to a lesser extent that form of prison.

Or, even better, and to express it as Tocqueville would, there is, today, a risk of the tyranny of the minorities. What Tocqueville said of the tyranny of the majority should be reversed, transposed, and henceforth expressed as the tyranny of these minorities. And perhaps that is the 'rational core' of the ultimately groundless accusations levelled against minorities when these accusations are limited to calling into question affirmative action and political correctness. Perhaps that is the real danger of identity politics. Perhaps it's from these minorities that are sacralised and praised to the skies that, once the great democratic revolution has come to the end of its course and finished deploying its 'irresistible and unknown' force, could derive, or has already derived, this evil spirit of conformism, this weight of the norm, this revulsion from singularity, this mistrust of freedom of thought and expression that Tocqueville's *Democracy in America* in its day attributed to the weight of the majority. Perhaps the crumbling of the American social fabric, the formation of these little capsules I saw juxtaposed from one end of the country to the other, bears witness to a lack of respect, not for the unified Whole, but for the diversified whole, and perhaps the genuine harm has been done not to Society, which can escape rather briskly from its Balkanisation, as we've seen, but to ordinary Americans who find themselves thus reduced to a simple, univocal adherence, all the more suffocating since it aspires to a form of naturalness, effecting better than any other method that panoptic reversal (everybody scrutinizing one person) that a great American actor spoke to me about in Washington. What is certain is that the danger does not derive, or derives to a lesser extent, from Americanness as such. What is certain is that, far from being that pure machine of alienation that the vilifiers of the Yankee way of life have denounced for a century, the stubborn, sometimes devout and almost religious will to become American has more of a tendency to act, in this context, as a tool of *dis*alienation, of emancipation, and, in fact, of deliverance. What I have observed and what seems quite undeniable upon investigation, at the risk of confusing what the entire Jewish and Christian traditions beseech us to distinguish from each other, at the risk of putting these two *opposite* notions of the *sacrality* of an origin or a source and the possible *sanctity* of a constitutional Text or charter of fundamental rights in the same bag of vague, ill-formed 'religiosity,' is this: in the dialectics of the two, in the vital and complex symbolic exchange that continues to occur between the possible sanctity of the Idea and the weighty sacrality of communities, the Idea is in the process once again of becoming, slowly but surely, the liberating principle that it had been for the Founding Fathers.

You can consider the problem from whatever angle you like. You can have a critical or positive vision of this principle, a Republican or Democrat notion, historical or forward-looking. You can, like me, refuse to conceal its dark nether side, its inevitable shadow. You can refuse to forget either the miserable ghettos of Los Angeles or the mothers of dead soldiers in Iraq, or, at the Fort Worth convention, the bovine stupidity of those who, in the name of the Second Amendment, support the free sale of weapons of war, or, of course, the millions of citizens living below the poverty level and going without health insurance. One detail remains, which hasn't, moreover, escaped the most recent slayers of the Yankee way of life (I'm thinking of that international league of terrorists for whom the poverty-stricken ghettos of Los Angeles are evidently not a harrowing preoccupation—I'm thinking of those jihadists about whom you can't say enough times that they aim to destroy what is best about the United States: freedom of speech and thought, equality, women's rights, democracy)—this basic yet decisive detail remains, then: in the sheer fact of being American, or at least expressing yourself like one and wanting to be one, there is a gentleness, a lightness, an element of freedom and, in a word, of civilisation, that makes this country one of the few countries in the world where, despite everything, you can still breathe freely today.

American Ideology and the Question of Terrorism

THE CURRENT STATE OF AFFAIRS

THE QUESTION OF terrorism.

This question has evidently become, over the years, one of the fundamental questions this country has had to tackle, and I see that aside from occasional remarks about reactions to the war in Iraq, aside from my pages about Guantánamo, or about the self-assuredness of Arabs in Dearborn, or about Orthodox Jews in Brooklyn worried about Israel, or, finally, about the obsession with security and the prevention of attacks in East Coast airports, I have scarcely touched on it.

A note on terrorism, then.

Some remarks on how the United States is experiencing its newfound vulnerability, echoes of which I kept hearing all throughout my journey, and how it thinks about it.

I finish this voyage with the feeling that to reckon with this new kind of threat, as well as the very particular kind of 'psychological shock' that Nechayev said is always the first aim of terrorism, Americans have three distinct lexicons, three possible kinds of discourse, each one to be inscribed beneath one of three major names on the intellectual scene.

The lesson of Francis Fukuyama, first of all.

Not, of course, that Fukuyama is a theoretician of terrorism.

But you remember the article—then the book—in which, after the fall of the Berlin Wall, he announced the 'End of History.'

That was Hegel's theory, who saw in Napoleon's 1806 victory at Jena the victory of French revolutionary ideals and the beginning of their universalisation.

It was Marx's theory, evoking the imminence of a classless society, about which he noted, in passing, that 'the new America,' with its way of allowing 'the greatest possible development of the worker's aptitudes,' offered the most precise foreshadowing.

It was the theory of Alexandre Kojève, who, in 1938, in his lectures on Hegel's *Phenomenology of Spirit* attended by so many of the future luminaries of the French intelligentsia—from Sartre to Bataille, from Lacan to Leiris and Merleau-Ponty—held that everything that has occurred since 1806 was 'only an extension' of the 'revolutionary power' contained in the two names Robespierre and Napoleon; that 'the two World Wars,' with their 'procession of big and little revolutions,' served only to align 'the obsolete civilisations of peripheral provinces' with 'the most advanced European historical positions'; and that these days no one knows anymore who—the 'Americans' (those 'rich Sino-Soviets'), or the 'Russians' and 'Chinese' (those 'Americans who are still poor')—best embodies the promise of a 'classless society' in the course of being fulfilled.

Well, that's Fukuyama's theory too, the fall of the Berlin Wall substituting itself for Napoleon's victory or the revenge of the proletariat. It's the theory this Hegelian intellectual uses when he explains that the prodigious events humanity is now witnessing are neither the mark of 'the end of the Cold War' nor the end of a 'special phase' in the post-1945 chronicle but the ultimate, culminating point of 'the ideological evolution of humanity'; and this thesis, taken seriously (and God knows America has taken it at face value!), will have an immediate, major consequence when it comes to the question of terrorism.

If, in fact, Fukuyama is right, if liberal democracy has triumphed not just over the most stubborn, but over the last of its adversaries, if the political and economic system that has been established in Prague, Berlin, Budapest, Sofia, Warsaw, Bucharest, and Moscow is not just one system among others but the 'final form of human government,' if the world, in other words, has truly entered this great era, this definitive maturity, the week of seven Sundays that was prophesied by his venerated masters but that he, Fukuyama, was the first to perceive clearly, then that means that History has exhausted its figures and ideals and that there is no place in this world for the slightest ideological or political questioning. Nothing can challenge the capitalist, liberal order that is in the process of imposing itself today.

There will, of course, be other events.

Humankind will continue to be restless, and various events will keep occurring.

But they will be events without surprise and without future. They will be sham events, ersatz events, illusions. They will be the last pirouettes of a History that, unlike the Devil, whose final trick was to have us believe that he didn't exist, will go to considerable efforts to convince us that it does exist. And terrorism, in this case, will be one of these efforts. It will be one of those groundless illusions, one of those events without consequence. It will be the symptom of that relentless persistence human history demonstrates when it makes us think it continues, whereas it has actually subsided into the fleeting insubstantiality of shadow plays. An epiphenomenon. A bloody but unimportant sign. A rearguard battle. A final showdown. A convulsion. A momentary lapse. A paper tiger. No reason to make a fuss over it. Nothing that would signal some sort of return of History. And surely no reason for one of those 'wars' that the West has, from the time History began, waged against all its previous adversaries.

The author of *The End of History and the Last Man* does not speak in these terms.

And I don't know of any other text by him that presents anything more than a circumstantial discussion of terrorism and how to react to it. But that is his position.

More precisely, that is the only position that is compatible with this theory of the End of History, while, conversely, regarding terrorism as epi-phenomenal is only conceivable from a theoretical position akin to Fukuyama's.

We have underestimated the importance and centrality of the Fukuyama way of thinking in contemporary American ideology.

All those who, here or there, are loath to turn the matter of terrorism into a tragedy, all those for whom the very idea of a war against Islamic fundamentalism seems a conceptual and practical absurdity, all those who find the image of the most powerful army in the world engaged in the mountains of Afghanistan hunting down an NGO of crime and its Ernst Jünger-like Saudi 'Chief Forester' bizarre or ridiculous, all those who think or pretend to think that the only realistic way to reply to al-Qaeda involves the police or the judicial system, all those people, whatever political kin they belong to, are supporters—full-fledged or unofficial—of a kind of 'Fukuyamaism'. They believe in a 'universal, homogeneous government,' one of whose first gestures will be, when it is established, to replace the old caste of warriors with a corps of police officers who will ensure the preservation of planetary order.

Then there is the Huntington solution.

Not the Huntington of *Who Are We?*, that xenophobic

book that, as we've seen, casts thirty million Hispanics, Mexicans especially, into the utter darkness of a shadowy barbarism.

But the other Huntington. The former National Security Council expert who, immediately after Fukuyama, in an article for *Foreign Affairs* and then in an influential book published a few years later, both copies his former student and contradicts him.

History is not over, he objects.

These few years devoid of significant wars, which have allowed you to launch your neo-Hegelian gospel, were merely a 'holiday from history.'

This world you and I both theorise about remains, and will long remain, a profoundly plural world, ripe for great crises, great upheavals, great wars.

And the principle of this plurality, the origin of this interminable, violent differentiation, the first and last motivating force that, ever since mankind has existed and as long as it continues to exist, moves History forward, is the clash not of consciences as in Hegel, not of classes as in Marx, not even of nations as in the theoreticians of European conservatism, but of those 'superior' totalities that he calls 'civilisations' and that are 'the highest level of cultural identity humans need to distinguish themselves from other species.'

That was Arnold Toynbee's theory in his monumental *Study of History*, as Marc Crépon has shown in his essay '*L'imposture du choc des civilisations.*'

It was Spengler's doctrine in his *Decline of the West*, and then, a dozen years later, in a lesser-known book, *The Years of Decision*, in which he imagined a twentieth century 'punctuated' by 'the rival plurality of civilisations' and, in particular, by the onslaught of 'the mass of peoples of colour' against 'all white people in general.'

It was the theory, finally, of Carl Schmitt, whom Huntington hardly ever cites but who, in Germany in the 1920s, as a prelude to the Reich's plans of European conquest and while he was elaborating his vision of politics defined as the art of distinguishing between 'friends' and 'enemies,' developed the same idea—that the world was divided into supranational units, each corresponding to a single historical tradition.

Well, that is Huntington's theory, and the principle behind his eight opposed 'civilisations,' namely: first, 'Western' (which he distinguishes from the second, 'Slavic-Orthodox'); third, 'Japanese' (not to be confused with the fourth, 'Confucian'); fifth, 'Indian' (he also says 'Hindu'); sixth, 'African' (as well as the seventh, 'Latin American'); and, finally, eighth, 'Islamic' (which may become allied with the 'Confucian' in an 'axis' whose consolidation is the principal danger threatening the West today). All are seen as so many noncommunicating, fatal entities engaged in wars either declared or latent.

If, in fact, Huntington is right, if the unifying principle of the human race is indeed 'civilisation identity' in the sense that he understands it, if the world is a theatre for this long ballet of civilisations clashing either to control territory or to promote their own version or concept of the Universal, and if, finally, of all the civilisations in contention, the Islamic one differs most from our own and is the most opposed to it, then the die isn't yet cast; the world isn't finished, and will never be finished, testing out solutions and striving to impose them. Islam is one of these tests, and terrorism is only the visible, early sign of it; and the war against terrorism must, conversely, be an all-out, long-lasting war against Islam.

Here again, I am not saying that Huntington expresses himself in exactly these terms.

And I know of no canonical text he's written on the subject. But that is certainly the gist of his argument.

And, just as certainly, it offers a theoretical matrix for all those in America or for all observers of it who think, first, that responding to terrorism is not a matter for the police but for the military; and, second, that if the target of this war is indeed al-Qaeda, that target is inscribed within a larger confrontation, to be fought without mercy or reservation, with an 'Islamic civilisation' irredeemably hostile to American and European values.

What is Huntington's influence?

As colossal as Fukuyama's.

I won't count his overzealous disciples who call for a crusade—he himself is far more prudent than that.

I will leave aside—although they can make use of Huntington's ambiguous declarations about the 'bloody frontiers' of Islam or his 'doubts' as to the sincerity of the 'patriotism' of Arab Americans, several of whom I met in Dearborn—the ultra-fanatics who want to see millions of suspect citizens expelled from the country.

But he was, after all, Charles Krauthammer's intellectual guide when the latter explained to Fukuyama the role he believed the war in Iraq was playing in the struggle against terrorism, despite the absence of a concrete link between Osama bin Laden and Saddam Hussein.

He was the inspiration for Norman Podhoretz when Podhoretz explained, in an article published in September 2004, that the world, and America especially, was engaged in a fourth world war, and that, faced with this, neither legal strategies nor carefully aimed reprisals made any sense.

And he inspired that whole faction of the neoconservatives (but only that faction, since we'll see that the neoconservative case in general is far more thorny and difficult to decipher) who made a global confrontation with Islam the central challenge of the new century.

He is the father, not always recognised, of that other part of American ideology where the excessively limited idea of an anti-terrorist policy reduced to simple police operations is contrasted with the idea of a total, global war, encompassing the earth, and waged against the whole of the Arab–Muslim world.

A brief political interlude.

One can articulate— again, as Marc Crépon did—four basic objections to Huntington:

The 'theoretical weakness' of his notion of a 'civilisation identity' informed by 'culture,' 'philosophy,' or 'religion'—without these different terms ever being actually delineated and without any priority clearly assigned among the three.

The naivety that consists, whatever term is used, in insisting on the exclusivity, the incompatibility, the essential and ontological foreignness, of these different civilisations, which have no choice, in effect, but to attack each other or else ignore each other.

Under this premise, what do we do with the connections and gateways between cultures? Aren't authentic civilisations intrinsically variegated, playing the twofold game of preserving identity while crossbreeding for difference? And, finally, what about those universal invariants that the first Lévi-Strauss disciple who comes along will tell you form the common basis of all the civilisations in the world?

The way, then, that this sort of ethnopolitics makes use of the worst relativism. If civilisations are what Huntington claims, if they are so hermetic and incapable of communicating, how can one help but conclude that some are fit for democracy and others not?

How can one not reserve human rights for civilisations in which they have already appeared and to which they are structurally connected? And aren't we right to worry about the regression that this idea implies in relation to the meagre progress made, in twenty or thirty years, toward a Kantian cosmopolitical principle—without resorting to New Age twaddle about world citizenship and universal brotherhood, aren't we justified in dreading the birth of a world where the very notion of interference in a humanitarian catastrophe or genocide would seem, as Huntington happens to say, definitely 'immoral'?

And then, regarding Islam itself, regarding this civilisation supposedly incapable of democracy, the empiric but decisive objection remains—namely, what the two great Egyptian political analysts (who both used the common pseudonym Mahmoud Hussein) call the 'southern side of freedom': the existence, in the lands of Islam, of moderate and modernist trends resisting from within the ideological teachings of fundamentalism; the reality (so contrary to the clichéd vision) of the great and ancient split separating the Islam of the Enlightenment from its false Salafist or Wahhabite twin; the absurdity, in other words, of lumping together in one single word and concept Massoud and the Taliban, disembowelled Algerian women and their jihadist executioners, or else Sayyid Qutb, who inspired contemporary Islamic fundamentalism, and the great Egyptian scholar Rifa'a Al-Tahtawi, who, after living in Paris from 1826 to 1831, returned home convinced that his country should be introduced to the ideas and values that enabled France to prosper…

Second political and theoretical interlude.
 I have four other kinds of objections to Fukuyama—this time on a different level, with different issues at stake:

The Kierkegaard objection: the system is one thing; subjectivity is another; and the closure of the former, its totalisation, or, to paraphrase Hegel, the capacity of absolute government to calculate, foresee, and integrate in advance dissent against it, will never get the better of the irreducible, irruptive, always new singularity of the latter—even if it's the atrocious singularity of the suicide bomber.

The Tocqueville objection: the levelling of conditions, of course; a classless society, granted; let's suppose that Kojève was right in announcing the reign of a humanity reduced to its needs alone and returned, for the first time, to that 'animality' I got a whiff of in the megalopolises of the West Coast and in the gilded hell of Las Vegas; even so, who can claim that the struggle for recognition stops? How can one so absolutely state that resemblance and similarity are the sources of proximity and peace? Isn't one of the lessons of *Democracy* precisely this, that hatred between those who are alike is the most implacable? And isn't that, incidentally, what the news teaches us when, from New York to Madrid, from London to Lahore and Karachi, it shows us those faces of terrorists formatted, Westernised, integrated into the very world they'd like to see perish along with them, and who, when all is said and done, look out toward us with the unsettling strangeness of mirrors?

Then the Hegelian objection: Did the author of the *Phenomenology* actually say what some of my coevals have him say? Where? In which texts? In what words, precisely? Isn't it rather Kojève, Hegel's great evangelist, that combination of Cagliostro and grand provocateur, philosopher and prankster, meta- and pataphysician, who, convinced that the master text was a coded text, read between the lines or, perhaps, dreamed it? And did Kojève himself always think this way? Didn't he eventually confess, in a note added to the second edition of his *Introduction to the Reading of Hegel*, that after a 'recent voyage to Japan,' he had 'radically changed his opinion'? And why didn't that American of Japanese origin, Fukuyama, draw all the consequences from his remorse? How—that is to say, through what bizarre denial—is it possible that Fukuyama did not devote more than a few lines (*The End of History and the Last Man*, end of chapter 29) to the enigmatic and beautiful page where, meditating on these signs of extreme civilisation in the Nō theatre, the art of flower arranging, the tea ceremony, in short, these 'unparalleled heights of Japanese snobbery' he had just observed in Tokyo, in the posthistorical country par excellence, in the only society known 'to have carried out the almost three-centuries-old experiment of living during the end of History,' Kojève concluded that this work on the given, this dialectics of subject and object, this struggle with the 'self' (all of which were, according to Hegel, History's pure motivating force) would continue? The shift in Kojève's opinion is decisive. For if the concept of the End of History collapses, then the historical event begins to rear its head. If the end of time has no meaning, then alterity begets its own meaning again. And if alterity—and the event—return to the stage of History, then terrorism once again becomes, alas, this likely wager, this sombre force, this intense and at times lethal negativity, this challenge.

Finally, an argument that isn't exactly Hegelian, but post- or hyper-Hegelian: Let us suppose, for the moment, that Hegel did say this. Let us suppose that this epoch of absolute spirit will in fact unfold, and that its main characteristic will be that the prodigious machine that turns two into one (which is called dialectics) is checked. There will be times, then, when those empty, aimless events Fukuyama described will occur and flow gently into the policed order of the world. But shouldn't we foresee, on the contrary, that it's the very fact that there will no longer be any dialectics there to welcome them into its matrix and extract from them, like the good grain of rye, their wholesome, fortunate positivity that will cause these events to actually become sharper, less diluted, impossible to stifle, harder? Because the beginning of the End of History signifies the beginning not of the end of time but of a new way for time to exist, and since the first characteristic of this new way is that things will no longer be systematically encompassed, transformed, and finally reduced, shouldn't we anticipate sudden occurrences that will be more ambiguous but also darker, devoid of solution or measure, and that, precisely because History is over, will have an unprecedented and trenchant radicality? In other words, isn't the entire paradox of Hegelianism its proclamation of a post-History that promises postevents endowed with a quantity of energy, a fissile violence, a force never before seen? And postevents that we can define only if we qualify as inherently 'tragic' the sombre ultimatum they issue to the world in which they are about to occur—the exact tenor, as much physical as metaphysical, of this megaevent that was the attack, for instance, on the Twin Towers and the Pentagon?

Thus we are back to the question of terrorism.

Let us suppose that, with this matter in mind, we mingle these two thoughts and philosophies with each other, mix these two series of political and theoretical arguments.

Let us suppose that we set against Fukuyama and Huntington's two rival and, in a certain way, twin systems their symmetrical and, on this precise question, possibly complementary forms of shortsightedness.

Let us suppose, in other words, that we decide to leave these two philosophies of the event—let us suppose that, one serving as a tool against the other, we decide to do away with two discourses, unequally cogent, but which have conjointly served as ideological magnets for more than ten years in America and that may well have fuelled the errors of perception, analysis, and strategy that have been committed since 9/11.

From this double series of objections and their more or less methodical combination, from this idea that the End of History is a joke, a chimera, an illusion of reason, a philosophical midwinter night's dream, a trick, and that the war of civilisations is yet another joke, another mirror chimera, Time that is taking its revenge over its impossible death, a ludicrously convenient idea, a fantasy, the new, even weaker version of that 'capharnaum of hypotheses' that Wittgenstein was already denouncing in Spengler—the following can be deduced.

History, contrary to what one system alleges, has more imagination than mankind, and is never done producing its new figures and new wars; but these wars are not civilisational ones of the kind Huntington sees emerging between Islam and the West.

Or rather: yes, in a sense, to that part of the Huntington theory that evokes a History that flares up again and does so with all the more gusto since it never, in fact, stopped unfurling; yes, if need be, to this scheme that was Hobbes's and Nietzsche's before it was Spengler's and Carl Schmitt's, of a clash not of naked interests but of world visions and ideas; yes, but only on the condition that you add that the only war of ideas that is relevant, the only clash of cultures or world visions that has meaning today, is not the clash between America and Islam, and even less between the West and the rest, but, in the heart of this rest, within the borders of this Islam, the clash of two Islams, embodied in the names of Massoud and the Taliban.

This opposition is a political one.

This position is the only one that, because it loosens the ideological and logical vise grip of these two major discourses, one that has trapped and hardened American ideology, allows us to grasp a hint of the complexity of reality.

For my part it is the position I have tried to articulate for over ten years, starting with investigations in the field in Pakistan, in Afghanistan, and in the black holes of Africa's forgotten wars.

But it is especially, in America, the position of a third family of intellectuals, who come from the left and who, for the most part, are still there—it's the position of a generation of American intellectuals whose itinerary intrigues me and that I refer to, for the sake of convenience as well as, perhaps, out of ignorance, under the name Michael Walzer.

I knew Walzer through his important book on just and unjust wars.

This book accompanied me during the time of the war in Afghanistan—the first one, the wretched one, the one that, in the beginning of the 1980s, let loose on the unarmed farmers of the Panjshir and Kabul a Red Army whose profound barbarism I still can't manage to fathom, even in hindsight, even when I know what we know today about the descendents of some of those whom we called at the time mujahideen.

And I found the book again ten years later in the heart of the Bosnian tragedy when, faced with a world that was 'irremediably divided' (in Walzer's words) between 'those who throw the bombs and those who receive them,' then faced with the unbearable 'shame of Srebrenica' (the words are still his, and they are impeccable), you needed some kind of help to think about this oxymoron—the idea of a morally necessary war—and then to emerge from the false debate between a warmongering on principle, which might already have been Huntington's view, and a diehard pacifism, which could have belonged to Fukuyama's disciples.

Today, Walzer is especially, in my mind, the author of some texts, on the international situation in general and on terrorism in particular, that I have read keenly, over the months, in various publications marked by fierce opposition to the war in Iraq, hostility to the right-wing administration of George W. Bush, and, however little meaning the word now has, globally oriented to the left.

He is at the centre of an intellectual galaxy whose shifting contours I can't precisely outline—I'm not even sure whether it perceives itself as such or not, and if so, to what point; but I can clearly see, nonetheless, how this galaxy is in the process of producing concepts on essential points that create rifts in what we'll have to call the Huntington-Fukuyama bloc.

First of all, it breaks from that culture of indulgence, excuse, and euphemism that, in the United States as well as in Europe, is the surest way of trivializing the horror of mass crimes against civilians. Terrorism, Walzer keeps repeating, is neither the weapon of the poor nor the revenge of the oppressed (truly poor people, the weakest of the weak, do not produce suicide bombers—consider Africa). Terrorism, he insists, is not the last resort of people who have exhausted other means of making themselves heard and advancing their just cause (9/11 occurred at the precise moment when the strategy to compromise on the Palestinian question was in the process of bearing fruit—Camp David, the 2001 Taba Conference). And as to the argument that holds that the Americans asked for and deserve what is happening to them, as to the devious analysis that posits that, because of their own crimes, they are the true origin of the crime that strikes them now, that is adding outrage to igno-rance, ignominy to stupidity. (So long as we're there, why not reproach blacks for racism? Jews for anti-Semitism? Why not follow this loathsome logic to its conclusion and announce that victims are always, everywhere, responsible for their own execution?)

Second, Walzer disposes of that other cliché, paradoxically linked to the deconstruction of the previous one since it's the rejection of the trivialisation, the loathing for indulgence and excuse, the decision not to get involved with the whys and ways of evil, that tends to generate it—he disposes of the idea of a meteoric terrorism without rationality or logic, without any cause at all, which boils down to series of isolated, simple, insane, desperate acts, thus evading all the known laws of Clausewitzian attraction: nothing is less certain, he objects, than the rather widespread idea of a 'post-Clausewitz' terrorism; for the terrorist may not have a *Ziel*, or 'target,' in the sense that Clausewitz uses the word—that is certainly the very principle of the blind attack, the indiscriminate strike—but there is another word in Clausewitz to express the target and the goal. According to Clausewitz, you might not have a *Ziel*, but you may still have a *Zweck*, which is the name for this other sort of goal, which is the 'strategic' objective; and isn't this precisely the case with religious zealots? Don't they have a Zweck, or even a double Zweck, which consists, on the one hand, in putting all their weight behind the war within the Islamic world and, on the other, in making life less viable, less breathable, in the free cities they abhor? You need to imagine bin Laden as a strategist, Walzer explains; you need to imagine him in his hideout, at that instant (which he says is 'difficult to reconstruct' but which he is 'sure actually took place') when, with his group of conspirators, he sat 'around a table' to 'discuss what had to be done,' among a number of possible options, and coldly chose mass murder. You need, once and for all, to get used to the strategic, hyper-Clausewitzian dimension of terrorism.

And then again, far from dehistoricizing the phenomenon, far from reducing it to some kind of lightning bolt that, as Bush uttered on the night of 9/11, had 'suddenly struck in the skies of our cities,' Walzer and his friends—I am thinking especially, here, of the texts and researches of Paul Berman—have the immense and ultimate merit of putting terrorism back into context. Its real context. Its larger context. That nonregional context that Milan Kundera says is essential to the proper appreciation of literature and that I am convinced is the only framework that restores historical phenomena to their proper scale, too. Islam? Yes, of course, Islam, says Berman. But also the Mussolini-like fascism that feeds some of the beliefs of the Christian Michel Aflaq, founder of the Iraqi Baath Party. And the eugenics of Alexis Carrel, the French Nobel Prize winner whom Sayyid Qutb, inspirer of the Muslim Brotherhood, explicitly claims to follow. And the Nazi Brown Shirts, for whom Hassan al-Banna, the founder of the movement, has never disguised his 'considerable admiration.' And then, quite bluntly, racism, anti-Semitism, the cult of violence, the love of death, the idea that history can only be written in blood—this disastrous opera of horror that hastened Europe to its ruin and now intoxicates the followers of bin Laden. We understand, when we read Berman, that the phenomenon is both strange and familiar. We sense men at once so remote and so close to us—barbarians, of course, but barbarians who eerily resemble us, barbarians who may well be our doppelgängers and who draw their strength from our worst qualities and our innermost, supremely shameful aspects. We say to ourselves, in other words, that here we are dealing with a new stage in an ancient revolution that began with Lenin, continued with Hitler and Mussolini, and that now manifests itself, with the bin Ladenist squadrons of death, in a chilling contemporary avatar. Then we realise—and this isn't the least merit of these texts—that our ideological patrimony, in this confrontation, is not as completely destitute as those people would like to believe who, by confining terrorism to its own limited context, turn it into an opaque, unintelligible, and consequently incurable occurrence. We are not this destitute, since, from our previous encounters, from our costly but undeniably victorious struggle against the former incarnations of the Beast, we have inherited a plentiful arsenal that is ready to serve again and which is called antitotalitarianism...

Maybe these authors have less in common than I tend to think. Maybe what separates them—in this domain and others—is more substantial than what unites them.

Maybe I should take into consideration that renowned 'Letter from America' entitled 'Reasons for Combat' that appeared in the immediate aftermath of the war in Afghanistan signed by sixty or so American intellectuals, including

Bernard-Henri Lévy

Fukuyama, Huntington, and… Walzer!

Maybe I should compare that text with yet another 'other left'—embodied by writers like Chomsky, Vidal, Boyle, and Sontag—that notably expressed itself, two weeks later, in a second letter, entitled 'Letter from Citizens of the United States to Their Friends in Europe,' that strove to invalidate the notion of a just war against terrorism.

In short, no doubt the American intellectual landscape is even more complex, multilayered, and contradictory than I feel at the end of this provisional and imperfect assessment of the current state of affairs—and maybe I'm in the process of conjuring up, of *dreaming*, this 'third system' endowed with an uncanny power, as it were, to work past the complicit opposition of Huntington and Fukuyama.…

Nonetheless.

There is, in this series of gestures, something strong and unusual.

There is, in this series of texts, a genuine theoretical attempt to take up the challenge that the onslaught of Islamic fascism hurls at thought.

There is, in this region of words and ideas that extends from Walzer's own journal, Dissent, to *The New Republic* and, surely, far beyond, an intellectual fever or turmoil or inventiveness that we are by and large ignorant of in Europe and that turns out to be one of the significant surprises of this investigation.

What I conclude is this: perhaps because they had the misfortune, this time, of finding themselves on the front line; perhaps because they had the terrible privilege of being, just this once, more brutally stricken in the flesh than their European allies; perhaps also because they benefit from an ideological tradition less crippled than our own by the weight of consent to earlier totalitarian systems; perhaps, in other words, because in this respect they are hiding fewer skeletons in their closets and don't need to exorcise a long history of indulging fascisms both Red and Brown, they are the ones, these American intellectuals, who are best placed today to think about this third fascism, this third-generation fascism.

With one reservation, possibly.

I still need to introduce one final nuance, one objection to this scenario.

It seems to me that following this gesture to its conclusion, completing this train of thought, fully exploring the intellectual consequences of this antifascist reading of the terrorist event, also requires that one reflect on terrorism's collateral effects on America.

It seems to me, to be precise, that no authentic reflection on this age of crime and terror, or on how we can eventually extract ourselves from it, can dispense with an analysis of those other three phenomena that, for the moment, appear on the landscape and are called torture, Guantánamo, and Abu Ghraib.

There's the rub.

Without aiming (with what right?) to lecture anyone, I have the peculiar and persistent impression that these are the three areas about which these same intellectuals, these spokesmen for the American antitotalitarian left, are, for the most part, the least convincing.

About Abu Ghraib, about the tortures inflicted by the paramilitary on Iraqi detainees who were defenceless and bereft of legal recourse, Michael Walzer did comment that they violated an 'essential principle of the theory of just war and the Geneva Conventions.' And, beyond his example, if we wanted to draw a comparison with France once again, if we agreed to reopen, for instance, the dossier of our war in Algeria and the state crimes it provoked, the exercise would probably show to America's advantage: on the one hand, censorship, newspapers seized, our journalists harassed or thrown in prison, French officials paid to keep their mouths shut for more than forty years now; on the other, information right away, Seymour Hersh's article reported on all the networks, images on the Internet, high government officials acknowledging the facts without delay, a great moment of transparency, a lesson in democracy. That said, has America settled its accounts with the gravity of what happened there? Has it performed the examination of conscience necessary to understand those atrocious scenes? Has it acknowledged the enigma, especially, of these grinning men and women equipped with cameras, as if they were at summer camp or on safari, filming one another as they humiliated and degraded their own prisoners? Has America reflected on what it took—long before Abu Ghraib, long before those images, in the innermost recesses of American society, in its intimate relationship to its own violence or to the culture of the 'enemy'—on what it took for these young Americans to become, in all innocence, torturers? Why, in short, wasn't there, in this same antitotalitarian movement, in this family of minds that wasn't prevented by its hostility to the Republican administration—far from it—from raising itself to the level of intensity set by the jihadist offensive, why wasn't there some equivalent of Susan Sontag's text, published in *The New York Times Magazine* just after the Abu Ghraib scandal? (A text whose impact was unfortunately diminished because of the author's previous declarations about the 'courage' of the suicide bombers.)

Guantánamo. Of course the American antitotalitarian left is outraged by Guantánamo. Of course the men and women I met all expressed their utter hostility toward the existence, on the edge of the country, of this unconventional prison at Guantánamo Bay. But there are more and less radical ways of expressing outrage. And if I heard a number of my interlocutors tell me that Guantánamo served no purpose, if I read dozens of articles reporting the fact that those imprisoned at Guantánamo were really just small fry and that the most egregious killers were secretly placed in even more appalling prisons under the surveillance of rogue states allied with the United States, if the theme, in other words, of appropriateness and effectiveness was a visibly popular one, I heard another key question posed less often, the question of pure principle that emerges from the very existence of such a lawless zone, barren of rights, neither inside nor outside the country, poised somewhere between hell and the real world, a zone where democracy's enemies are fought with undemocratic methods. For once again, there are two possibilities. Either we believe that America is at war—in which case these detainees must benefit from prisoner-of-war status and from the protections accorded by the Geneva Convention. Or we subscribe to the End of History, to police treatment— and then all the rights normally granted to prisoners by common law need to be recognised. But this intermediate condition, this statutory monstrosity, the fact that Guantánamo's prisoners, having neither the rights of combatants nor the rights of criminals, finally have no rights at all, these limitless detentions with no publicly stated charges, these systematic infractions of all the principles of that great government of law that is the American federal government—this is a scandal that has nothing to do with considerations of appropriateness, and I have not heard it denounced clearly enough. How many people are there in the United States who have spoken out loudly and firmly against taking liberties with liberty, even in the name of effectiveness? Who among these politically aware citizens who had the courage to accept the idea of a just war against the adherents of jihadist fascism is truly conscious of the fact that accepting Guantánamo, tolerating a state of emergency with the excuse that it's a state of war, letting the rigor of judicial rules be slackened (even if it's at the margin) when the entire value of these laws lies in that they absolutely and formally cannot be limited—who is aware that this is just like inserting a worm into fruit, or a virus into a computer program? Who among them is fully conscious that, for America as for any democracy, this is the source of a crisis that could lead anywhere?

And finally, as for torture, it's possibly even worse. Once again, we are familiar with it in France. Once again, during the same Algerian War, we witnessed, in France, a raging intellectual battle focused especially around Henri Alleg's book on torture, *La Question*. Except that the difference, this time, was that most of the intellectuals in France were united in their complete and absolute rejection of this practice. In the United States, on the other hand, we have seen a whole surreal discussion develop around the 'circumstances' that could make methods permissible that, at the level of principle, remain absolutely intolerable. Here, we find a major judge, Richard Posner, mobilizing a Bentham-like utilitarianism to define cases where the evil that is torture can be used to avoid the greater evil of a civilian massacre. There, we find another lawyer, Harvard law professor Alan Dershowitz, using all the full supply of both good sense and sophistry to lead us into the aporia of the terrorist who has just hidden a 'ticking bomb' that will explode within an hour if he isn't forced to say where he hid it. Next, it's a neolibertarian, Robert Nozick, whose twenty-year-old text has been unearthed because it supposedly demonstrates that torture is indeed acceptable when it is part of a larger plan (once again) to save innocents. And last, it's Walzer who also republished a text, from the 1970s, in a collection edited by Stanford Levinson, which pretends to pose in new terms the age-old problem of 'dirty hands' set forth by Sartre, Camus, and Machiavelli (sic); it's Walzer himself who declares, in an interview with the British journal *Imprints*, that he wants leaders 'to accept the rule' but that they should be 'smart enough to know when to break it.' He goes on to say: 'And finally, because they believe in the rule, I want them to feel guilty about breaking it—which is the only guarantee they can offer us that they won't break it too often.' And it's Walzer again who, in *Dissent*, introduces a staggeringly pointless debate between opponents (not always intransigent) and supporters (always cunning) of this concept of torture as a last resort…

For this debate is not a worthy one.

It is undoubtedly *the* blind spot of an intelligentsia stunned—understandably, it goes without saying—by the shock of 9/11.

And it's the critical point where, for my part, I would dissociate myself from a family of minds whose fundamental choices are otherwise so close to my own.

American intellectuals may remain trapped in this blindness, sunk in the black hole of this casuistry and in another culture of excuse—one that copies the very culture that Walzer condemns as excusing terrorism, that condemns without condemning, while in fact condoning, those exceptional zones and procedures to which a democracy at war is always wrong to consent. If so, their criticisms remain partial, and they will only half keep their antifascist promise.

Or else they will emerge from it, they will follow their intellectual and moral courage to the end and draw all the consequences, absolutely all, from the historical decision to renew the antitotalitarian pact required by the new threats; in other words, they will both wage implacable war against terrorism and also indefatigably defend the rule of law—then, yes, America would once again show the way by providing us, through its intellectuals, with a lesson in democratic daring and lucidity.

Has America Gone Mad

NOW LET US tackle the trial of America as such.

Let us take on the accusations of fundamentalism, neocon-servatism, and imperialism, all viewed as representing the worst the world has to offer and proving the utterly, profoundly, criminal nature of this country.

That's not exactly the image I formed of this country.

And, since we've reached the end of this investigation and since the documents of the case are all, so to speak, out on the table, I owe my reader—and perhaps myself a few final clarifi-cations.

Fundamentalism.

It's *the* word that comes up most often in an overwhelming majority of commentaries—even the ones that aren't tena-ciously hostile—on contemporary America.

And there are, in my own account, a number of scenes (the Willow Creek sermon; the creationist helicopter pilot from Las Vegas convinced there were 'two theories' about the formation of the Grand Canyon; my notes on the crusade of moral values in America's heartland) that unquestionably veer in that direction and convey a rather disturbing image of these evangelical churches, so significant in the life of the new America.

That said, let's be serious.

And let us begin, once again, at the beginning.

Don't all democratic nations have their laboratories? Don't they all have the symbolic and actual places where they were born and took shape? Well, in America's case, these places are the great Protestant churches. That's what the Pilgrim fathers indicated when, inspired by the Scriptures, they announced their aim to create a 'City upon a Hill.' That's what the Founding Fathers repeated, as when George Washington emphasised in his inaugural speech that 'every step by which they have advanced' to an 'independent nation' 'seems to have been distinguished by some token of providential agency.' That's what his disciples and believers asserted when they turned Washington, just after his death, into the 'Aaron,' the 'Moses,' of this new exodus from Egypt that was to produce the country. And that is especially what one discovers when one tries—as Huntington does in the most acceptable part of his book and as Tocqueville did before anyone—to examine the genealogy of values that form the American democratic ethos. Individualism? Directly inspired by the one-to-one relationship, typically Protestant, between the believer and his Lord. Freedom of conscience? Linked to the practice of reading the Scriptures without a priest, armed only with reason and good sense. The taste for free debate? The practice of it? The multiplicity, precisely, of the readings; the theological impossibility of resolving this multiplicity and choosing between right and wrong interpretations. The ideology of advancement by merit? The indifference—asserted very quickly, and so characteristic of this country—to hierarchies of birth or nature? A secular version of the responsibility of the believer summoned to answer, alone before God and before God alone, for his failure or success on this earth. The very organisation of the government, the network of associations that, for Tocqueville, was the clearest sign of the brilliant vitality of the system? Still the example of churches; the importation, into the life of the citizen, of a kind of community first experienced in the contemplation of New England meetinghouses. Tolerance, finally? That principle of tolerance theorised by John Locke in his 1689 'Letter Concerning Toleration,' then, a century later, by Thomas Paine in his *Age of Reason*? Half a century before Locke and a century and a half before Paine, it was already the obsession of the passengers on the *Mayflower* and it's an obsession that comes directly, whatever anyone may say, from this omnipresence of chapels—at the time they were called 'sects'—which, by their very diversity and sheer number, were forced to compromise and accommodate everyone. ('If you have two religions in your countries,' Voltaire wrote in the article on 'Tolerance' in his *Philosophical Dictionary*, 'they will cut each other's throat'; but if, as in America, 'you have thirty,' then, yes, 'they will dwell in peace.') Too bad for the lovers of simple ideas: religion in America was not the grave of democracy, but its cradle. Of course, democracy would also later proceed from the Enlightenment—but it proceeded first of all from Protestant evangelism.

Contrary to commonly held ideas, contrary to what knee-jerk anti-Americans drivel on about, this religion, if you consider it over the course of time, is not synonymous with extremism. It is, of course, in some cases. It may, particularly in the South, have committed the terrible mistake of identifying with the worst, that is to say, with Jim Crow laws and with racism. And it is undeniable that, in the antiabortion activists, in the hyperpuritans who expect heavenly thunderbolts to strike down homosexual couples, or in those factions who believe that the welfare state is evil since it goes against God's sovereign distribution of wealth and fate, a feeling of remaining faithful to the teachings of the Scriptures can play a decisive role. Just as undeniable, though, was the role of the churches and, often, of *the very same churches*, in the civil-rights movement of the 1950s and '60s. Just as undeniable is the fact that when Martin Luther King, Jr., announced that he had a dream, his dream—he immediately went on to specify—was 'deeply rooted in the American dream,' and his aim was to reveal 'the glory of the Lord' so that 'all flesh shall see it together'; to allow 'Jews and Gentiles, Protestants and Catholics,' 'all of God's children,' to 'join hands' and 'let freedom ring… from every village and every hamlet' while thanking 'God Almighty.' Just as undeniable, later on, is the fact that it was as a professed Baptist—excuse me, a 'born-again'—as fervent as his successor, George W. Bush, that President Jimmy Carter spoke when, in the name of his own vision of a reconciliation between the sons of Abraham, he sponsored the historic agreements at Camp David; and the fact that, in the North, it is around the massive non-denomination-al churches that the benevolent networks of solidarity are organised that connect believers with a variety of humanitarian campaigns for increasing awareness (like Bono's campaign for awareness of AIDS in Africa). Is this what the lady at the Washington airport was telling me when she reproached me for my caricature-like impression of Willow Creek? Yes, in a sense. And in this sense, she wasn't wrong. Not that I would take back any of what I said about the unease I felt there. But let me be more specific. What I reproach these churches for is their banality. It's their propensity for turning God into some kind of 'good guy,' friendly and reassuring, free of problems, watching over a sterile universe, bereft of anguish or negativity. It's the idea of an insipid God, devoid of mystery, whose aims, although previously impenetrable, are now becoming as familiar as those of a near neighbour or friend. What I reproach them for (still linked, as the history of religions teaches us, with the crisis and failure of transcendence) is their methodical and, at times, obsessive puritanism; their dream of burning vices and vanities at the stake in all the crossroads of America; their hunt for sexual deviance; their obsession for transparency and confession; their wish to squeeze repentance out of some governor accused of taking advantage of his assistant, or some senatorial candidate whose wife was suspected of visiting a 'sex club,' or some director of a Catholic periodical forced to resign after it was revealed that, twenty years ago, when he was a college student, he had had inappropriate relationships with girls—all this seems to have become a new national pastime. But, in the end, puritanism is not fascism. And I would never let myself go so far as to say that, in a country where more than nine citizens out of ten declare they believe in God and a number of them in the Devil, in an America where Kerry seemed as good a Christian as Bush and where opponents and supporters of the death penalty, antisegregationist activists and those nostalgic for southern order, pacifists and warmongering hawks, all share the same faith and congregate in the same churches—I would never say that, in this country, a fervent, even 'fundamentalist' Christian is, by definition, a fascist.

The overhasty reasoning that, because American presidents swear their oaths on the Bible, because they end their inaugural speeches with the phrase—unthinkable in a country like France—'So help me God,' because banknotes bear the maxim IN GOD WE TRUST (which, by the way, contrary to what is often repeated, is *not* the motto of the country, which remains, as we know, the Virgilian, republican *E pluribus unum*), and, finally, because a large majority of voters are swayed, now more than ever, by their faith and the faith of candidates seeking office, leaps to the conclusion that this country does not enjoy the polite secularism we pride ourselves on in France. What, after all, is secularism? It is not, as we know, agnosticism. Nor is it atheism. And it is obviously not a separation of individuals from churches. It is the utterly distinct separation of churches from government institutions. It is the command given to every state not to favour one faith over another. Likewise, and symmetrically, it's the command given to citizens to believe in whatever they are partial to so long as their faith remains a matter of their own conscience and tolerates the conscience of others. But it is in no way a systematic hostility toward religion in general. Even less so since, as historians know, there is a Christian genealogy of secularism that dates back to the doctrine of the two powers promulgated fifteen centuries ago by Pope Saint Gelasius I. This twofold obligation not to prom-ulgate an official religion, and thus to guarantee the equality and freedom of all religions, is very precisely what emerges from both the Declaration of Independence and the American Constitution (where no reference is made in the latter to either Providence or God). It's what Article VI of the Constitution guarantees ('no religious test shall ever be required as a qualification to any office or public trust under the United States'), as well as the First Amendment ('Congress shall make no law respecting an establishment of religion, or prohibiting the free exercise thereof '). And it's what Thomas Jefferson himself confirmed, so solemnly, when in his 1802 letter to the Danbury Baptist Association he calmly, firmly reasserted the complete separateness of the two realms (the first article of the Bill of Rights should be understood, he said, as 'building a wall of separation between church and state'). America is a secular country. America, contrary to myth, is, in the strict sense and from its very beginnings, faithful both to the doctrine of the two powers and to the neutrality of the state in matters of religion. France has fought for secularism. It has won its secu-larism after centuries of confusion and wars of religion. Its cel-ebrated separation of church and state was, truly, a separation, a *scission*, with all the brutality, political infighting, and even massacres (like the St. Bartholomew's Day Massacre) that the word entails. The Americans did not need to separate from anything. The wall of separation, to speak like Jefferson, was raised from the beginning. They were born secular, whereas we French had to become it.

All right, you might say. But what about today? What about secularism in this dawn of the twenty-first century, in the era of Mel Gibson, with millions of new Pentecostal Christians believing that the times of waiting are over and that the hour of Armageddon is approaching, the battle of the End of Days? What about Jefferson's 'wall' in the era of these born-again Christians who believe the world, like them, is on the verge of rebirth and that there isn't a second to lose in preparing the house of God for the ultimate event? Here, of course, we need to tread carefully. Here, obviously, there are temptations. And no doubt we should start to worry when we see the Republican administration pouring hundreds of millions of dollars into support groups for the destitute that are clearly impregnated with religious ideology; or when the most powerful of all born-again Christians of the present age decides to name a ninth judge to the Supreme Court who could be swayed, as a large faction of the public prompts him, to swing the Court majority toward restricting those abortion rights acquired with an extremely narrow margin thirty years ago, by means of a ruling establishing that 'the foetus is not alive till after the period of quickening'; or else when unbridled Huntingtonians entertain the idea that it's with Islam itself that born-again Christianity is entering into conflict. All right. Although the associations in question may well be of Christian inspiration, they are not, at least for now, actually religious institutions. And as for that 'Islam' upon which the apostles of the clash of civilisations wish to declare total war, honesty requires us to admit that President

Bush himself often makes it a point to stress the respect he feels for Islam, in its moderate version; he frequently mentions the satisfaction he experienced the day Muzammil H. Siddiqi, the imam of the Washington Islamic Center, provided him with a copy of the Koran…. A question of tactics? Evidently. Duplicity? Perhaps. But also, and it would be absurd to deny it, a sign of an ideological power struggle that shows the opponents of secularism to be at a greater disadvantage than is usually thought (see, as evidence of this, the literature of ultra-conservatives like David Limbaugh, shouting to whoever will listen that Christians are the true persecuted victims in contemporary America). Proof that the compromise negotiated by the Founding Fathers is resisting the slings and arrows of time fairly well, once again (never forget that the God mentioned in the Republican and Democratic conventions, the inaugural speeches, the houses of Congress, is a purposefully abstract God, almost deistic, and, at core, consensual, recognised by all American faiths, Christian or not). Or proof, if you prefer, of the solidity of a tradition that, even if it were tempted to slacken on the nonintervention of religions in the affairs of state (roughly, the legacy of the Enlightenment), would not give way on that symmetric, and symmetrically formational, requirement of the principle of secularism: nonintervention of the state in matters of religion (roughly, Protestant separatism, especially in its Methodist and Baptist forms). The result, in any case, leaves little room for doubt. That there exists another kind of secularism in America, profoundly different from the French model, is likely. That it should be called by a different name—perhaps we might use the word *secularisation* for this American-style secularism—is possible. But what is certain is that American monotheism—that is to say, once again, the underlying equality of revelations, convictions, and faiths—is a founding component of this model of secularisation, and this model is still going strong.

Messianism, finally: that odd conviction that holds that the American people is a chosen people, born under the sign of the Universal and elected by God to build here, on this land promised to it, a new kind of nation, freed from the corruption, rottenness, and aberrations of old Europe. And with it, this other, connected certainty, according to which this magnificent people, this indispensable nation, this new Jerusalem, this third Rome, this Canaan of modern times, has received a mandate to show the way to the rest of the world and guide it on the paths of freedom. This is the most problematic aspect of American religiosity. This is what, personally, makes me most uncomfortable. And I do mistrust the idea that there could be a community on this earth, of whatever kind, whose leaders believe themselves endowed with a direct line to the Almighty, and feel assured, when they act, of doing Right and Good: I mistrusted it when it was Holy Russia that, proletarian or czarist, thought itself invested with this role of leading the world to its salvation; I mistrusted it when it was the little nations of central Europe, Christian and crucified, who, after 1989, used this great tale of suffering to legitimise their demands for identity; I mistrust it, in France, when the idea takes on the face of colonial universalism; and I like it no more—need I say so?—when, in the Near East, it cripples intelligence and nourishes hard-line extremists; I always mistrust it, in fact it terrifies me, when it is embodied in religious zealots who seek to impose the Sharia on 'Jewish' and 'Crusader' nations; well, I can find no reason to applaud either when three hundred million Americans are told they're commissioned by Providence and that whatever they undertake is marked by a seal of excellence and exception. But all the same… Here, I would articulate two objections as well. Two series of questions and, hence, of objections. To begin with, do we have to pretend that we're just discovering what we've known since the birth of America? Can we ignore the fact that this exceptionalism, this theme of holy birth and heaven-granted mandate, is a constant, powerful theme that has always pervaded the national philosophy? Can we obliterate, or try to obliterate, the fact that this great providentialist and legendary account, this modern manifestation of the myths of foundations and ancient cities, can be traced, described in the same words, with the same extraordinary fervour, by so many of the intellectuals who have formed the ideological and moral backbone of the country (Walt Whitman, Reinhold Niebuhr, Thomas Paine, and even the Melville of *Clarel*)? Wasn't the neoconservative intellectual David Brooks entirely right, in a word, when he pointed out to me in New York, not without malice, that it's a recurrent theme for all American presidents, up to and including the ones we think of in Europe as being most beyond suspicion (Wilson and his declarations on America's universal mission; Roosevelt; Kennedy; Carter; Clinton, in 1999, in his State of the Union speech, when he said, 'Now is the moment for this generation to meet our historic responsibility to the twenty-first century'; and so forth)? Second, is it legitimate to use the same concept, and the same catchphrase, 'fundamentalism,' to designate these various and diverse forms of messianism? Do we have the right, as detestable as present American politics seem at the moment, to equate the sin of pride of a nation that regards itself as the reincarnation of the ancient Hebrews crossing that avatar of the Red Sea that is the Atlantic with the purifying mania of those zealots of God (and sometimes those godless zealots) who want to either convert the world or blow it up? Is it acceptable, or honest, to overlook the gaping chasm—not just political but also metaphysical—that separates religions that still take into account the hypothesis of original sin and radical evil and the natural limits they impose on all aims, even democratic ones, of reshaping society (and that's the case, despite everything, with most American churches) from religions that trade in sin suppression, in the methodical concealment of the negative constituents of the human, and, hence, in an all-powerful and all-consuming desire for purity (roughly, the different variations of radical Islam)? In short, inscribing an equal sign between a small-minded redneck who believes he's entrusted with the responsibility of spreading the good democratic word throughout the world and a commando of suicide bombers united in a brotherhood of terror and mass murder—isn't that the first step in this culture of euphemism and banalisation from which we must so urgently free ourselves? The answer, for me, leaves no room for doubt. And, in turn, leads to the question of neoconservativism.

Neoconservatism.

The species isn't a new one and, considering the current rhythm of decomposition, it might even be a fossil when these lines appear.

It dates back—if we are to believe good paleontologists—to the already distant era when a certain number of left-wing and even extreme-left-wing thinkers began to wonder about the dead ends of socialism.

Species is not quite the word.

We should say, rather, *clique*, *breed*, or *swarm*.

We should find words to designate these murderers, these despots, these enemies of the human race, these slaughterers of children in the Sahel, these Dr. Strangeloves, this academy of crime.

We should find the right tone (like the giant antiglobalisation demonstrations that rightly enough decried the deaths in the American war in Iraq but never mentioned the two million other civilians gassed, buried alive, killed with pickaxes or shovels, or tortured to death under Saddam Hussein's dictatorship) to describe this neoconservatism that, like Zionism before it, is in the process of turning into the supreme insult, the incarnation of evil, the synonym for whatever is basest in this world—including, in fact, Zionism itself, which relinquishes its most-wretched status only because these neocons, these con-scienceless, fierce psychopaths, also happen to be, as if by pure chance, the unconditional allies of Israel....

What are we to make of this?

Who exactly are these sorcerers' apprentices, these princes of darkness, these mercenaries of vileness, these superhawks, these vampires?

The first point that strikes you when—like my fellow Frenchmen Daniel Vernet and Alain Franchon, in their essay 'L'Amérique messianique'—you take the trouble of reading them or, as I have done, meeting them is that they practice, or claim to practice, a politics of ideas. You can disagree with these ideas. You can find them absurd, naïve, even dangerous. You can think—as I do—that the very notion, for instance, of going to war in Iraq as a response to the al-Qaeda attacks on Manhattan and the Pentagon was a considerable mistake. But the fact is there: here we have the only example, I reckon, of a major modern country adding considerations drawn from Thucydides or Leo Strauss to its diplomacy. It's the first time in a long while that this supposedly materialistic, pragmatic country has (to par-aphrase Valéry) the politics of its thought and the thought of its politics. And I think that listening to the former second in command at the Department of Defence quote Plato and Aristotle, observing him engage in a war with a theory in his knapsack, even a vague one, on natural rights and on history, takes us beyond those generations of 'wise men' who thought that politics had nothing to do with ideas since politics must be practiced with nothing but self-interest at stake.

The second rather striking and, here again, undeniable char-acteristic is that the wars these people waged, the three or four military operations they have led or inspired (Bosnia and Kosovo, Afghanistan, Iraq) ended up, each time, with the fall of a dictatorship. Here, too, you can object. You can judge that the 'smart' bombs so dear to Albert Wohlstetter, their master, took heavy tolls in Kabul and Belgrade. In the case of Iraq, you can wonder if there didn't exist other methods besides setting off this pandemonium to overthrow the regime. But the end result was the same. What is undeniable is that a neoconservative is someone whose enemies are called Saddam Hussein, Mullah Omar, and Milosevic. Would we rather return to an era when American Cold War diplomacy made friends with the entire gamut of tyrants on the planet so long as they sided with America in its power struggle with the Soviet Union? And, in the particular case of Iraq—having agreed, I repeat, that the war was a political mistake, granted that it did not attenuate the pressure of terrorism in the least, that it aimed at the wrong target and did so at the wrong time—in the case of Iraq, then, if we absolutely had to decide and between two evils, choose the lesser one, which would you deem, morally, was the least evil: Bush, Sr., inviting the Kurds and Shiites to rise up but not moving his finger the day when, having listened to him, they rose and were massacred, or Bush, Jr., undertaking, under the influence of these neoconservatives, to capture Ali Hassan al-Majid, otherwise known as Chemical Ali, the man responsible for the poison-gas attacks on the Kurdish town of Halabja, along with other deeds the international community discreetly closed its eyes to?

These people have a third passion that also contrasts strongly with the political customs of the past decades. Perhaps they harbour the same ulterior realpolitik motives as the traditional right. Perhaps, in Iraq, as well as in their innermost depths, they had no concern other than making a show of force while also— which wouldn't, by the way, have been an outright crime— securing oil supplies for their country. But at least they're taking the trouble to talk about democracy too. At least they're asserting that democracy isn't set aside for white people, Christians, and Westerners. And, not content with saying so, not content with proclaiming, like good disciples of Leo Strauss, that they loathe relativism and don't see why the Iraqis might not be capable of exercising universal suffrage and representative and parliamentary democracy, the fact is that they have made their actions agree with their words. The fact is that once Saddam was overthrown and the oil wells secured, once the first goals of the war were achieved and their enemies made to witness American determination and power, they took the strategic option to remain in the country in order to support, for a time at least, the process of national and republican reconstruction. Here again, the question is, at bottom, simple. Would an American army adept at hit-and-run tactics, washing its hands of the fate of liberated peoples, have been better? Once the war was over and won, should we have preferred racists and cynics thinking that the other cause, the cause of democracy, is, in principle, a hopeless cause, since the validity of human rights expires at the Western border?

You can—as I have done, once again—offer all kinds of reproaches vis-a-vis these neocons.

You can accuse the neoconservatives of being bad politicians, angels rushing in, strategists without tactics, incapable of devising ways to realise their ideas.

You can consider them naïve when they fantasise about human-rights charters parachuting like packages of food or medicine into countries they know nothing about.

You can think that this wish to export democracy at bayonet point is merely the reverse form of the permanent revolution of their youth and that they've never fully left their original Trotskyism.

You can wonder: What's the use of breaking with Marxism and, beyond Marxism, with the historicism that constituted its secret code only to encounter it all over again under the guise— more human certainly, less barbaric, but not intrinsically more reasonable—of democratic messianism?

Recalling the global lie of those so-called weapons of mass

destruction that were never found, you can wonder if their familiarity with great texts didn't also give them a taste for the 'necessary lie' theorised—one of them ingenuously explained to me—by Machiavelli, Benjamin Constant, and Plato in Book III of *The Republic*.

Alternatively, and so long as we're on the subject, you can regret that they aren't truly radical and that, when the tyrant named Putin threatens to 'do away with the last Chechen,' or when the torturer-government is called China and the issue at stake has to do with the occupation of Tibet, when the neocons have to deal, in other words, with an enemy more serious than the ruined government of the Taliban or the bankrupt army of Baathists, they prudently file their grand principles away in the cabinet of ideologies and dreams.

Finally, you can reproach them—and this was my position during my conversation with Bill Kristol, in Washington, D.C.—for believing that they're compelled, as soon as they provide their support to a president's foreign policy, to back his choices in domestic policy and, brashly overlooking the rules of independence of spirit that their masters should have instilled in them, for sacrificing their differences of opinion to the simplistic concept of a party line that no one in reality is forcing them to toe; you can reproach them for having deserted that other front line—that being, at home and abroad, the fight against chronic poverty, social exclusion, and discrimination of all sorts.

But what you can't do is transform them into paragons of immorality and vice.

What is both unfair and absurd is to ignore the progress— yes, I did say *progress*—represented by the emergence of a generation of political leaders for whom the question of what the ancients called the 'nature' of regimes is worthy of being regarded as one of the key parameters of well-conducted international initiatives.

If I were an American, I would probably have been one of

the people who, during this journey and especially during the last presidential campaign, argued for the real progress it would be to appoint an authentic liberal as the head of the State Department. Someone faithful to the spirit of the Enlightenment and to the values of old Europe, skilful at multilateralism and the culture of compromise, revolted by the practices of the *kapos* at Abu Ghraib and by the very existence of detention centres in Guantánamo Bay. But since things are the way they are, since the political debate, in America as well as elsewhere, consists in choosing not between good and evil but between an evil and a lesser evil, intellectual scrupulousness obliges me to distinguish what, in Pittsburgh for instance, the wordless dialogue between a Henry Kissinger and a Christopher Hitchens distinguished no less irreducibly (in the heart of what worldwide progressivism registers under the all-purpose heading the 'American Right'): a real politician without principles from a rational antifascist.

For there are, actually, vastly different ways to think about the relationship of America with the rest of the world.

There are four, at least.

Or, more precisely, there are, at the core of what our intellectual lethargy goes out of its way to conflate as the 'American Right,' two factions amounting to four main positions and attitudes.

There is a first faction made up of those who, when Rwanda is sinking, when Sarajevo is burning, when Europe is living under the Nazi or Communist heel, declare, like Secretary of State James Baker about Bosnia in 1992, that America doesn't 'have a dog in this fight' and, consequently, sees no reason to get mixed up in it. (That's the traditional isolationist position; it's what Walter Russell Mead calls 'Jeffersonian,' from the name of a famous president, apostle of a prudent, guarded foreign policy, eager, as Mead wrote, to avoid 'entangling alliances' and to 'strengthen' the model of the elected nation rather than export it.) Then there is the faction that contradicts them and replies, No, that is simply not viable; a great power always has a dog in all the fights of the world, and America of all countries cannot afford to lose interest in what's happening on the planet. (That's the position of the anti-isolationists; from right to left, among both Republicans and Democrats, that's the school of people who, whatever their reasons are, do not think the United States should act as though it were an immense island, cut off from the world, freed from concern for the other; that's the great family of people who are sometimes called—wrongly, however, since the paradigm is more general and reaches much further back—'Wilsonians.')

And, in the midst of this second family, among those who believe America cannot escape its global destiny, there is a second principle of division that gives rise—according, still, to the same typology of Walter Russell Mead—to three opposing subfamilies. Hamiltonians, who like to think of themselves as pragmatic and believe that the country should intervene only in the name of its economic and commercial interests. Jacksonians (after the energetic populist Andrew Jackson, president from 1829 to 1837 and thus a contemporary of Tocqueville's journey), who insist that the country is justified in acting only when its vital interests are attacked, but add that the goal then is to strike very hard and promptly retreat—to demonstrate power and, mission accomplished, go home. And then the Wilsonians (in the narrow sense), who think that striking, demonstrating power, exacting revenge, can be necessary but is never enough—in brief, they object that none of the other schools are really worthy of a great democratic country: against the Jacksonians, they object that the sheriff strategy, the 'In Guns We Trust' of the Far West extended to international relations, is beneath the dignity of the American creed; against the Hamiltonians, they protest that commerce, however noble and respectable, could never be the last word, either in universal history or in the manner in which the elected nation is supposed to intervene; and, last, against the Jeffersonians, they claim that while of course they share their 'exceptionalist' hypothesis and adhere just as ardently to the idea of the providential nation whose virtues must be preserved with all possible strength, still, noblesse oblige—and defending the sanctuary, protecting the fort, saving the American laboratory from the risks of invasion or corruption, carrying out all of this, in a word, entails the moral obligation to share some of America's wonders with the world. Neoconservatives are the most recent manifestation of this last school….

The question, contemplating the latter, is rather straightforward.

Among all these factions—as distinct, let me emphasise, as the European ideological families are from one another—are we absolutely certain that the last one is the least worthy of our respect?

Of these four parties, often unnamed, but whose arguments pervade the entire political history of the country, profoundly permeate, in fact, all of its official factions and matter at least as much as the split between the red states and the blue states, or between the Democrats and the Republicans, are we truly convinced that the fourth—the family of pure Wilsonians, supporters of a Kantian, elected, universal nation, whose true aim in war would be to distribute democratic values everywhere—is the most shameful political beast America has produced?

Of these four major sensibilities that either join together (the Hamiltonians Condoleezza Rice and Colin Powell allying with the Jacksonians Dick Cheney and Donald Rumsfeld), or wage a merciless ideological war against one another (the Jeffersonian Pat Buchanan trumpeting the treason of George W. Bush, who, according to him, has gone over to the side of neoconservative Wilsonianism and its militant Zionist wing), or else succeed one another, or even cohabit in one single mind (George W. Bush, actually, beginning his first term in a Jeffersonian fashion, shifting to Jacksonianism after 9/11, and in effect converting, during the Iraq War, to a moderate Wilsonianism, preferring the policy of the missionary to that of the sheriff; or even Woodrow Wilson himself, who, at the beginning of the First World War, when he declared that the United States was 'too proud to fight,' wasn't very far from a Jeffersonian position, but who, in 1917, went over to the side, if I dare say it, of pure and multi-lateralist Wilsonianism)—of these four poles of discourse and practice that deserve to be isolated as carefully as, at the conclusion of a renowned French classification, the legitimist right wing, the Orléansist right wing, and the Bonapartist right wing were, or even (since speaking of 'right wings' involves beliefs that once again pervade the space shared by both right and left and hence is too simplistic) the liberal, Christian, social democratic, and Communist traditions, is it sensible to act as though only the last one merited detestation and opprobrium?

My conclusion, as you can deduce, is quite clear.

It is based not on prejudice but on investigation, observation, and listening.

I am not one of them.

My heroes, my friends, the people I identify with, the people who most strongly impressed me throughout this journey are named Barak Obama, Hillary Clinton, Morris Dees, Jim Harrison, Norman Mailer.

But I still believe that it took all the thick ignorance of European anti-Americanism to have this fourth family—a family that, I insist, possesses the dual merit of both practicing a politics of ideas and reaching back to the internationalist ideas of democratic principles—be synonymous with the stupidest and most inhuman right in the world.

And, at last, the question of imperialism.

We're familiar with the critique, so hackneyed it's become

tiresome, of an America that's grasping and gluttonous, devoted to worshipping the Golden Calf, concerned only with imposing its inferior products, its lowly culture, its law.

We are familiar, even in America, with a political and intellectual class obsessed for three centuries (and more so after Leo Strauss) with the myth of the grandeur and decadence of the Romans, with the impulse to depict itself as a threefold Rome where the empire of images and culture (Los Angeles) thrives to reinforce the military empire (Washington) that is itself at the service of the capitalist and financial empire (New York).

And, finally, we are familiar with the latest variations on the same theme. We know the antiglobalist rants about this monstrous imperialism, extending even beyond America, that, not content with inundating the world with its degenerate, criminal commodities, not content with starving people or, worse, poisoning them, not content with having no other aim but capturing for the profit of its oligarchies the principal sources of raw materials—especially oil—that are the property of other countries, still has the nerve (and herein lies all the ignominy both of its 'fundamentalist' apostles and of the Wilsonian messianism of its 'neoconservatives') to disguise its conquests as 'humanitarian interventions,' to rebaptise its wars as 'peacekeeping operations,' and to take advantage of terrorism as a miraculous surprise, allowing America to reshape global order, to discourage and prevent any vague impulse for a new political leadership capable of competing with it, and ultimately lending a face to this enemy that has receded ever since the collapse of the Soviet Union: yesterday Iraq, today Iran, tomorrow a China whose demonisation is already being plotted by the two connected strands of neo-Straussian Machiavellianism and academic orientalism…

The problem is that the facts are there, and that if the American nation has been capable of the worst as well as the best, if the country of Truman, Nixon, and, now, George W.

Bush has made mistakes and, in some cases, committed crimes, if it organised the fall of Salvador Allende in Latin America and supported Greek, Spanish, and Portuguese dictatorships in Europe; if it has, in other words, been somewhat unfaithful to the messianic mandate it claims for itself after God himself supposedly granted it, the facts are there, and, as the writer Alexandre Adler demonstrated in *L'Odyssée Américaine*, they complicate the oversimplified vision of America as a big bad wolf feeding on the blood of the peoples of the world.

Fact: the Americans, in the course of their history, have been infinitely less colonialist than the English, the French, the Dutch, the Spanish, and, of course, the Russians.

Fact: America's power, that notorious and satanic superpower that we in Europe tend to perceive as the result of a shady scheme, is, always or almost always, the fruit of our European shortcomings, the price of our renunciations, our failures.

Fact: most of America's recent interventions, most of the operations that caused it to secede from the systematic isolationism that constitutes, in the Jeffersonian tradition, the sharpest divide in their relations with the rest of the world, stem either from the Jacksonian desire to respond to an attack (you can, as I'll say one last time, think it counterproductive and absurd to respond to the attacks on Manhattan and the Pentagon by counterattacking Baghdad—but that there was an attack in the first place is not, alas, deniable) or from the Hamiltonian need to regulate and police the flow of international commercial transactions (this was one of the impulses behind the First Gulf War and the decision to fly to the aid of Kuwaiti oil), or else stem again from the Wilsonian sentiment of being accountable not just for world order but for a 'natural law' that international organisations were not capable of enforcing. (Isn't that the whole reason for the decision to get involved in Bosnia, then in Kosovo, after so many prevarications?) Never was a wish for conquest the motivating force. Never did these operations end in a lasting occupation. When the Saudis asked for the Dhahran air base to be evacuated in 1954, when General de Gaulle asked, later on, in March 1966, for the evacuation of the Châteauroux Air Depot, and when the Philippine Senate asked for the Clark Air Base at Subic Bay to be closed in 1991, each time, the empire obeyed and decamped.

Another fact: America has an unparalleled air force (as I witnessed at the Colorado Springs academy). It has (as I saw in Norfolk) a flotilla of submarines that would have enraptured Stephen B. Luce, Alfred T. Mahan, and the supporters of the strategic theories of the Naval War College a century ago. Beyond this, their land army, the forces that should be the spearhead for the imperial wars of today and tomorrow, the troops that are meant to serve in the pacification of conquered territories and, right now, of Iraq, are mediocre, unprofessional, under-equipped, and poorly trained. Isn't half the Iraqi expeditionary corps composed of non-Americans who signed up for military service to speed their process of naturalisation? Aren't the most sensitive missions—for instance, the protection of government buildings and the U.S. embassy—entrusted to hired mercenaries recruited by private security companies? is this really the imperial army of modern times? Is this the vanguard of a long march in which Baghdad is just the first stop? For anyone keen to draw parallels with the ancient world, for those obsessed with Theodor Mommsen, Edward Gibbon, and Fustel de Coulanges, America resembles great imperial Rome less than it does Athens in decline, which Plato blamed for having privileged the oar over the shield and spear—or even commercial Carthage, which, on the eve of the Third Punic War, had become incapable, says Flaubert in *Salammbô*, of maintaining both a fleet and an army of mercenaries....

Another fact, or rather a series of other facts that are scarcely compatible with the idea we usually have in Europe of an empire: the odd displacement, first of all, of which I saw an example at the Mall of America in Minneapolis and whose result is that most conventional manufacturing activity is carried out in Third World countries; the fact that the banks, the state governments, the Treasury Department, the businesses, and hence the pension and retirement funds in a country that, in principle, is a dominant country are all dependent on a colossal foreign deficit that is itself financed by the economies the empire theoretically dominates—on Indian, Russian, Japanese, and Chinese assets especially. One is confronted, then, with the extreme unconventionality of a model that gathers its sturdiness both from the conviction among the dominated—including China and India—that it's in the U.S. banks, the U.S. financial system, and the dollar that the best return on their assets lies, and from the other, linked conviction that the rest of the world must continue to send its elite, its researchers, its future executives, its businessmen, to be trained, until further notice, in American universities, scientific institutions, and companies; in short, this paradoxical system, unique in history and, in reality, extraordinarily fragile, that makes America's strength dependent on the strength of the confidence that is daily invested in it, that is to say, to be precise, on the strength of confidence that Americans themselves have in the confidence the world lends them, or rather (and disregard the apparent circle) on this culminating point that is the strength of the confidence the rest of the world has in the continuing confidence the Americans have and will have in the confidence that the rest of the world will continue, they hope, to have in them—but until when?

Not counting, finally (and this, too, is a fact), that the obsession with imperialism, this reduction of universal history to the duel of the American Hydra with the angels who resist it, this grand dualistic and paranoid tale where everything amounts to conspiracy, everything has meaning, and where it's not the peculiarities of the so-called empire, its restraint, its retreats, its Carthaginian qualities, its ways of occupying without occupying and deploying armies not of hoplites but of helots who, as in all paranoid logic, turn into their opposite and assume an 'imperiality' all the more criminal since it has become insidious and imperceptible—not counting, then, that this fixation has an ultimate effect that, to my eyes, is no less pernicious and that consists in hiding, discrediting, throwing into the oubliettes of nonmeaning and non-knowing, a whole other scene of contemporary history: the one that neither fights America nor submits to it; that isn't especially pro- or expressly anti-imperialist; the one that mixes together all the microstories of massacre or genocide that, no matter how much you search for them, never turn up in the great categories created by anti-imperialist progressivism and that, although they're at the origin of the most terrifying wars, although these wars cause deaths not in the thousands but in the hundreds of thousands and even millions, suddenly cease to be of interest to anyone...

I am not saying, of course, that there are no imperialist temptations in the United States.

We know but too well how a taste for extreme power develops in those already powerful to dismiss the possibility of seeing this administration, or any other, seized by the hubris I mentioned earlier, which Plato wrote is the opposite of peace, more so than *polemos*.

Besides, I do not like this method of 'punishing' the supporters of a diplomatic position other than America's own.

I do not like the autistic arrogance of the upholders of a unilateralism that previous administrations, even Republican ones, took heed to avoid. Detestable, too, and of ill omen is the cynicism with which, at the height of the Iraq crisis, a handful of government officials tried to exploit old Francophobic prejudices that are scarcely any better than French anti-American clichés.

And then, beyond current events, there are signs indicating that the America of President Wilson, the one that invented the

League of Nations and promoted the United Nations, is playing faster and looser with international law, its institutions, its criminal courts, its conventions, its Kyoto Protocol—the signs are numerous, and they so corroborate one another that you obviously can't rule out seeing the new Carthage wind up one day trying to resemble Rome a little.

But this temptation toward imperialism is still, for now, just a temptation.

And we have to admit that, placed side by side, all this yields quite a unique combination of power and reticence, concern and indifference, for the rest of the world, but also (and this is most disturbing) strength and weakness, authority and latent precariousness, a capacity to impose its law that is currently unequalled, and a premonition of the day (which could come at any time) when the oppressed, the world populations, or, quite simply, a rival power will become aware that the hegemony of the master is supported only by the force of the desire, self-interest, and consensual submission of its supposed vassals. We have to admit that all of this yields a regime of domination, an imperial model that can no longer be accounted for by the two opposing but circumstantially complicit doctrines currently in fashion, the ones arising from either Marxism-Leninism (imperialism, the final stage…) or from Leo Strauss (the great Jewish intellectual, contemporary of Franz Rosenzweig, who, in order to continue preaching—against Rosenzweig—'Jerusalem *and* Athens,' needed to believe, and have his disciples believe, that the site of empire had just shifted from Germany to America).

So then, to understand this mixture, I can see only two possible methods—arising from two different sides of the political spectrum.

The one proposed by the modern theoretician of liberal thinking in the French sense—Raymond Aron, who, in *Peace and War: A Theory of International Relations*, uses Paul

Morand's phrase for America: an 'involuntary empire.'

And another, introduced by the Italian intellectual Toni Negri, founder at the end of the 1960s of a radical left-wing group and author more recently of one of the most stimulating meditations on modern mechanisms of domination (*Empire*, co-written with the American literary critic Michael Hardt and commented on by the French essayist Yann Moulier-Boutang).

An empire, Negri says, that is a response—and not the other way around—to the emergence of what he calls 'the multitude.'

An empire and a multitude that, in the eyes of this impenitent Spinozan, are like the two attributes—slightly unsymmetrical, since the multitude comes first—of one single substance, which is the actual substance of the world.

And a definition of imperiality that exceeds all schemas, based on the idea—outmoded, according to him—of a leading nation that, by expanding, could produce the terms of central conflict that it would later be able to arbitrate, then dominate.

There is no centre to the new empire.

No beating heart or thinking head in the sense of Rosa Luxemburg, Bukharin, Hilferding.

Or rather yes, of course there are heads. Organs of control. But they are banks and mafias. Global summits like the G7 and G8. Multinational firms, like Microsoft, that are dragged into court for having infringed precisely on the former sovereign power of the fallen imperial state. Terrorist organisations whose empire over the financial system and over our lives threatens to increase. Massive trade unions. Opinions. Yes, public opinion itself participates in this diffuse imperiality when it is organised and strong. It's no longer this particular nation that's ruling. Or that one. Or any nation specifically. No nation has or will any longer have the power, by expanding, to create and secrete its empire. A delocalised empire, since it's contemporary with a polycentric, postnational, deterritorialised world.

I'm thinking one last time of that curious, and curiously

recurrent, debate on the imminent decline of the American empire.

I'm thinking of Paul Kennedy's argument, joining with the spirit of Montesquieu in his *Considerations on the Causes of the Greatness of the Romans and Their Decline*; and I'm thinking of the counterargument of those who, observing that a very long time passed between the fulminations of Petronius and Juvenal and the beginning of the actual end of the Roman Empire, and between Pericles' warnings and the defeat of the Delian League, followed by the destruction of the Long Walls, conclude that the American empire has some fine days yet left to unfold.

That's the whole debate, in fact, that we should be able to settle.

America is neither Rome at its height nor the conquered Rome of the last days.

It's neither the Rome of Augustus nor that of newfangled cults and barbarian attacks.

All that for the simple reason that America's Roman moment has already passed; and it's the very idea of turning Rome into an allegory for the modern city or, conversely, of describing the modern empire, American or not, as based on the model of the ancient imperial city that we need to start ridding ourselves of.

Let me make myself clear.

Various nations, and America in particular, are of course party to empire in this new sense, this empire that is at once without core and without border and that, like the world according to Nicholas of Cusa, has its centre everywhere and its circumference nowhere.

Better: just as American culture recoils from the old definition of empire, so some of its themes—the myth, for instance, of the frontier; this idea of a frontier that's open, flexible, and always receding, which was, and remains, so powerfully constitutive of American spirit and optimism—tally, on the other

hand, rather well with this new imperiality, one of whose characteristics is precisely the absence of frontiers.

Better yet: if we agree to take an interest not in the structure
but in the phenomenology of this neo-empire, if we admit that
from Marx to Negri the characteristic of an empire remains,
whatever its principle may be, to unify and, so to speak, globalise
the world by producing subjects with increasingly similar
desires, and if we mean to take an interest in the very particular
type of human produced by this imperiality and characterised,
let us say, by subservience to Commodity, Technology, and
Entertainment, then we will need to admit that this type of
human triumphs with particular vividness in a number of scenes
of American life I was able to observe in California and Texas,
at the Des Moines fair, and in the brothels of Las Vegas.

Still…

I'm not so sure…

And that's exactly where things once again become complicated.

I remember the Catholic Texan, a believer in home
schooling, who wanted to snatch his children out from under
the steamroller of dominant thinking. I remember those Belles
of the Lord, admirable in their elegance and extravagance at the
huge black Pentecostal church in Memphis. I think of those
signs of differentiation and, thus, singularisation that I kept
observing and that I've often spoken about. I think of all those
other irregulars who don't belong to the Church of Minority
Studies and whom I likely haven't mentioned enough—I think
of those young and not-so-young neo-urbanites who save an
endangered building in a ghost town near the Great Lakes; I
think of those friends of urbanism and, thus, of civilisation I saw
defending the architectural heritage of Savannah and enriching
Chicago's; I think of those neopioneers who, on the contrary,
are leaving the cities to reinvent postmodern methods of prairie
living, in Wyoming, Colorado, and Oregon; I think of all those,

here and there, who make it a rule, almost a moral duty and a nonconformist principle (but, paradox of paradoxes, here we find nonconformists en masse), to remain aloof from the great communitarian masses, that is to say, from the machines of programmed stupefaction that are typically television, commercial brands, and the major civic religion of sports; I think of all those Americans I saw, everywhere, in all classes of society, jumping out, once again, of the ranks not, as Kafka said, of murderers but of cattle stamped 'American Way of Life'; and, thinking of them, thinking of all those living deniers of a society marching as one single man toward the horizon of a nihilism it would strive to impose on the rest of the world, I tell myself that here, too, America has a real head start on its own caricature, and that it might be in the process of morphing into the seat not of empire but of a reaction to empire; I tell myself that it's the anti-imperial counterreformation that might be beginning in the United States…

One thing, in any case, seems clear to me.

No paradigm is more ill-suited for the actual state of this America than the Roman paradigm.

No model tells us less about America's concrete situation than this imperial, Latin model that Leo Strauss imported from his native Germany but that, transplanted into the Washington of his neoconservative disciples, suddenly has no meaning.

It had a meaning under Charlemagne, under Charles I of Spain, under the Hapsburgs, under Wilhelm II, under Napoleon and Hitler, under the czars of the new Rome that Holy Russia always sought to be—but it no longer has any meaning in this latest avatar of modernity that, for better or worse, is America.

Of this implacable and often invisible power that the modern empire has become now that it no longer represents the ultimate stage of state power; of this eyeless and originless panopticon that no longer offers us the name of a suspect, the head of a guilty man, or the map of a Bastille on a silver platter every morning, now that it is no longer the 'master'— a notion that is a pure signifier, about which Lacan would say (and about which I myself wrote, almost thirty years ago, in *Barbarism with a Human Face*) that it is the other name if not for the world then at least for all that, in this world, works toward the enslavement of men—America is not the demiurge; it is no longer, if it ever was, the mastermind; you can no longer say either that it is the malignant nucleus of empire or that it is the empire of evil; or else, yes, you may well say so, but if you do, then you'll need to resign yourself to understanding nothing whatsoever about empire, evil, and America.

Index

Index

Index

Index

Index

About the Type:

This book is set in Bembo, a font cut in 1495 by former goldsmith Francesco Griffo for the Venetian printer Aldus Manutius who wished to publish a small tract as a favour—De Aetna by Cardinal Pietro Bembo, on the latter's visit to the vulcano. Set in the new face, words were more inviting and easier to read than in previous available designs. Light and harmonious in weight, the elegant beauty and legibility of its stems ensured that the type's popularity instantly spread to France, Holland, Germany and the rest of Europe's printing centres. Having influenced typeface design for centuries, the classic type was revived in its orginal shape in 1929 by the foundry Monotype—whose designers added the italics—restoring its popularity for a modern generation of typesetters.